THE SUTHERLAND ESTATE, 1850–1920

SCOTTISH HISTORICAL REVIEW

MONOGRAPHS SERIES

No. 18

CURRENT AND FORTHCOMING VOLUMES

THE SUTHERLAND ESTATE, 1850–1920

Aristocratic Decline, Estate Management and Land Reform

ANNIE TINDLEY

EDINBURGH UNIVERSITY PRESS

For Mum, Dad and Jen

© Annie Tindley, 2010

Edinburgh University Press Ltd
22 George Square, Edinburgh
www.euppublishing.com

Typeset in 10 on 12pt ITC New Baskerville by
Servis Filmsetting Ltd, Stockport, Cheshire, and
printed and bound in Great Britain by
CPI Antony Rowe, Chippenham and Eastbourne

A CIP record for this book is available from the British Library

ISBN 978 0 7486 4032 4 (hardback)

Contents

Acknowledgements

I was very fortunate to have as my Ph.D. supervisor Dr Ewen Cameron; his continuing support for and interest in my research, as well as his valuable suggestions and encouragement, deserves my warmest thanks. He oversaw my undergraduate degree and later encouraged me to think about post-graduate research, and his support through many applications, reports and references, not to mention drafts of this book, has been instrumental to my getting this far, as has his good humour and kindness.

I am grateful to the Caledonian Research Foundation through the Carnegie Trust for the Universities of Scotland for funding the research for this book. A large number of institutions and individuals have helped make the course of my research run smoothly, including Staffordshire County Record Office, the National Archives of Scotland, the British Library, Highland Council Archives, the National Archives and the Bodleian Library, Oxford. Special mention must go to Lord Thurso of the Sinclair of Ulbster estates, the Macdonald estate, Armadale Castle, Skye and MacLeod of MacLeod estate, Dunvegan, Skye, who all generously allowed me access to their estate archives. Chris Whealing, estate manager of the Sutherland Estates, has also been unfailingly helpful and shown an encouraging interest in the history of the estate he now manages. Lastly, but most importantly, I would like to thank the staff of the National Library of Scotland, particularly Mrs Olive Geddes, curator of the Sutherland papers, without whose expertise this book would be much the poorer. I would also like to give a special thanks to Mr Alec O'Hara, assistant curator, who made the days pass a great deal easier in the North Reading Room and whose good humour I trespassed upon so much.

My colleagues at Glasgow Caledonian University are a model of encouragement and support for early career academics, and my thanks go to them. Likewise, thanks are due to Dr Andrew Newby, Dr Andrew Mackillop, Professor Jim Hunter, Dr John MacAskill, Dr Ron Callander, Mr Geoffrey Baggott and the examiners of my Ph.D. thesis, Professor T. M. Devine and Professor Eric Richards, for encouragement, discussion and scrutinising draft chapters. All of the errors contained in this book are, of course, my own.

This book could not have been completed without the support of family and friends; I would specially like to thank Katharine Glover for countless kind words; Elena Aldegheri for taking the piss heroically for twelve years; Kirsteen Mulhearn for copious amounts of wine, and Joanna Duncan for her support and faith in me. I owe an immeasurable debt to my family: to my mother, Linda, for her rock solid, if occasionally bemused, support; my father, Roger, for picking a fight about crofters with me ten years ago, and to my sister Jay, for thinking crofters were people who fixed roofs and never reading beyond this page – I salute you all!

The most thanks though, and love, are for my husband, Colin Campbell, who has not only demonstrated patience and good humour in the face of eight years' worth of research and writing on Sutherland, but repeatedly visited Sutherland with me over the years; rain, midges and all. He has kept me going with a killer combination of wine, homemade curries and that handsome grin – thank you my dear.

Introduction

> The direct descendants have been as a race respectable and even useful; but their fortunes have been beyond their deserts, and we must end as we began, by pronouncing the Gowers the luckiest among the great English houses.[1]

Lucky or not, the Leveson-Gowers, earls and dukes of Sutherland, were a force to be reckoned with in the nineteenth century. Fascination about them is understandable; they were among the top rank of British patrician landowners through most of the nineteenth century, their position based on a seemingly unshakeable bastion of wealth.[2] By 1850, the 2nd Duke of Sutherland was the largest landowner in western Europe: in the far north of Scotland the Sutherland estate covered roughly 1.1 million acres, almost the entire county, with a population of nearly 25,000. Although the northern estate is the focus of this book, the family also owned substantial landed estates in England; in Yorkshire, Shropshire and Staffordshire, as well as a broad portfolio of sometimes exotic investments in a huge range of ventures.

In addition to this vast landed wealth, the Sutherlands have generated enormous, and generally hostile, public controversy, the roots of which can be found in the Sutherland clearances of 1807–21. Although many Highland estates carried out clearances in the first half of the nineteenth century, it has been the Sutherland clearances that have come to symbolise the perceived injustice and cruelty of the policy, for a number of reasons.[3] Firstly, the rigorous ideology and defence of the clearances was notable in a Sutherland context; James Loch, estate commissioner from 1812, was an articulate defender of the policy, in parliament and in print, particularly of their 'Improvement' ethos.[4] Secondly, the sheer scale on which the clearances took place on the estate makes them stand out, and lastly, the infamy surrounding Patrick Sellar, clearance agent and sheep farming tenant, permanently tainted the clearance story in Sutherland. His methods,

---

[1] J. L. Sandford and M. Townsend, *The Great Governing Families of England*, vol. I (Edinburgh, 1865), 275.

[2] E. Richards, *The Leviathan of Wealth: the Sutherland Fortune in the Industrial Revolution* (London, 1973), 3–18.

[3] E. Richards, *The Highland Clearances: people, landlords and rural turmoil* (Edinburgh, new edn 2008), 153–4.

[4] Richards, *Highland Clearances*, 157; J. Loch, *An Account of the Improvements on the estates of the Marquis of Stafford* (London, 1820); *Hansard Parliamentary Debates*, 3rd series, 81 (1845), 412–13, 1455–61.

culminating in an accusation of and trial for culpable homicide, entered clearance mythology and the estate never cleansed itself of the infamy generated by this controversial experiment.[5] One of the central themes of this book is the impact of the clearances, financially, practically and ideologically, on the family and estate policy, particularly after 1882.

The second main theme of this book is of changing estate management policy and philosophies in the period. This links directly into the role of and relationships between the Sutherland estate staff, the crofting and large tenants on the estate, and government agencies in the region. The personal sinews of estate management, the key personalities of the period, and the way in which external political and governmental changes in the Highlands impacted upon them, are the framework of this book. Very little has been written on Highland estate management in the post-1860 period; the model used here has been the work of Eric Richards, which deals with the Sutherland estate, using its archive as a principal source, in the period 1780 to 1855.[6] This book is an attempt to continue the narrative and investigation started by Richards. The present study attempts to clarify some over-simplifications regarding the Sutherland estate management through decades of huge change and occasional acute crisis. The common contemporary assumption that the Sutherland estate management was a monolithic and efficient structure is challenged; its deficiencies, fractures, and, sometimes, its complete breakdown under both internal and external pressures are exposed.[7] The Sutherland estate needs to be regarded as a complex, elaborate, hierarchical structure, prone to breakdown and faction fighting and sometimes ill equipped to deal with the problems facing all Highland estates in the period.

Additionally, the aim of the current study is to put the Sutherland estate into its wider Highland context, principally through current academic debates on the Highland land question, the Crofters War, the role of agencies such as government and the churches and the impact of Irish land agitation in the region in this period.[8] In many of these existing studies, the position and response of Highland estates, including the Sutherland estate, with some honourable exceptions, is deduced without the benefit of using

---

[5] E. Richards, *Patrick Sellar and the Highland Clearances: homicide, eviction and the price of progress* (Edinburgh, 1999), 352–68.

[6] Richards, *Leviathan of Wealth*.

[7] E. A. Cameron, *Land for the People? The British Government and the Scottish Highlands, c.1880–1925* (East Linton, 1996), 196; see Appendix for a complete description of the estate management, 1850–1920.

[8] J. Hunter, *The Making of the Crofting Community* (Edinburgh, 1976); E. A. Cameron, *Land for the People? The British Government and the Scottish Highlands, c.1880–1925* (East Linton, 1996); A. G. Newby, *Radicalism, Ireland and the Scottish Highlands, c.1870–1912* (Edinburgh, 2007); A. W. MacColl, *Land, Faith and the Crofting Community: Christianity and social criticism in the Scottish Highlands, 1843–1893* (Edinburgh, 2006); I. M. M. MacPhail, *The Crofters' War* (Stornoway, 1989); T. M. Devine, *Clanship to Crofters' War: the social transformation of the Scottish Highlands* (Manchester, 1994).

estate papers.[9] This book looks at these debates from the perspective of one of the most important, certainly the largest and richest, Highland estate.

The third and last theme of the book follows David Cannadine's thesis of the 'decline and fall' of the British aristocracy from c. 1880.[10] This has developed into a key historiographical debate among historians working on landed aristocratic and gentry families, and has been a central framework used in this book. The picture of decline painted here matches that described more generally by Cannadine – in the family's once colossal wealth, their territorial dominance, and in their political and social influence – and is one that has been explored in other great aristocratic families and among the class in general.[11] The Sutherlands were able to manage the decline of their economic and social position fairly well, although this was less the case for their political power, which they lost at central and local levels from the mid-1880s.[12] The decline of the Sutherland family broadly matches that of other great patrician families such as the Westminsters and Devonshires: decline, but not complete eradication.[13] As in those families, the cushion of investments and land was large enough to facilitate a financial re-structuring in the early twentieth century, mainly via land sales, which enabled the Sutherland family to service its debt and survive into the twenty-first century with 100,000 acres and Dunrobin Castle to its name. A detailed investigation into this process will be central to this book.

The Sutherland Estate, 1850–1920

For most of the nineteenth century, the dukes of Sutherland consistently enjoyed an annual income of roughly £120,000, but the sources behind this income changed over the century. In 1833, the 2nd Duke had £1.1 million invested in government stocks, but by 1850 this figure had dropped to £506,046: he had spent half a million pounds in under twenty years, principally on building and improving the five family houses and supporting his

---

[9] The work of Cameron is an exception; Cameron, *Land for the People*, 4, 12–13.

[10] D. Cannadine, *The Decline and Fall of the British Aristocracy* (London, 1990), 25–32.

[11] For example, Cannadine, *Decline and Fall*; A. Adonis, *Making Aristocracy Work: the peerage and the political system in Britain, 1884–1914* (Oxford, 1993); A. Adonis, 'The Survival of the Great Estates: Henry 4th Earl of Carnarvon and his dispositions in the 1880s,' *Historical Research*, 64 (1991); D. Cannadine, *Aspects of Aristocracy: grandeur and decline in modern Britain* (London, 1994); D. Spring, 'The role of the aristocracy in the nineteenth century,' *Victorian Studies*, 4 (1960); A. Adonis, 'Aristocracy, Agriculture and Liberalism: the politics, finances and estates of the third Lord Carrington,' *Historical Journal*, 31 (1988); M. Cragoe, *An Anglican Aristocracy: the moral economy of the landed estate in Carmarthenshire, 1832–1895* (Oxford, 1996); J. S. Donnelly, *The Land and the People of Nineteenth century Cork: the rural economy and the land question* (London, 1975).

[12] The political aspect of the 'decline and fall' of the Sutherlands has been examined elsewhere; A. Tindley, '"The Sword of Avenging Justice": Politics in Sutherland after the Third Reform Act,' *Rural History*, 19 (2008), 192–3.

[13] Cannadine, *Decline and Fall*, 135–6.

relations.[14] The clearances also dented the family's finances: the northern estate generated no income between 1811 and 1833, and on top of this, £60,000 of capital was spent.[15] The broad picture of ducal expenditure up to c. 1850 is completed when land purchases totalling £554,000 are added.[16] When the 3rd Duke inherited the estates in 1861, therefore, his income was still £120,000 per annum, but a greater proportion of this sum came from estate rentals, a potentially more temperamental revenue. Luckily for the 3rd Duke, the 1850s and 1860s saw rentals from sheep farming in the north rise considerably and when these began to fall away in the 1880s, sporting rents made up the shortfall.[17] The 3rd Duke continued the traditions of his forebears, despite a reduction in the more secure sources of his income, and made unrestrained capital outlays on grand projects that generated little or no return.[18] The 4th Duke, faced with a shrinking base of capital, low land prices, a depressed agricultural sector and the consequences of decades of unremunerative spending by his forebears, began, along with many other landowners, to sell land to free up capital, which was then invested in more productive ventures.[19] He sold 170,000 acres of land in Sutherland between 1898 and 1913, and used the proceeds to buy land in Canada, which he thought would give him a higher return. Unfortunately for the family coffers, it did not, and the land was sold off by the 5th Duke between 1913 and 1920, at the same time as he put nearly 450,000 acres of Sutherland up for sale.[20]

A breakdown of the income generated by the Sutherland estate itself is necessary to set the policies and activities of the ducal family and estate management in context.[21] There were a few significant trends in the rental income of the estate over the period 1850 to 1920; the significant increase in the rental between 1850 and 1882, from £35,717 to £69,612, was directly attributable to increased rents from large sheep and arable farm tenants. The high point of rental income from the Sutherland estate was 1882; by 1886, the total had dropped slightly to £65,852, and by 1898, just before

---

[14] E. Richards, 'An Anatomy of the Sutherland Fortune: income, consumption, investments and returns, 1780–1880', *Business History*, 21 (1979), 46, 52–3.

[15] Richards, *Leviathan of Wealth*, 231–2.

[16] Richards, *Leviathan of Wealth*, 16, 216, 232; Richards, 'An Anatomy', 55.

[17] Richards, 'An Anatomy', 54, 62.

[18] Large investments were made in the railway infrastructure of Sutherland in the 1860s (£254,064), and in the great land reclamations in the 1870s (£220,000): Richards, 'An Anatomy', 54; 5th Duke of Sutherland, *Looking Back: the autobiography of the Duke of Sutherland* (London, 1957), 32–3.

[19] Cannadine, *Decline and Fall*, 133–4.

[20] 5th Duke, *Looking Back*, 58–9; Cannadine, *Decline and Fall*, 108.

[21] For all the following figures, see: NLS, Acc. 12173, Dunrobin Rental Abstracts, 89 (1862), 94 (1867), 99 (1872); Acc. 10853, Dunrobin Rental Abstracts, 81 (1882), 85 (1886), 92 (1893), 97 (1898), 105 (1906), 113 (1914); Acc. 12173, Tongue Rental Abstracts, 114 (1862), 119 (1867), 124 (1872); Acc. 121273, Scourie Rental Abstracts, 140 (1862), 145 (1867), 150 (1872).

the 4th Duke made his first land sales in the region, the rental was down to £59,257. In 1918, just before the most significant land sales, the total rental had dropped slightly again to £58,643. Overall, the estate rentals started to grow from the end of the Highland famine period in the mid-1850s, up to the early 1880s, at which point the dominating trend was one of decline, although not of a catastrophic nature. An explanation for this overall trend can be found when a more detailed breakdown of the estate rentals is presented; throughout the entire period 1850 to 1920, what the estate termed 'large rents' propped up the overall rental to an extraordinary degree, especially from the 1880s. In 1862, for instance, large rents – sheep and arable farms and shooting lets combined – made up 84% of the total rental. Small rents, that is, crofters' rents, contributed just 16% and 30% of that figure was in arrears. By the 1880s and later, this trend was not only confirmed, but even more pronounced; in 1886, large rents made up 88% of the total rental and of the crofters' rents, 45% were unpaid. Although some of the crofters' arrears can be explained by the political agitation sweeping across the Highlands in the 1880s, in fact, the estate rentals demonstrate that crofters' arrears at all times were rarely less than 20%, and in 1914 stood at a staggering 59%. Crofters' arrears on the Sutherland estate therefore were a chronic and permanent problem facing the management, as this book will make clear.

A brief examination of demographic trends in Sutherland is also necessary, given that ideas about population, migration, emigration and congestion were central to the debate about the Highland Question throughout the whole period covered by this book. [22] The effect on population levels generated by the clearances, famine and emigration was not as immediate as might be expected: the population of Sutherland peaked in 1861 at 25,246, and then began a determined march downwards. The most striking decline in population came between 1901 and 1921, by which time the population of the county had shrunk to 17,802.[23] This broad picture disguises more extreme decreases in some parishes: Assynt, for example, saw a 44.2% decrease in population between 1891 and 1921, with Durness close behind with a 36.8% decrease. That the poorer and more marginal parishes were most affected by population decline is perhaps not as surprising as some other steep population decreases in the central and eastern parishes, particularly Rogart (32.7%) and Loth (39.2%).[24]

[22] R. N. Hildebrandt, 'Migration and Economic change in the northern Highlands in the Nineteenth century, with particular reference to 1851–1891', unpublished Ph.D. thesis (University of Glasgow, 1980), 336–7; M. Anderson and D. J. Morse, 'High fertility, high emigration, low nuptuality: adjustment processes in Scotland's demographic experience, 1861–1914, Part II,' *Population Studies*, 47 (1993), 326.
[23] *Census of Scotland*, 1911 (Edinburgh, 1912), 2233; *Census of Scotland*, 1921 (Edinburgh, 1923), 1874; Hunter, *Making of the Crofting Community*, 107–8.
[24] *Census of Scotland*, 1911 (Edinburgh, 1912), 2231; *Census of Scotland*, 1921 (Edinburgh, 1923), 1868.

This steep decline was a source of urgent concern to government agencies in the Highlands. In the 1850s, the government had been keen to manage de-population; it was felt that the Highland famine had highlighted a 'redundant' population in the region which had to be removed, via emigration, to improve the position of those who remained. In this view, the Sutherland estate management was in agreement: along with most Highland estates they wished to see the poorest, cottar class assisted to emigrate by government and the more prosperous crofters to remain, to prop up the rental roll.[25] By the 1910s and 1920s, however, the government was deeply concerned by the haemorrhage in population and attempted to stem the flow of de-population in an unqualified way, especially in Sutherland, which saw some of the most extreme decreases in population.[26] Essentially, the government and estate management were in agreement in their views on population management from the 1850s, but from 1910 this changed as the government became increasingly exercised by the absolute population decrease taking place.

In order to unpick the complexity of the estate management, an essentially estate-centric approach has been taken, the Sutherland estate papers being by far the most important and influential source used. Central to this book, aside from the estate's relations with its crofting tenants and the government, has been the structure of the management of the estate, the mechanics of policy formation and implementation and life on the ground for the estate staff. The Sutherland estate papers expose the cogs and wheels of a vast estate turning in a way that leads to very different conclusions about Highland estate management commonly found in other sources. Additionally, this book has been structured chronologically in order to make sense of both the enormous size of the estate archive and to maintain a sense of coherence as regards the estate staff and policy in a rapidly changing social and political context. The final chapter takes one crofting township in Sutherland and examines its history in detail between 1850 and 1910 as an illustration of many of the key themes of this book.

The principal problem in using the Sutherland estate records in depth was the danger of developing a myopic estate-centric view. There has been much comment in Highland historiography over the use of particular types of sources and how their use identifies the perspective of the historian in a manner labelled by Cameron as 'sectarian.'[27] Dependence in the present study on the Sutherland estate papers can be defended on two counts: firstly, the archive of a Highland estate the size of Sutherland contains records of huge diversity. From financial records to personal papers, inter-

---

[25] T. M. Devine, *The Great Highland Famine: hunger, emigration and the Scottish Highlands in the Nineteenth Century* (Edinburgh, 1995), 247–9.

[26] Cameron, *Land for the People*, 203–4.

[27] Cameron, *Land for the People*, 9–15; A. Mackillop, *More Fruitful than the Soil: army, empire and the Scottish Highlands, 1715–1815* (East Linton, 2000), 2; Hunter, *Making of the Crofting Community*, 4–5.

nal correspondence between estate management personnel to letters to and from government agencies and both large and small tenants, there is much in the Sutherland archive that is not strictly 'landlord' in content.[28] Secondly, aside from a few key works already mentioned, analysis of the affairs, structure and philosophies of landed estates and landowners in the later nineteenth and early twentieth centuries has been either neglected or based on other types of sources.

Papers of other Highland estates have also been used to set the Sutherland estate more securely into its contemporary Highland context. Five sets of papers have been examined; those of the Cromartie estate in Ross-shire, the Macdonald, MacLeod and Kilmuir estates on Skye and the Sinclair of Ulbster estate in Caithness.[29] The estate papers of three key Skye landlords were chosen for two reasons. Firstly, the extent of the financial limitations or embarrassment of these estates makes them a useful contrast to the Sutherland estate, where the dukes' income was not so heavily dependent on the estate rentals. Secondly, the Skye estates were, like the Sutherland estate, unpopular and vilified by the crofting community and the wider public, for both the extent of their clearances in earlier decades and their treatment of crofting tenants up to and during the Crofters War. They, therefore, provide both a useful contrast to and comparison with Sutherland. The Ulbster estate was chosen as a contrast to the Sutherland estate; although the land there was similar to that in much of eastern Sutherland, and the estate had fewer financial problems than the Macdonald estates, they also had far fewer crofting tenants. What this meant for policy formation and investment strategy provides an interesting contrast with the Sutherland estate. The Cromartie estate was actually part of the Sutherland empire up to 1893, brought into the family by the 3rd Duke's first wife, Anne Hay Mackenzie.[30] The upper estate management was therefore the same as that in Sutherland, creating some common ground between the two estates, but also highlighting some key differences, principally that of the precarious financial position of the Cromartie estate.[31]

A range of other sources has been used to broaden the perspective of the book generally and to put the Sutherland estate more firmly into its geographical and political context, including contemporary newspapers, both 'crofting' and 'landlord' in view. Principally, however, it has been government records that have provided the other main perspective on the estate. These include Parliamentary papers, ranging from the records

---

[28] O. Geddes and A. Tindley, 'Who Owns History – archivists or users? The Sutherland Estate Papers: a case study', *Scottish Archives*, 13 (2007), 27–9.

[29] National Archives of Scotland [hereafter NAS], Cromartie Estate Papers, GD 305; Armadale Castle, Macdonald MSS, Skye; Sinclair of Ulbster MSS, Thurso; Highland Council Archives, D123, Kilmuir Estate MSS; Dunvegan Castle, MacLeod of MacLeod MSS.

[30] E. Richards and M. Clough, *Cromartie: Highland life, 1650–1914* (Aberdeen, 1989), 378.

[31] Richards and Clough, *Cromartie*, 246, 248, 252–5.

of the Crofters Commission (1886–1912), the Congested Districts Board
(1897–1911), and the Scottish Office.[32] The use of these records has led to
consideration as to how the estate, the Sutherland crofters and the government interacted and dealt with one another, and has exposed the possibilities for conflict, given the different pressures and desires driving the three
groups. It is the records of the estate management which are central to this
book, however, in all their complexity and contradictory perspectives.

---

[32] NAS, AF67 Crofting Files; AF42 Congested Districts Board Files; Papers of the High Court
of Justiciary, JC26; Papers of the Sheriff Court of Dornoch, SC9/47.

CHAPTER ONE

'The condition of its peasantry is wonderfully higher in every respect': The Sutherland Estate, 1850–70[1]

Introduction

While acknowledging pockets of economic crisis, the decades between the end of the Highland Famine and the start of the Crofters War in 1882 have been tentatively labelled by Hunter as a 'period of relative prosperity'.[2] Economic recovery after the famine, helped in turn by rising agricultural prices and stricter estate policies as to subdivision of crofts, led to slowly improving living standards for most of the crofting population of the Highlands.[3] For British agriculture as a whole this period has been seen as a golden age of high prices, investment in the new technologies of 'high farming' and increasing rental income.[4] Other historians present a more pessimistic view of the crofting economy, however, pointing to the fragility of this economic recovery, most famously in the downturn in 1880–1, which has been identified as a major impetus for the outbreak of agitation in 1882.[5] One of the key concerns of both Highland estate managements and central and local government was the fact that since the famine, the numbers on poor rolls across the region had been increasing, instead of decreasing.[6] The Sutherland estate's responses to these seemingly intractable problems will be examined in this chapter. The attitude of the estate management towards the small tenants saw very little change, however; being a combination of exasperation, anger, fear and as a burden, both financial and social, on their landlord.[7]

---

[1] National Library of Scotland [hereafter NLS], Sutherland Estates Papers, Acc. 10225, Policy Papers, G. Loch to Peacock, 14 Dec. 1868.

[2] J. Hunter, *The Making of the Crofting Community* (Edinburgh, 1976), 119–20; T. M. Devine, *Clanship to Crofters' War: the Social Transformation of the Scottish Highlands* (Manchester, 1994), 200, 206–7.

[3] Hunter, *Making of the Crofting Community*, 107–11.

[4] G. E. Mingay, *Land and Society in England, 1750–1980* (London, 1994), 195–6.

[5] T. M. Devine, *The Great Highland Famine: hunger, emigration and the Scottish Highlands in the nineteenth century* (Edinburgh, 1988), 83–104. This included a collapse in sheep farming incomes: W. Orr, *Deer Forests, Landlords and Crofters: the Western Highlands in Victorian and Edwardian times* (Edinburgh, 1982), 13–17.

[6] PP 1859 *Thirteenth Annual Report of the Board of Supervision for the Relief of the Poor in Scotland*, vi.

[7] W. E. Vaughan, *Landlord and Tenant in Mid-Victorian Ireland* (Oxford, 1994), 104.

The response of the crofters and cottars of the estate to continuing economic difficulties and estate management policy will also be considered, particularly through agitation. Although on nothing like the scale seen in the 1880s, crofter agitation was a fairly regular occurrence on the Sutherland estate from the 1850s. For instance, in April 1851, Evander McIver, the Scourie factor, wrote to James Loch, commissioner for the Sutherland estates, reporting rebellion among the crofting tenants of Elphin, Assynt:

> When I think of the very awkward position in which we are placed, with the law set at defiance and the people who did so glorying in it, and wholly disregarding our authority and wishes, and when I reflect on the dangerous tendency which allowing the people to have the upper hand and no legal notice taken of them, I cannot but look to the future with doubt and apprehension.[8]

The origins of this dire proclamation can be found in the preceding January, when McIver suggested that as the Elphin crofters were in arrear of rent, a portion of their common grazing should be removed and added to Cromault sheep farm, which would additionally 'stimulate the tenants of these townships to pay more punctually'.[9] Summonses of removal were issued in early February 1851; to McIver's surprise and Loch's consternation, the sheriff officer who was sent to Elphin to serve the summonses was promptly deforced.[10] Fear of attracting unwanted and unfavourable publicity precipitated a loss of nerve on the part of the 2nd Duke and Loch. No further legal action was taken and the grazing was left for the Elphin people.[11]

By June, McIver wrote that 'the spirit displayed at Elphin is fast spreading in the district, and I fear we are to reap bitter fruits from the passiveness with which the Elphin people were treated for their illegal and violent conduct'.[12] Another pasture dispute, this time with the township of Achniskill, blew up when McIver tried to annex a section of the township's pasture to the Inn at Rhicoinich. McIver was sufficiently concerned to go to Achniskill himself, and found that 'all the men were absent but the women turned out with violence and virulence which I have never seen and I saw the best course was to leave them and to apply to the legal authorities'.[13]

---

[8] NLS, Sutherland Estates Papers, Dep. 313, 1181, McIver to Loch, 25 Apr. 1851.
[9] NLS, Dep. 313, 1181, McIver to Loch, 3 Jan. 1851.
[10] NLS, Dep. 313, 1181, McIver to Loch, 28 Mar. 1851. Deforcement is a Scottish legal term, meaning a legal official has been physically prevented from carrying out his duties; E. Richards, *The Leviathan of Wealth: the Sutherland fortune in the Industrial Revolution* (London, 1973), 272.
[11] NLS, Dep. 313, 1181, Loch to McIver, 24 Jun. 1851; Loch to Duke, 24 Jun. 1851; Richards, *Leviathan of Wealth*, 272.
[12] NLS, Dep. 313, 1181, McIver to Loch, 20 Jun. 1851.
[13] NLS, Dep. 313, 1181, McIver to Loch, 20 Jun. 1851.

McIver believed that the violence seen in Achniskill was a direct result of the lenient approach the upper estate management had taken towards the Elphin deforcers and felt that an example had to be made to save the estate from further violence:

> One of them [an Achniskill tenant] told the ground officer blood must be shed before they would yield – nothing but the strong arm of the Law put in force with decision will arrest the feeling now so common in the minds of the people of this district, and if I am to continue in it, I cannot undertake to carry on my duties unless assisted in punishing those who display such a spirit.[14]

This was the first occasion on which McIver would threaten to resign in his fifty-year tenure as Scourie factor, though it would not be the last. McIver felt that nothing less than the rights of property and his authority to enforce them was at stake, but Loch was less certain. He saw the necessity for decisive action, but was wary from the bitter experiences of the 1810s of both bad publicity for the estate and the long-term impact of the removal policy: 'there is no doubt that the people must not be permitted to perpetually violate the law, but it requires us on the other hand to be very careful not to unite them in a common interest to oppose it'.[15] McIver eventually resolved the dispute, reporting in October 1851 that 'after considerable delay and negotiation which required to be conducted with care and tact, I have without appearing to interfere got the Achniskill tenants to send me the enclosed letter [of capitulation]'.[16] It had taken the estate management over nine months to resolve a minor grazing dispute with one township of small tenants.

This chapter has begun with this controversial, but not uncommon, episode because it illustrates a number of key patterns in the Sutherland estate management. The first of these is the ducal family's increasing aversion to the clearance policy, particularly when it was resisted; concern to protect their fragile public image was, by 1851, more important to them than maintaining crofter discipline. Secondly, continuing adjustments to tenancy boundaries initiated by the estate management generated low level but frequent conflict with the small tenants. Although there were no clearances on the scale seen in the early nineteenth century, regular adjustments were made, creating numerous flashpoints throughout the period. Thirdly, frequent inter-managerial conflict, most commonly between the upper management of commissioner and duke and those 'on the ground', factors and ground officers, was endemic and clearly detrimental to the efficient running of the estate. Fourthly, the actions of the Achniskill crofters, both in their tactics in opposition to estate policy and their desperate

---

[14] NLS, Dep. 313, 1181, McIver to Loch, 20 Jun. 1851.

[15] NLS, Dep. 313, 1181, Loch to McIver, 24 Jun. 1851; Richards, *Leviathan of Wealth*, 261; Vaughan, *Landlord and Tenant*, 112.

[16] NLS, Dep. 313, 1516, McIver to Loch, 21 Oct. 1851.

economic position, were replicated across the whole of the estate.[17] This chapter will consider these issues of estate management philosophies and practice, and the impact of continuing economic problems in the region, for the estate, crofters and sheep farming tenants.

'Holds up the management to public condemnation': the Sutherland Estate staff and finances[18]

This section will examine two key aspects of the Sutherland estate; its financial structure and the duties and responsibilities of its staff. The 1850s saw a high turnover of staff, at the top level of commissioner and among the factors: such a widespread change would not be repeated until the 1880s, and the process would be fraught with tension and bitterness. How new factors were recruited and what their duties were will be outlined, as will their attitudes towards their role and status, and the many tenants, both large and small, that they managed.

The Sutherland estate management was a complex structure; at the top was the duke of Sutherland, who delegated most of the day-to-day running of his estates, businesses and investments to his commissioner.[19] The commissioners were far more than land managers, however; they were influential men in their own right, exemplified by the Loch dynasty, which ran the Sutherland estates in England and Scotland from 1812 to 1879. Both James Loch and his son and successor to the commissionership, George Loch, were MPs, and both trained for the Bar.[20] James Loch developed an elaborate style of management in which he was immersed in every aspect of estate management and the ducal finances: no detail was too small for him.[21] Although such minutiae as poaching cases and building repairs could easily have been left to the factors, he was also arbiter on much more important issues.[22] James Loch did not have a happy contemporary reputation and was described as 'a man of iron will and seemed to carry out his views with despotic authority.'[23] This was not only the view of the crofters, or interested observers, but at times the factors too.[24] All action taken by the factors or ground officers had to be sanctioned by the commissioner, from bringing actions against crofters in the Small Debt Court, to the creation

---

[17] Agitation periodically flared up on other Highland estates in this period, which has generally been considered by historians as peaceful: for instance, Highland Council Archive [hereafter HCA], Papers of Christie and Ferguson, solicitors, Kilmuir Estate MSS, D123/1v, William Fraser to Alex. Macdonald, 3 Mar. 1865.

[18] NLS, Dep. 313, 1542, Crawford to Loch, 17 Oct. 1859.

[19] See Appendix for a full description of the estate staff, 1850–1920.

[20] Richards, *Leviathan of Wealth*, 19, 23.

[21] Richards, *Leviathan of Wealth*, 25–6, 32.

[22] NLS, Dep. 313, 1182, J. Loch to 2nd Duke, 3 Jun. 1852.

[23] J. Mitchell, *Reminiscences of my Life in the Highlands*, vol. II (1884: Newton Abbot, 1971), 93.

[24] E. Richards, *The Highland Clearances: people, landlords and rural turmoil* (Edinburgh, new edn 2008), 154–5.

of a new boundary or road or the administration of large tenancies. The factors were the eyes and ears of the commissioner, who would usually travel to Sutherland only once a year with the ducal family to deal with business in person. The very structure of society was part of the commissioner's remit and both James and George Loch worried about the wide social and economic gap between a high proportion of impoverished people and the large tenants, principally sheep farmers. As James Loch pointed out to the Dunrobin factor just before his death in 1855,

> The result of the exclusive management has been to draw too strict a line of demarcation between the Gentry and the people. This is not a safe state of things . . . You have frequently referred to the injury done among the people by the doctrines inculcated on them by the worst portion of the Press. My belief is that this effect can hardly be over-rated and that very unsafe opinions have been industriously propagated among them, and that it has only been checked and kept in order by the real esteem in which the Duke is held.[25]

James Loch had overseen the great clearances of the early nineteenth century and latterly, emigration in the wake of the Highland Famine.[26] According to Loch's clearance ideology, both the estate and the small tenants should have benefited economically and socially.[27] But any progress had been slow and fragile, as amply demonstrated by the Highland Famine. Such an event should not have occurred in Sutherland: the clearances were intended to prevent exactly that kind of catastrophe from happening.[28] By the time of his death, James Loch had come to realise that the clearances, with all the accompanying bad press coverage on the ducal family, had failed as a permanent solution to the problems of the county. Indeed, by the 1850s, he regarded the crofters on the estate as socially and politically alienated:

> I have for years been convinced and have stated that conviction to those in power, that there is no feeling of attachment to the Constitution or the present order of society among the working classes of the towns and villages in the north of Scotland. It is the natural turn of their minds, they are great readers and their local press is of the worst description, tending as far as it dares to preach socialism and its accompanying doctrines.[29]

---

[25] NLS, Dep. 313, 1222, Loch to William Gunn, 22 Mar. 1855; Richards, *Leviathan of Wealth*, 31.

[26] Richards, *Leviathan of Wealth*, 19.

[27] J. Loch, *An Account of the Improvement on the Estates of the Marquis of Stafford in the counties of Stafford and Salop and on the estate of Sutherland* (1820), 60, 168.

[28] NLS, Dep. 313, 1182, Loch to 2nd Duke, 11 May 1852; Richards, *Leviathan of Wealth*, 155–6.

[29] NLS, Dep. 313, 1179, Loch to 2nd Duke, 13 Aug. 1850; Richards, *Leviathan of Wealth*, 275. Loch is probably referring to the *Northern Ensign*, a paper which was fiercely and consistently critical of the Sutherland estate's policies.

By the 1850s, there were fears among the upper estate management that any residual clan loyalty to the house of Dunrobin had evaporated.

George Loch continued the practices developed by his father when he became commissioner in mid-1855. He was, however, eager to improve upon his father's methods and impressed upon the factors the necessity of his being kept informed of every detail of management: 'I labour under considerable difficulty in consequence of there being no method by which I may be kept informed of all matters of interest and importance occurring on the estate.'[30] Loch instituted a system of weekly ground officers' reports and fortnightly factors' reports, so that this difficulty could be rectified.[31] One of the most important roles of the commissioner was to supervise and direct the estate factors. The factors were well educated and experienced individuals, all having held posts on other estates before being appointed to the Sutherland management.[32] They were as a rule never locals and were not usually native to the Highlands, it being thought by the ducal family and commissioners that an outsider would bring a more balanced approach. They tended to be equal to or above Sutherland society, including the large tenants and the rest of the small 'middle' class of the Highlands; ministers, doctors and teachers.[33] The job was extremely demanding; the Tongue factor, John Horsburgh, ruefully wrote in 1859 that 'in these bustling times the office of a Highland factor cannot well be anywhere a sinecure'.[34] Aside from the Scourie factorship, which Evander McIver took up in 1845, both the Tongue and Dunrobin managements saw a staff turnover in 1859. Such a significant change gives a useful insight into the duties expected of a factor, their relationship with the upper management, their initial reactions to their duties and social circumstances in Sutherland and their changing attitudes over time.

John Horsburgh had been Tongue factor since 1837; in 1857 he began considering his retirement, a process that became increasingly painful and fraught with tension.[35] Often, well-established factors found it hard to adjust to new colleagues, especially superiors, and when George Loch took the commissionership in 1855, problems had arisen. Horsburgh wrote a letter of resignation in January 1859, and on being requested to give his reasons, made it clear that it was to George Loch's intrusive and controlling style of

[30] NLS, Dep. 313, 1223, G. Loch to William Gunn, 25 Nov. 1855.
[31] NLS, Dep. 313, 1223, Loch to William Gunn, 25 Nov. 1855; Vaughan, *Landlord and Tenant*, 107.
[32] E. McIver, *Memoirs of a Highland Gentleman: being the reminiscences of Evander McIver of Scourie*, Rev. G. Henderson (ed.) (Edinburgh, 1905), 33–8, 57, 59; Vaughan, *Landlord and Tenant*, 110.
[33] Richards, *Leviathan of Wealth*, 248; Hunter, *Crofting Community*, 121–2; J. S. Donnelly, *The Land and the People of Nineteenth Century Cork: the rural economy and the land question* (London, 1975), 173, 175, 178, 184.
[34] NLS, Dep. 313, 1541, Horsburgh to McIver, 25 Feb. 1859.
[35] NLS, Dep. 313, 1541, Horsburgh to 2nd Duke, 19 Jan. 1857.

management that he objected: 'I made it both my pleasure and my duty loyally to recognise and uphold your authority as Commissioner ... but while I did so, I never ceased to feel that I had, like yourself, been bred to business and that I could not under any circumstances consent to be reduced to the position of a mere sub-factor.'[36] Initially, Loch requested Horsburgh to reconsider, and Horsburgh took the opportunity to list his demands:

1. My position as factor of the Tongue district to continue as it was under the late Commissioner and the appointment and dismissal of all subordinates to rest as heretofore with me.
2. A few weeks leave of absence in each year to be allowed for relaxation and the maintaining of health.
3. My salary to be raised from £400 to £500.[37]

Although his salary was comparatively respectable (the local doctor's annual salary was only £100, for example), Horsburgh felt it did not reflect his workload.[38] Financial considerations and his indifferent health were important reasons given for his retirement, but the main sticking point seems to have been a breakdown in relations with George Loch. In a letter to the duke, Horsburgh identified the inherent tension in the relationship between factor and commissioner: 'the change in the whole mode of managing the estate adopted by your present Commissioner which I believe to be in some respects injurious to the interests of the proprietor and destructive to the proper status and usefulness of the factors'.[39] The thorny issue of the preservation of the factors' status by the upper management would recur through the decades.

Horsburgh was replaced in mid-1859 by John Crawford, allowing George Loch an opportunity to direct his ideas about status more satisfactorily than he had been able to manage with Horsburgh. In August 1859, Loch wrote to Crawford outlining his principal duties, stressing that his most important field of activity would be relations with the large and small tenants.[40] Loch did not predict any difficulties with the first group:

it is a great pleasure to be able to state that the tenants of the large farms are gentlemen of the highest respectability and position. The Duke studies at all times to treat them with high consideration and seeks to induce them to interest themselves in the affairs of the County, and to take an active part in public business.[41]

---

[36] NLS, Dep. 313, 1541, Horsburgh to Loch, 20 Jan. 1859.
[37] NLS, Dep. 313, 1541, Horsburgh to Loch, 8 Feb. 1859.
[38] S. Blackden, 'From Physicians' Enquiry to Dewar Report: a survey of medical services in the western Highlands and Islands of Scotland, Part I,' *Proceedings of the Royal College of Physicians Edinburgh*, 28 (1998), 62.
[39] NLS, Dep. 313, 1541, Horsburgh to 2nd Duke, 4 Mar. 1859.
[40] NLS, Dep. 313, 1339, Loch to Crawford, 26 Aug. 1859.
[41] NLS, Dep. 313, 1339, Loch to Crawford, 26 Aug. 1859.

Of Crawford's relations with the small tenantry, George Loch was not so sanguine, 'that branch of your management which relates to the lotter [i.e. crofter] population, is, in many aspects, the most important, as it is certainly the most difficult'.[42] Loch laid out the basic philosophy of the ducal family and upper management; the promotion of the social and economic circumstances of the small tenants, keeping well within the laissez faire ideologies of the time:

> The only object which the Duke of Sutherland has in view as regards these people, is the promotion of their moral and material well being – all the managements, all the regulators of the estate . . . have that end in view and no other. It is not the Duke's belief that the prosperity of a people can be established on any secure footing that does not rest on independence of character and persevering industry – he aims, therefore, rather at encouraging these qualities . . . [rather than] giving direct assistance, which only induces the people to lean on others for support, in place of relying on themselves.[43]

It was made clear to Crawford from the moment of his appointment that ducal funds were not limitless, especially where the crofters were concerned.[44] Along with the other two factors, any proposed expenditure had to be approved by Loch and the duke and listed in detailed annual estimates submitted to them.[45]

Crawford's first impressions were positive: 'on the whole the people are much more comfortable or at least have the means of considerable comfort within their reach than I was prepared to expect . . . their condition as a class will compare very favourably with any other Highland population, or in fact with that of many parts of the Lowlands'.[46] As Crawford settled into his post, however, he became concerned about the low standard of agriculture displayed by the crofters, particularly in the stocking of common grazing and their farming methods.[47] Crawford reported that the crofters did not drain or fertilise their arable land properly, annual cropping resulted in pitiful returns and lack of forward planning in the storage of feed crops meant stock starved to death in the spring of every year.[48] Maintaining a positive outlook, Crawford stated he would, 'try to instruct and guide the people so as to induce them to adopt some improvement . . .

[42] NLS, Dep. 313, 1339, Loch to Crawford, 26 Aug. 1859.
[43] NLS, Dep. 313, 1339, Loch to Crawford, 26 Aug. 1859; Donnelly, *The Land and the People*, 199.
[44] NLS, Dep. 313, 1339, Loch to Crawford, 26 Aug. 1859.
[45] R. Perren, 'The effects of the agricultural depression on the English estates of the dukes of Sutherland, 1870–1900,' unpublished Ph.D. thesis (University of Nottingham, 1967), 19–20.
[46] NLS, Dep. 313, 1339, Crawford to Loch, 12 Sep. 1859.
[47] Hunter, *Making of the Crofting Community*, 113–14.
[48] Hunter, *Making of the Crofting Community*, 118–19.

from their peculiar habits, this will take time and persuasion'.[49] More worrying, however, was the crofters' management of common grazing ground, which was universally overstocked due to congestion and the practice of landless cottars setting up home on the common pasture. Crawford soon identified this problem and laid it out, with all its consequences, to Loch:

> I am led to believe that this system – for it is quite a system – of families with inadequate means taking in brothers, sisters or other relations as also parcelling out their lot . . . has existed for a long time . . . There is no doubt a hardship in turning out these people, but they ought never to have been there . . . in doing which [i.e. evicting] he [i.e. the factor] leaves several without a home, full of bitter feelings of discontent and the would be philanthropist catches up the echo of dissatisfaction and holds up the management to public condemnation, for which the people are themselves to blame.[50]

Crawford foresaw other managerial difficulties. Firstly, he expressed distaste at the use of eviction as a tool in the factor's armoury, but crucially, quickly recognised that his concern would be nothing to that of the crofters or the radical press.[51] Secondly, Crawford gradually began to see his position and duties as opposed to the crofters: at best they needed to be educated, at worst, evicted. Crawford soon became convinced that only education could improve the social condition of the Sutherland crofters: 'education is the best appointed axe with which to strike the fatal blow – prepare the minds of the young for taking advantage of the various openings for business and trade and they will as it were instinctively go out beyond their native homes for employment'.[52] Crawford identified a 'surplus population' that he wanted to see emigrate in a 'voluntary vacation', encouraged by education.[53] This represented a notable hardening of attitude towards the poverty-stricken crofters in his management. When, in early 1860, Crawford reported to Loch that he expected widespread suffering in the spring among the crofters, he attributed this to poor crop management and reluctantly accepted Loch's suggestion that the duke provide hay *gratis*, 'and this, not so much to help them out of their difficulty – for they deserve to feel it – so as to prevent loss of rent afterwards through loss of their stock now'.[54]

This attitude had clearly set in by the following year, when Crawford

[49] NLS, Dep. 313, 1542, Crawford to Loch, 12 Nov. 1859.
[50] NLS, Dep. 313, 1542, Crawford to Loch, 17 Oct. 1859: Crawford blames 'the people' for subdivision, but other Highland estates strictly enforced bans on subdivision, for example the Argyll estate; Devine, *Great Highland Famine*, 279–80.
[51] Richards, *Leviathan of Wealth*, 261.
[52] NLS, Dep. 313, 1542, Crawford to Loch, 6 Jan. 1860.
[53] NLS, Dep. 313, 1542, Crawford to Loch, 28 Feb. 1860; Richards, *Leviathan of Wealth*, 264, 271.
[54] NLS, Dep. 313, 1542, Crawford to Loch, 28 Feb. 1860.

wrote to Loch explaining the large volume of small rent arrears, which stood in 1862 at 30%.[55] Crawford began by blaming his own inexperience: 'I have no doubt but that the increase in the arrears . . . arose from my imperfect knowledge of the people, and consequent inability to discriminate in the pathetic appeals made to me.'[56] The bulk of the blame, however, Crawford laid at the feet of the crofters, the root of the evil lying in 'long cherished improvidence, added to habits of the most untidy and even degraded, which convey the idea of poverty greater than what really exists'.[57] A palpable sense of frustration had set into Crawford's tone, and would dog his career until his retirement in 1885. The factor's relationship with the small tenants was fraught with tension and a mutual lack of understanding of language, agriculture and landscape: 'I am astonished to observe the pertinacity with which they put forth their claims to the soil on which they first saw light, as if there could be any distinction peculiarly attached to Sutherland, more than any other county in Scotland.'[58] Crawford saw this attachment to the land as an obstacle for necessary economic and social reform, through improved management of lots and voluntary emigration.[59]

The ducal family of Sutherland was one of the richest landowning families in Britain, but despite this, James Loch was consistently concerned about the economic performance of the Sutherland estate.[60] As he wrote to the duke in 1850, 'the condition of the expenditure on the Scotch estate, must likewise go under revision. That estate is in an anomalous position, mainly expending the whole revenue on it, which no other landlord could do, and leaving none for himself.'[61] The entire annual rental of the estate, which in 1856 stood at £35,717, was ploughed back into the estate in improvements, maintenance and supporting the small tenants.[62] How did this income break down? Essentially, a small number of large sheep farm and shooting tenants paid the bulk of the rental income, and a large number of small tenants paid nominal rents for their tiny plots. In the Tongue management, fourteen large sheep farming tenants paid a total of £5,864.15.0 per year, with Patrick P. Sellar's Strathnaver let bringing the estate £1,178 per

---

55 NLS, Acc. 12173, 114, Tongue Rental Abstracts, 1862.

56 NLS, Dep. 313, 1542, Crawford to Loch, 8 Jan. 1861.

57 NLS, Dep. 313, 1542, Crawford to Loch, 8 Jan. 1861.

58 NLS, Dep. 313, 1542, Crawford to Loch, 28 Feb. 1860; C. W. J. Withers, '"Give us land and plenty of it": the ideological basis to land and landscape in the Scottish Highlands,' *Landscape History*, 12 (1990), 46–7, 52–3.

59 NLS, Dep. 313, 1542, Crawford to Loch, 28 Feb. 1860.

60 D. Cannadine, *The Decline and Fall of the British Aristocracy* (London, 1990), 710.

61 NLS, Dep. 313, 1188, Loch to Duke, 28 Jan. 1850; E. Richards, *Patrick Sellar and the Highland Clearances: homicide, eviction and the price of progress* (Edinburgh, 1999), 362.

62 NLS, Acc. 12173, 80, Dunrobin Rentals, 1856; 104, Tongue Rentals, 1856; 129, Scourie Rentals, 1856; Loch's concerns pale into insignificance when compared with some other Highland estates; the debt on the Macdonald estate, Skye in 1850 stood at £209,521.15/- on a rental of just £12,725 per annum; Armadale Castle, Macdonald MSS, 4667/1 'State of rentals' Nov. 1850; Devine, *Great Highland Famine*, 83.

annum alone, his brother John Sellar's Bighouse farm a further £830 and
Melness sheep farm £640.[63] In contrast, 704 small tenants collectively paid
only £1,759.18.6 per year, with most rents falling between £1 and £2 each.[64]
Similarly in the Dunrobin management, most small tenants paid between
£2 and £5 for their plots, like John MacKay of Acharandra who paid 19/- for
10 acres in Dornoch parish. At the other end of the scale, Patrick P. Sellar's
Morvich and Culmaily let brought in £1,028 per annum.[65] The Scourie
management also followed this pattern, with thirty-five large tenants and
583 small tenants, most of whom paid under £3 per year in rent.[66] Out of
a total rental of £35,717, only £3,923 or 16.2% was paid by small tenants,
and many of these were periodically in arrear.[67] Loch could see only one
solution if the estate was to become self-supporting: 'unless some material
reduction is adopted the painful alternative of a forced reduction may
have to be resorted to at some future period'.[68] Lord Stafford's marriage
to Anne Hay Mackenzie, proprietrix of the ailing Cromartie estate, added
another financially troubled estate to the ducal books, increasing Loch's
fears.[69] Some efforts at reducing expenditure were made at Loch's insist-
ence, but the famine made this difficult, and overall, Loch was unsuccessful in curbing either ducal or estate expenditure.[70] That the ducal family
remained among the top ten richest aristocratic families in Britain was in
spite, not because, of their unprofitable acres in the north of Scotland.

'There will not only be destitution, but actual starvation': the Sutherland crofters, 1850–70[71]

Small tenants made up the greatest proportion of the population on the
Sutherland estate, and this was reflected in the amount of time and effort
the estate management spent on policy formation relating to them. As the
period covering the late 1850s and 1860s has been labelled one of 'relative prosperity' by some historians, an improving economic picture might
be expected.[72] There is some evidence that conditions were stabilising in

[63] Richards, *Patrick Sellar*, 361–2; Patrick P. and John Sellar were two sons of the infamous clearance agent and sheep farmer Patrick Sellar.
[64] NLS, Acc. 12173, 104, Tongue Rentals, 1856.
[65] NLS, Acc. 12173, 80, Dunrobin Rentals, 1856.
[66] NLS, Acc. 12173, 129, Scourie Rentals, 1856.
[67] NLS, Acc. 12173, 80, Dunrobin Rentals, 1856; 104, Tongue Rentals, 1856; 129, Scourie Rentals, 1856.
[68] NLS, Dep. 313, 1188, Loch to Duke, 28 Jan. 1850.
[69] NLS, Dep. 313, 1184, Loch to Duke, 9 Jan. 1853; E. Richards and M. Clough, *Cromartie: Highland life, 1650–1914* (Aberdeen, 1989), 246, 248, 252–5, 378.
[70] NLS, Dep. 313, 1216, Loch to Gunn, 12 Jun. 1850; Richards, *Leviathan of Wealth*, 270, 294–5.
[71] NLS, Acc. 10225, Policy Papers, 211, McIver to Loch, 8 Dec. 1862.
[72] Hunter, *Making of the Crofting Community*, 87, 111; Devine, *Clanship to Crofters' War*, 200; Devine, *Great Highland Famine*, 285.

Sutherland after the famine, especially in the eastern side of the county, but for those living in the north and west, the economic picture was more troubled.[73]

In February 1856, the 2nd Duke wrote to Horsburgh, worried by reports of severe weather and the potential destitution it might spark. Horsburgh was quick to reassure him: 'it is true that we had a heavy fall of snow – a severe storm in short; but to the smaller class of tenantry and cottars in this part of the county, it has fortunately brought no peculiar hardship or suffering'.[74] The duke's concern was understandable; a bout of severe weather was often enough to tip the crofting community in Sutherland into destitution, but this did not happen after 1855, even in the poorest management, Scourie. In 1854, McIver cheerfully reported that 'the district is very healthy, and the people have an abundance of food. We have much cause to be satisfied and thankful when we compare our present position with what it was a few years ago.'[75] For McIver, the memory of the Highland Famine, which had hit the Scourie management particularly hard, was still fresh, and he knew better than any of the other factors how close to the edge of absolute poverty the crofters subsisted. Still, the late 1850s seemed to show significant improvement, as McIver was happy to admit. He saw the evidence of this in the rash of improvements crofters made to their lots and thought that this should be encouraged by the estate, 'to wean them from . . . slothful habits.'[76]

Despite the improving economic picture, McIver was concerned about the growing volume of 'surplus' population in his management; the famine and its aftermath had seen one-sixth of the west coast population emigrate, but now he saw a recovery and was worried, 'every year's experience convinces me that we have so many people who will not go away and cannot be removed if it were wished, more should and more must be done to better their condition – for if not stimulated and taught to improve by their landlord, they have not the energy or the ability or the means to improve as they ought for themselves'.[77] This view was not shared by Loch, or the other factors; they felt that the ducal family had done enough for the small tenants in the famine years, and objected to the principle that the proprietor should take sole responsibility for any relief: that was what the Poor Boards were responsible for: 'suppose however for a moment that suffering did exist, I cannot but entertain grave doubts of the expediency of a proprietor stepping in . . . and relieving the Boards of a burden falling, by Act of Parliament, upon them.'[78]

Despite McIver's worries, there seemed little for the estate to be

[73] Devine, *Great Highland Famine*, 295.
[74] NLS, Dep. 313, 1540, Horsburgh to Duke, 28 Feb. 1856.
[75] NLS, Dep. 313, 1186, McIver to Duke, 17 Jan. 1854.
[76] NLS, Dep. 313, 1520, McIver to Loch, 26 Aug. 1856; Devine, *Clanship to Crofters' War*, 201.
[77] NLS, Dep. 313, 1520, McIver to Loch, 11 Jul. 1856; Richards, *Leviathan of Wealth*, 273.
[78] NLS, Dep. 313, 1540, Horsburgh to Duke, 28 Feb. 1856; A. Blaikie, 'Accounting for

concerned about in the late 1850s. This was especially the case in the Dunrobin management, which sent in uniformly positive reports about the condition of the small tenantry, including the cottar population.[79] This was a period of improving living standards, helped by wider availability of alternative employment possibilities. The east coast fishing was doing well in the early 1860s, with 'an abundant supply of herrings taken all along the coast, furnishing a good supply of food, as well as excellent baits for cod fishing'.[80] Other forms of employment were available to the east coast crofters, such as labouring on railway building projects, including the duke's own Sutherland railway.[81] One key indicator of improving circumstances for crofters was the increasing trend of reclamation and improvement of their lots, which Peacock approvingly reported: 'the open weather of the past winter has afforded the industrious able-bodied workers among them ample opportunity of improving their lots, by draining and trenching new land'.[82] Unlike McIver, Peacock did not foresee difficult economic circumstances for the crofters in his management.

The factors invariably blamed any poverty on the people. Horsburgh pointed to the extraordinary determination with which the small tenants would remain on their tiny patches of land, which discouraged them from emigrating out – the only solution to the congestion and poverty of the region in his view: 'in Sutherland all deem it essential that they should occupy a portion of this soil, and they cling with remarkable tenacity to the patches which gave them birth'.[83] In Assynt, McIver was continually surprised by the squalid, filthy housing and poor social conditions: 'I came away often much disgusted and grieved to find them so careless as to personal cleanliness of any kind . . . they appear only to think it necessary to use water when going from home to Church.'[84] Aside from motivating the people to wash, the factors were concerned about the radicalising influence of Free Church ministers in Sutherland. Crawford never saw eye to eye with the Rev. James Cumming, Free Church minister of Melness, due to his outspoken attacks on estate policy. As Crawford pointed out, 'a man of this type can never do good under any circumstances but in the midst of a prejudiced and ignorant people, may do an amount of harm which a long future and much labour may not easily remedy'.[85] Cumming and his Free

---

poverty: conflicting constructions of family survival in Scotland, 1855–1925', *Journal of Historical Sociology* 18 (2005), 205.

[79] NLS, Acc. 10225, Factor's Correspondence, 273, Peacock to Loch, 9 Jan. 1862; 277, Peacock to Loch, 14 Mar. 1863; 283, Peacock to Loch, 27 Jul. 1864.

[80] NLS, Acc. 10225, Factor's Correspondence, 277, Peacock to Loch, 14 Mar. 1863; Devine, *Clanship to Crofters' War*, 201–2.

[81] NLS, Acc. 10225, Factor's Correspondence, 278, Peacock to Loch, 9 May 1863.

[82] NLS, Acc. 10225, Factor's Correspondence, 274, Peacock to Loch, 13 May 1862.

[83] NLS, Dep. 313, 1540, Horsburgh to Loch, 17 Apr. 1856.

[84] NLS, Acc. 10225, Policy Papers, 212, McIver to Loch, 19 Apr. 1871.

[85] NLS, Dep. 313, 1542, Crawford to Loch, 4 Jan. 1861.

Church colleagues would continue to be a thorn in the side of the estate well into the 1880s.[86]

McIver's predictions of economic trouble for the crofters came true in the early 1860s in the Scourie management. The root problems of an increasing population, and lots too small and poor to fully subsist upon, had created a fragile economy. As he had warned Loch, the crofters were entirely dependent on imported meal and so were slaves to market prices; the whole edifice of crofting society in Scourie was vulnerable to economic downturn: 'bear in mind that the increase in the population leads to a yearly increasing consumption of food, that at the present rate of improvement the increase of people will far outstrip the increase of food produced. Recollect also that these people have no leases, no means, no knowledge, that they are at present very dependent on their landlord.'[87] This statement was as close as McIver came to blaming the vulnerable state of the crofting economy on the clearance policy of earlier decades, but his immediate priority in 1861 and 1862 was to prevent actual starvation in his management.[88]

The destitution of the early 1860s began in the same way the famine had a little over ten years previously – the failure of the potato crop: 'the material condition of the people is less satisfactory this year than last, owing to large purchases of meal . . . and the almost total failure of the potato crop and a less than average corn crop this year . . . Since 1848 there has not been produced so little food for the people of this district.'[89] Added to this was a poor year for the fishings, unseasonably bad weather and the failure of other crops. McIver dreaded a repeat of the famine conditions of the late 1840s, and the upper management dreaded the potential political and financial cost of another economic disaster. The duke and Loch were unwilling in early 1862 to start any extraordinary relief effort for the Scourie people; after all, there had only been one winter of hardship: 'the Duke of Sutherland has decided to abstain altogether from interference in cases of want or destitution, and leave all that to be dealt with by the Parochial Board'.[90] McIver was unhappy with this situation, and begged Loch to 'arm me with some authority to give some employment as a test in some cases'.[91] This was rejected, however, and McIver's worst fears started to come true by the winter of 1862, when he reported to Loch the seriousness of the situation: 'the potatoes are quite a failure all over this district.

---

[86] NLS, Acc. 5931, Papers of Rev. James Cumming, 'Observations of our Land Laws', Mar. 1883; A. W. MacColl, *Land, Faith and the Crofting Community: Christianity and social criticism in the Highlands of Scotland, 1843–1893* (Edinburgh, 2006), 127, 164–5, 167–8.

[87] NLS, Dep. 313, 1520, McIver to Loch, 26 Aug. 1856.

[88] Devine, *Clanship to Crofters' War*, 206.

[89] NLS, Acc. 10225, Policy Papers, 211, McIver to Loch, 27 Dec. 1861.

[90] NLS, Acc. 10225, Policy Papers, 211, McIver to Loch, 24 Jan. 1862.

[91] NLS, Acc. 10225, Policy Papers, 211, McIver to Loch, 24 Jan. 1862; J. S. Donnelly, 'The Irish Agricultural Depression of 1859–64', *Irish Economic and Social History* 3 (1976), 33, 46–7.

Many tenants have already consumed all that grew on their lots . . . I am therefore warranted in concluding that in these circumstances and after so severe a year as the last there will be a very large importation of food and also of seed necessary to maintain the people.'[92] McIver knew that the upper management were not willing to expend money as charity; they had after all done just that in the late 1840s and this had evidently failed to prevent another breakdown in the crofting economy a decade later.[93] Instead, McIver argued that the duke should provide employment and wages for the people, mainly on roads in Assynt, and this the duke finally agreed to in December 1862. McIver was able to 'rejoice' at this decision, and it came not a moment too soon, as McIver pointed out, 'that if work be not provided there will not only be destitution but actual starvation'.[94]

The winter of 1862 was the lowest point for the Scourie crofters, but conditions did not materially improve until 1865, a situation in which McIver found it 'really difficult to keep cheerful or in good humour'.[95] Poor weather in late 1863, plus another failure of the herring fishing, meant that by the spring of 1864, McIver had to request seed for 'the poorest'.[96] One of the results of this spate of destitution was that small rents were paid very irregularly and the volume of arrears shot up. McIver wearily pointed out that 'the means of the people have become so reduced by the recurrence of bad crops and fishings in past years that this is not so much to be wondered at'.[97] The situation began to improve after 1865, but the fragility of the economy on the west coast was again painfully demonstrated in 1868–9, when conditions sank to the lows of 1862, McIver reporting, 'many complaints of starvation – and I do believe there never was more scarcity of food or more actual pinching and suffering'.[98] McIver convinced the 3rd Duke to start a land reclamation project at Clashmore, Assynt to provide employment for local destitute crofters, the long-term results of which are explored in Chapter six.

That the late 1850s and 1860s heralded a period of relative prosperity can be accepted for the Sutherland estate, with a heavy emphasis on 'relative'; relative as to the climate, the availability of employment opportunities, and the vagaries of fish migration patterns and potato disease. There was a slow improvement in material conditions for crofters in Sutherland, especially slow on the west coast, but this progress could be reversed with frightening speed by a poor season or two.[99] McIver had seen the worst effects of the

[92] NLS, Acc. 10225, Policy Papers, 211, McIver to Loch, 13 Nov. 1862.
[93] Richards, *Leviathan of Wealth*, 263, 267.
[94] NLS, Acc. 10225, Policy Papers, 211, McIver to Loch, 8 Dec. 1862.
[95] NLS, Acc. 10225, Policy Papers, 211, McIver to Loch, 2 Oct. 1863.
[96] NLS, Acc. 10225, Policy Papers, 211, McIver to Loch, 15 Mar. 1864.
[97] NLS, Acc. 10225, Policy Papers, 211, McIver to Loch, 20 Nov. 1864.
[98] NLS, Acc. 10225, Policy Papers, 212, McIver to Loch, 17 Mar. 1869.
[99] Agricultural depression also hit Ireland in the early 1860s, with similar results for small tenants there; Donnelly, *The Land and the People*, 200.

famine in Sutherland in the late 1840s, and lived in dread of the situation recurring, heralding bouts of crushing poverty for the crofters.[100] The estate's response was to wait until the last possible minute before doling out aid, desperate to break the dependency of the crofters on their landlord.

In the 1860s, Loch attempted to address this difficulty by establishing a poor house for the county, which he believed would be a much more effective 'test' of poverty than that attempted by the Boards. The idea of a poor house had been mooted a decade earlier by his father, James Loch: 'it would certainly be advantageous to repress the increasing desire to be put upon the poor roll . . . the feeling of disgrace that attached itself to getting Parochial relief had disappeared entirely'.[101] It was precisely this difficulty of an ever-increasing poor roll in Sutherland and the financial burden this represented to the duke as the largest ratepayer that George Loch wanted to resolve. All poor relief in Sutherland was granted as outdoor relief, which had led to a 'present state of things not only extremely disadvantageous in a financial point of view, but they are still more mischievous as regards the social and moral condition of the people'.[102] Loch argued that a bad example was set to the people, and that friends and relatives of paupers, who should have supported the destitute among themselves, encouraged them to take poor relief instead. This had fairly predictable results: 'a rapid decline among the people of all those qualities of vigour and virtue, which are founded on self-respect and on a confidence in the efficacy of perseverance and action'.[103] In 1862, for instance, a total of 1,001 people (811 of whom were female) were on the poor roll in Sutherland, out of a total population of 24,157, costing the ratepayers £5,211.11.4.[104] As by far the largest ratepayer in every parish in the county of Sutherland, the duke and estate management were keen to come up with a consistent policy to deal with the widespread poverty and occasional destitution of the small tenants. Loch argued that the only way to stem the flood of pauperism in Sutherland was to introduce the 'check imposed by the Poor House', which would also have the benefit of helping those really infirm or destitute.[105]

---

[100] Richards, *Leviathan of Wealth*, 271; Devine, *Great Highland Famine*, 295.

[101] NLS, Dep. 313, 1181, J. Loch to 2nd Duke, 27 Oct. 1851.

[102] NLS, Dep. 313, 1339, Loch to 2nd Duke, 7 Jun. 1859; this view was expounded by the Board of Supervision of Poor Relief also, which wanted to see a reduction in outdoor relief in favour of an extension of the more supervised care provided by indoor relief: A. Paterson, 'The Poor Law in Nineteenth Century Scotland', in D. Fraser (ed.), *The New Poor Law in the Nineteenth Century* (London, 1976), 190–1.

[103] NLS, Dep. 313, 1339, Loch to 2nd Duke, 7 Jun. 1859.

[104] PP, 1863, *Seventeenth Annual Report of the Board of Supervision for the Relief of the Poor in Scotland*, 100, 154.

[105] NLS, Dep. 313, 1339, Loch to 2nd Duke, 7 Jun. 1859; the Board of Supervision agreed with this view; PP 1859 *Thirteenth Annual Report of the Board of Supervision for the Relief of the Poor in Scotland*, vii–ix; S. Blackden, 'The Board of Supervision and the Scottish Parochial Medical Service, 1845–95', *Medical History*, 30 (1986), 147.

The factors put their support behind a poor house, with some qualifications. Crawford argued that a poor house was needed to 'relieve a burden now heavily pressing on property', but argued for a more holistic approach towards lifting the small tenants out of poverty: 'in connection with a poor House, any well devised scheme of improvement of property . . . so as to afford the means of earning a livelihood to all able and willing to work, would, I apprehend, act most beneficially'.[106] In September 1861, all of the Parochial Boards of Sutherland agreed to the principle of combining to build a poor house for the county at Swordale, near Bonar Bridge.[107] As in many other Highland parishes, each Parochial Board alone could not possibly aspire to its own poor house, but had to agree to combine with neighbouring parishes to raise the necessary funds.[108] This process was relatively simple in Sutherland, where the largest heritor owned almost the entire county, reducing the potential friction between the Boards, all of which were chaired by estate factors.

Once this agreement had been reached, however, difficulties arose. Loch began to get cold feet over the amount of capital that would be needed to build the poor house, as he confided to Peacock, 'the large total makes me feel anxious about the experiment in its merely pecuniary aspect'.[109] Despite this, the poor house went ahead, the total cost of £6000 split between the twelve Sutherland parishes.[110] It was first opened to inmates in 1865; by 1868, Peacock could happily report that 'the Poor House Test has been satisfactorily applied in a great number of cases in this county – the result being a considerable decrease in the annual expenditure'.[111] Despite this positive report, the poor house did not succeed in redressing the balance between outdoor and indoor relief in the county. In 1867, for example, only four out of the fifty poor house places were occupied, and by 1886, although the number had risen to

---

[106] NLS, Dep. 313, 1542, Crawford to Loch, 6 Jan. 1860; O. Checkland, *Philanthropy in Scotland: social welfare and the voluntary principle* (Edinburgh, 1980), 315–16.

[107] NLS, Dep. 313, 1342, Loch to Crawford, 24 Sep. 1861; National Archives of Scotland [hereafter NAS], HH23/10, Minutes of the Board of Supervision, 30 Oct. 1862, 6 Nov. 1862, 27 Nov. 1862. Other Highland parishes had built combination poor houses along the same principles: NAS, HH23/8, Minutes of the Board of Supervision, Skye, Islay, Thurso and Black Isle combination poor houses.

[108] Blackden, 'Board of Supervision,' 156–7, 162; Paterson, 'Poor Law in Nineteenth Century Scotland', 179, 181; M. A. Crowther, 'Poverty, Health and Welfare', in W. H. Fraser and R. J. Morris (eds), *People and Society in Scotland vol. II 1830–1914* (Edinburgh, 1990), 272, 274.

[109] NLS, Acc. 10225, Policy Papers, 79, Loch to Peacock, 9 Apr. 1865; NAS, HH23/10, Minutes of the Board of Supervision, 2 Apr. 1863, 22 May 1863.

[110] PP, 1867–8, *Twenty-Second Annual Report of the Board of Supervision for the Poor in Scotland*, 249; R. MacLeod, 'The Sutherland Combination Poor House', *Transactions of the Gaelic Society of Inverness*, 63 (2004), 295.

[111] NLS, Acc. 10225, Factor's Correspondence, 297, Peacock to Loch, 7 Jan. 1868; NAS, HH23/12, Minutes of the Board of Supervision, 19 Oct. 1865, 18 Oct. 1866; HH24/32, Minutes of the Chairman of the Board of Supervision, 19 Oct. 1865.

eighteen, less than half of the capacity of the poor house was utilised.[112] Contrary to the hopes of the estate, outdoor relief was cheaper at 1/- per week to the 8/- per week it cost to maintain a pauper in the poor house in the 1880s.[113] Additionally, it made no impact on the widespread poverty and destitution prevalent on the estate; indeed, little progress was made on this front until well into the 1930s. The estate management had built a poor house to control the 'tide of pauperism' in Sutherland; this was an unattainable goal given the range of causes and extent of poverty in the county. It also undermines the argument that this was a 'period of relative prosperity', at least for the western and northern portions of the estate. The crofting economy had recovered from its atrophy in the late 1840s, but was still vulnerable, with most of the small tenants still living in poverty.

Small tenant arrears were the weeping sore of the Sutherland estate finances, and would remain so beyond the First World War. It was a matter of almost constant correspondence between the factors and the upper management, both of which were at a loss to deal with them.[114] Although only a small proportion of the total rental income of the estate came from crofters, the issue of arrears exercised estate staff considerably because the arrears symbolised both the chronic poverty of the population and the ultimate failure of both the clearance policy and estate discipline.[115] Crawford was appalled by the situation, giving Loch the example of,

> A man living at Strathy Point, who occupies five and a quarter acres of land, all improved, at annual rent of 4/- and he and four of his family are in receipt of relief from the Parish funds, while an able bodied son and two daughters live in family with him and partly supported by the produce of the lot. There are other cases of a similar character. The whole of the lots in this township are large, the rents nominal and the result is a den of pauperism requiring three times the amount of rental of the place in the shape of relief.[116]

Crawford's frustration was palpable. He blamed this situation on 'the largeness of the lots and the inability of the original occupiers to manage them, thus opening a door for relations and others to come in and settle down,

---

[112] PP, 1867–8, *Twenty-Second Annual Report*, 238 and PP, 1886, *Forty-First Annual Report of the Board of Supervision for the Relief of the Poor in Scotland*, 220; MacLeod, 'Sutherland Combination Poor House', 297, 300.

[113] MacLeod, 'Sutherland Combination Poor House', 301.

[114] Hunter, *Making of the Crofting Community*, 73; Vaughan, *Landlord and Tenant*, 113.

[115] Between 1862 and 1872, crofters' rents typically represented 14–16% of the estate's rental income and arrears stood between 20 and 30% of that; NLS, Acc. 12173, Dunrobin Rental Abstracts, 89 (1862), 94 (1867), 99 (1872); Acc. 12173, Tongue Rental Abstracts, 114 (1862), 119 (1867), 124 (1872); Acc. 12173, Scourie Rental Abstracts, 140 (1862), 145 (1867), 150 (1872).

[116] NLS, Acc. 10225, Policy Papers, 172, Crawford to Loch, 11 Sep. 1863.

and ultimately becoming a charge on the property'.[117] Not only were the crofters a burden on the poor roll, they consistently failed to pay their rents year after year without any obvious cause.[118] The estate's response to rent arrears was to take a few of the defaulters in each management to the Small Debt Court in the hope of setting an example to the rest.[119] The estate management rarely evicted crofters for non-payment of rent because it was so widespread, and small tenant arrears became a permanent fixture in the estate rental books.

A further intractable and worrying problem, and one intimately linked to that of small rent arrears, was the issue of the cottar population. The factors and Loch identified the root of poverty in Sutherland in these unfortunates, who were not only poverty stricken themselves but were accused of dragging down the living standards of neighbouring crofters. Crawford certainly argued this link existed: 'I should like to do something towards having the rights of property respected and endeavouring if possible to point to some principle by which the tide of pauperism might be stopped; and to do this one must strike at the root of the unquestionable evil which produces much of it . . . those perverse habits [squatting] of the people.'[120] The cottars also created problems for the large tenants in the county, who complained to the estate management when cottars' stock trespassed on their pasture.[121] McIver suggested a decisive policy in dealing with the issue: 'the more firmly and decidedly these people are dealt with by us the better for themselves and for the well being of the estate on which they are placed'.[122] The difficulty of course was, what was the policy to be? 'The cottars of whom you speak, ought certainly to be removed, but so, in fact, ought all cottars – for the existence of this class of squatters is unfair to the tenantry who pay a rent,' wrote Crawford. 'They are in fact mere trespassers, and there is a more summary mode of removing them, under orders from the Sheriff.'[123] But cottars and squatters represented up to 20% of the entire population, and summary removal or interdict for trespass was not a viable solution.[124] Crawford suggested a range of measures, including evicting any tenant who allowed a cottar or lotter onto their land, was in receipt of parochial relief, or unable to pay their rent. He also suggested

---

[117] That is, subdivision of lots; NLS, Acc. 10225, Policy Papers, 172, Crawford to Loch, 11 Sep. 1863.

[118] For example, NLS, Acc. 10225, Policy Papers, 172, Crawford to Loch, 1 Jan. 1864.

[119] For example, NLS, Acc. 10225, Policy Papers, 126, Loch to Crawford, 7 Jan. 1868; M. Cragoe, 'The Anatomy of an Eviction Campaign: the General Election of 1868 in Wales and its aftermath,' *Rural History*, 9 (1998), 179.

[120] NLS, Dep. 313, 1542, Crawford to Loch, 26 Feb. 1861.

[121] NLS, Acc. 10225, Policy Papers, 81, Loch to Peacock, 29 Jun. 1866; Dep. 313, 1333, John Sellar to Horsburgh, 4 Nov. 1856.

[122] NLS, Dep. 313, 1524, McIver to Loch, 5 Mar. 1858.

[123] NLS, Acc. 10225, Policy Papers, 131, Crawford to Loch, 23 Mar. 1873.

[124] Richards, *Leviathan of Wealth*, 274; Devine, *Clanship to Crofters' War*, 200; Devine, *Great Highland Famine*, 291–2.

that 'parties refusing to comply with well considered estate regulations, or who are ring leaders in mischief or in exciting insubordination I would at once and without hesitation remove'.[125]

This long-standing problem reveals two vital points about the estate management. Firstly, the fact that large numbers of cottars had been allowed to live on subdivided or common land points to a key failure of estate discipline. Other estates, most notably the duke of Argyll's, ruthlessly controlled subdivision with eviction; the Sutherland estate appears to have lost its nerve for eviction, a prisoner of its own clearance history and reputation.[126] Secondly, the principle of upholding the rights of property was seen as equally important as dealing with the practical problem itself.

Large-scale eviction of cottars was no longer a realistic policy option; by the 1850s, James Loch was no longer as certain of the long-term success of the clearance policy than he had once been, although he was as punctilious as ever in defending it from visitors or the radical press.[127] One of the most striking failures of Loch's plans was the expectation that crofters would take up fishing as their principal form of employment. By the 1850s, Loch had admitted defeat: 'there are a good many south side boats at Brora, catching and curing immense quantities of cod, the natives looking on . . . the lotters are employed in sowing their land – another proof that the union of Crofter and fisherman is not to be expected'.[128] Nevertheless, Loch was proud of his achievements and always liked to hear praise, as in 1850 when two visiting American sportsmen told him that 'you spoil the people. You put within their power all the comforts of life so cheaply, that they don't work as they ought, they spend half their time doing nothing . . . they were better clothed in every way than the peasantry of the south.'[129] Despite occasional, and qualified, praise like this, the catastrophe of the famine and related emigration could be considered proof of the failure of the clearance policy. Loch himself admitted defeat in the west coast management, but maintained that the small tenants' standards of living would have been even worse if they had been allowed to continue living inland.[130]

George Loch was still less sure of the wisdom of the clearance policy, and he collected information as to the process of clearance, the changing number of tenants in Sutherland, and the tenants' 'progress', both social and economic, to refute recurring claims in the press about the cruelty and failure of the policy.[131] As a rule, the factors were less concerned about the

---

[125] NLS, Dep. 313, 1542, Crawford to Loch, 26 Feb. 1861.

[126] Similarly to the Sutherland estate, the Matheson estate on Lewis was unable to control subdivision of holdings, with grave long-term results; Devine, *Great Highland Famine*, 8, 10, 238–42, 279–80.

[127] Richards, *Leviathan of Wealth*, 274–8; Donnelly, *The Land and the People*, 199.

[128] NLS, Dep. 313, 1182, Loch to 2nd Duke, 11 May 1852; Richards, *Leviathan of Wealth*, 286.

[129] NLS, Dep. 313, 1179, Loch to 2nd Duke, 16 Aug. 1850; Richards, *Patrick Sellar*, 355.

[130] Richards, *Leviathan of Wealth*, 272.

[131] NLS, Dep. 313, 1524, McIver to Loch, 16 Sep. 1859.

public image of the clearances, being convinced that they had done overall good for the people, despite the fact that 'the people themselves were at first great opponents'.[132] McIver argued that public opinion in the matter should be disregarded, as most people were 'not sufficiently informed as to the actual condition of persons and things on Highland estates to be able to form correct opinions or to arrive at safe conclusions'.[133] McIver pointed to the 'peculiar and opposite ideas' held by the uninformed public and asked: 'are we on that account [to] cast our convictions to the winds and be guided wholly by what the public think and say? Surely not.'[134] Loch and the ducal family, however, were never entirely convinced by this, possibly because of the London social circles they moved in, via the royal court, parliament and the clubs, and the ducal family's personal distress at being labelled cruel clearing landowners.

This issue re-appeared during the 1868 election campaign for the Wick Burghs seat, when George Loch and the Sutherland estate management came under attack in the pages of their old enemy, the *Northern Ensign*.[135] This echoed the 1852 election campaign undertaken by his father for the same seat, which he lost due to his local reputation as the architect of the clearances.[136] Loch responded by putting together a short pamphlet attempting to demonstrate through facts and figures the success of the clearance policy. As Loch wrote to Peacock, 'something must now be done to correct the mistakes so prevalent as regards Sutherland . . . that will alike vindicate the memory of those who have gone and establish the claims of those who exist, to having been and being actuated by earnest conscientious desire to promote the welfare of Sutherland'.[137] Loch's factors were very supportive of this action, upset by the 'dastardly attacks' made on Loch and the ducal family.[138] Despite these efforts, the estate management and ducal family were shadowed by their reputation in the following decades, and the issue would rear its head in a particularly destructive way in the 1880s.

Congestion and land hunger were at the root of crofter and cottar grievances in Sutherland and began to be translated into numerous petitions to the estate requesting extensions of land for their townships. The first came in 1856 from cottars in Dornoch, perhaps because the east coast had avoided the worst of the ravages of the famine of the late 1840s and the original clearances had long past.[139] The Dornoch cottars requested more

[132] NLS, Dep. 313, 1524, McIver to Loch, 22 Feb. 1858.
[133] NLS, Dep. 313, 1542, McIver to Loch, 22 Mar. 1858.
[134] NLS, Dep. 313, 1542, McIver to Loch, 22 Mar. 1858.
[135] E. Richards, 'The Military Register and the Pursuit of Patrick Sellar', *Scottish Economic and Social History*, 16 (1996), 40, 54–6.
[136] Richards, *Leviathan of Wealth*, 275.
[137] NLS, Acc. 10225, Policy Papers, 85, Loch to Peacock, 14 Dec. 1868.
[138] NLS, Acc. 10225, Policy Papers, 174, Crawford to Loch, 18 Dec. 1868.
[139] NLS, Dep. 313, 1224, Loch to Peacock, 7 Apr. 1856.

pasture, a request that both Peacock and Loch were happy to consider and eventually grant.[140]

The bulk of the petitions for more land, not surprisingly, came from the north and west of the county, where the greatest numbers of cottars were concentrated and where the quality of the land was much poorer. None of these requests was granted, as they were generally more ambitious in scale, and requests for the same small farms or portions of land would, in many cases, recur well into the twentieth century.[141] Two such cases were the farm of Melness near Tongue, which fell out of lease in 1866, and Unapool, a portion of grazing in Achmore farm in Assynt, in 1859. McIver was absolutely set against giving small tenants any more land in Assynt, and put his point across to Loch in no uncertain terms: 'to give a sheep farm such as Achmore to a set of small tenants would be downright madness – they would never make it pay and could not pay the rent which a sheep farmer of skill and management could afford which this farm under proper management would produce fine stock [sic]; it would under small tenants produce infirm sheep.'[142] McIver also did not want to encourage the crofter population to expand: 'we have too many people already in Assynt and to give Unapool in addition to them would only be increasing the difficulty and entanglements which a large population create'.[143] McIver also made the point that the overall value of Achmore farm would depreciate if Unapool were removed from it, and with no guarantee that the crofters would be able to pay the rent for it, McIver dismissed the request.[144]

Another unsuccessful petition was submitted by the Melness crofters in 1866 for a portion of grazing from Melness sheep farm, which covered an enormous 81,000 acres.[145] The 3rd Duke was inclined to grant their request for two reasons; firstly, because Crawford and Loch were concerned that high sheep prices would put off potential bidders for the lease, and secondly, as a test of this type of crofter request. Crawford worked passionately towards denying this whim: 'I would most earnestly recommend His Grace not to dismember so valuable a farm as Melness with the view of trying an experiment which is certain to end in disappointment and loss.'[146] He shared McIver's view that the small tenants were incapable of managing large areas of grazing, principally because they did not have enough stock to make use of it.[147] Crawford also raised the point that such an action would effectively be a reversal of the clearance policy, and as such an admission of defeat:

[140] NLS, Dep. 313, 1224, Loch to Peacock, 7 Apr. 1856.
[141] NLS, Acc. 10225, Factor's Correspondence, 273, Peacock to Loch, 8 Mar. 1862.
[142] NLS, Dep. 313, 1524, McIver to Loch, 16 Sep. 1859.
[143] NLS, Dep. 313, 1542, McIver to Loch, 30 Sep. 1859.
[144] NLS, Dep. 313, 1542, McIver to Loch, 30 Sep. 1859.
[145] *Scotsman*, 21 Dec. 1865; *Inverness Courier*, 21 Dec. 1865.
[146] NLS, Acc. 10225, Policy Papers, 173, Crawford to Loch, 5 Apr. 1866.
[147] NLS, Acc. 10225, Policy Papers, 173, Crawford to Loch, 5 Apr. 1866.

I believe it would be a great misfortune were His Grace to yield to the sentimentalism of those who would advocate the subdivision of sheep farms for benefit of the small tenantry or any other class. However well the country was suited for these people when living in a semi-barbarous state, now that the change has been effected, both for their good and the Proprietor's – I may say for a national good – it would be the subversion of a right principle and an evil of no small magnitude to go back and unsettle the public mind on a question which everyone capable of forming an unbiased judgement, believes to have been adjusted on a sound basis.[148]

Crawford need not have worried; in May 1866, a serious offer was made for Melness, and all talk of helping the crofters ceased at once.[149] The new tenant, Donald Mackay had signed the lease by July 1866.[150]

The estate's relationship with its large tenants, either sheep farmers or, increasingly, shooting tenants, was vitally important, both financially and socially. The estate management saw the large tenants as providing a good agricultural, social and moral example to the mass of crofters on the estate, or 'the influence of a better class among so many poor ignorant and unreasonable people', as McIver put it.[151] Resident large tenants were always preferred for this reason, and for their contribution to local administration.[152] A Sutherland Farmer's Club was set up and run together with the estate, and deference was given to the tenants' views as to land management and social matters.[153] The relationship did not always run smoothly, however, and disagreements over the renewal of leases, deterioration of land, stock management and rent reductions flared up from time to time, usually when the market for sheep and wool was depressed.

After a severe winter in 1860–1, Crawford wrote to Loch claiming that many of the losses suffered by the large sheep farmers could have been prevented by better stock management: 'non residence and want of proper attention to the necessities of a hill stock . . . are the principal causes of the loss now experienced . . . they mostly seem averse to all innovation on their routine of management'.[154] It was not just in situations of temporary difficulty that Crawford saw much to criticise; the large tenants had allowed the quality of the grazing ground to deteriorate over the years, a lapse that led to demands for rent reductions.[155] The fluctuating state of sheep and

[148] NLS, Acc. 10225, Policy Papers, 173, Crawford to Loch, 5 Apr. 1866.
[149] NLS, Acc. 10225, Policy Papers, 36, Mackay to Crawford, 14 May 1866.
[150] NLS, Acc. 10225, Policy Papers, 173, Crawford to Loch, 25 Jul. 1866.
[151] NLS, Acc. 10225, Policy Papers, 211, McIver to Loch, 19 Oct. 1866.
[152] NLS, Acc. 10225, Policy Papers, 211, McIver to Loch, 19 Oct. 1866.
[153] NLS, Acc. 10225, Factor's Correspondence, 293, Peacock to Loch, 27 Mar. 1867; Richards, *Patrick Sellar*, 352.
[154] NLS, Dep. 313, 1542, Crawford to Loch, 1 May 1860; Richards, *Patrick Sellar*, 353; *North British Agriculturalist*, 11 Apr. 1860.
[155] NLS, Acc. 10225, Policy Papers, 171, Crawford to Loch, 2 Aug. 1861; W. Orr, *Deer Forests*, 14.

wool prices throughout the 1860s were also a problem; a raft of sheep farm leases were due to expire between 1868 and 1871, just as the market was falling, and Loch feared that the consequences would be severe for the estate.[156] The sheep farmers were lobbying for rent reductions, which Loch thought unfair, given that the market could improve at any time, and that many sheep farmers had made significant fortunes over the decades.[157] Instead, the upper estate management allowed some farms to fall out of lease to allow a land reclamation experiment to go ahead, and converted others to deer forests, let out under lucrative shooting leases.[158]

'The difficulty and entanglements which a large population create': conclusion[159]

It is clear that the estate management's relationship with the bulk of its small tenants was an often troubled one, riddled with misunderstanding and tension, despite slowly improving economic conditions through the 1850s and 1860s. The early 1850s were a difficult time for the crofters and cottars; when faced with the economic catastrophe of the famine, many chose to emigrate, especially from the west and north coasts.[160] Although conditions did improve, especially on the east coast, periodic food shortages and real destitution continued to plague the small tenants in 1862–5 and 1868–9. The fragility of the crofting economy was a matter of intense concern to the estate management, both practically and ideologically. Clearly one of the central planks of the clearances – to make the small tenants economically self-sufficient – had failed.[161] This failure was also of practical concern, as the management feared a future of cyclical economic crisis, in which the estate would have to step in and bail out the crofters at considerable extra expense.

Evidently, the clearance policy had failed, especially on the west coast, which defied all attempts at improvement. Although many crofters found employment in the fishing industry, many more depended entirely on their tiny plots of poor-quality land, which underwent further processes of sub-division and squatting. The estate failed to recognise the uncertain nature of the fishing industry, and the common problems of debt, which were unavoidable for crofter-fishermen with no capital. Too frequently, a poor fishing season combined with low prices for agricultural goods or a bout of poor weather could push the crofting population to the brink of destitution over the course of a few months.[162] There was palpable frustration among

---

[156] NLS, Acc. 10225, Policy Papers, 85, Loch to Peacock, 8 May 1868; Orr, *Deer Forests, Landlords and Crofters: the Western Highlands in Victorian and Edwardian times* (Edinburgh, 1982), 14.
[157] NLS, Acc. 10225, Policy Papers, 85, Loch to Peacock, 8 May 1868; Orr, *Deer Forests*, 15.
[158] NLS, Acc. 10225, Policy Papers, 175, Crawford to Loch, 4 Nov. 1871.
[159] NLS, Dep. 313, 1542, McIver to Loch, 30 Sep. 1859.
[160] McIver, *Memoirs*, 79; Richards, *Leviathan of Wealth*, 267–70.
[161] Richards, *Leviathan of Wealth*, 273.
[162] Richards, *Leviathan of Wealth*, 274.

the estate staff at this uncertain economic picture, especially as the large sheep farming tenants, benefiting from high market prices, were doing so well in the 1860s.[163] Often, the crofters' problems were blamed on idleness, conservatism and ignorance, and, most often of all, on their unaccountable habit of dividing their already tiny crofts among family members.[164] The non-payment of rent was the most obvious and frustrating consequence of the crofters' poverty, but there was very little that the estate management could do in practice about small tenant arrears.

The estate management also faced periodic crofter agitation over relatively minor issues. Agitation was most common in the Scourie management, especially in Assynt, the poorest and most densely populated parish in Sutherland. There were no large-scale clearances in Sutherland after 1852, but even small additions of common grazings into sheep farms could spark a reaction in crofting townships. Insecurity was fundamental to crofting life, a problem not helped by the managerial tactic of issuing summons of removal for minor rule-breaking.[165] All of these rules were, it was felt by the estate, for the crofters' own benefit, but due to mismanagement and misunderstanding, the crofters failed to recognise this.

The estate management was facing another problem by the late 1860s, however, one which was potentially much more damaging for its finances. The great sheep farming magnates of the county had long been the mainstay of the estate rental; the 1850s and 1860s had on the whole been good years for them, with high prices making fortunes for some.[166] But by the late 1860s, many of the Sutherland estate's sheep farm leases were due to end and the estate was having trouble attracting new tenants.[167] Although prices were high in 1869 and 1870, a depression in 1868 had scared off many tenants, and the recovered prices put off potential tenants due to the huge sums of capital required to take over sheep stocks.[168] This meant Loch and the 3rd Duke were in a position to institute a radical and expensive scheme to keep sheep farmers attracted to Sutherland: land reclamation.

---

[163] Orr, *Deer Forests*, 14–15.

[164] Hunter, *Making of the Crofting Community*, 115.

[165] Hunter, *Making of the Crofting Community*, 116.

[166] Orr, *Deer Forests*, 13–14.

[167] Staffordshire County Record Office [hereafter SCRO], Sutherland Estates Papers, D593, K/1/8/10, G. Loch to Sir Kenneth Murray, 12 Jul. 1869; Orr, *Deer Forests*, 22.

[168] Orr, *Deer Forests*, 15.

CHAPTER TWO

'A failure in every sense of the word': The Sutherland Reclamations, 1869–93[1]

Introduction

In 1869, George Loch started making enquiries into the potential of reclaiming arable land from the wastes and bogs of Sutherland. He addressed his initial enquiries to two Ross-shire men, William Mackenzie, factor on the Ardross estate, who was well known for his reclamation works there, and a small landowner, Kenneth Murray of Geanies, also highly regarded for his experience in the field. Loch made clear what the reclaimed land would be necessary for:

> These questions must be determined not only with reference to the intrinsic qualities of the land itself, but to considerations bearing upon the interests of the sheep farmers of which it now forms a part. How far, for example, it will be for the advantage of these sheep farms to have additional arable land attached to them?[2]

The total acreage of arable land in Sutherland was disproportionately small; out of a total 1,207,188 acres, only 28,711 were under cultivation and this meant that the large sheep farmers were obliged to send their flocks into Caithness and Ross-shire for winter feeding, as sufficient crops could not be grown locally.[3] The reclamations, using the most modern agricultural technology and theory, aimed to create neat and productive fields from land lying in a 'state of nature', by removing all stones and other obstacles, ploughing it over, fertilising it and cropping it, so that Sutherland sheep farmers would no longer have to line the pockets of farmers and suppliers from outside the county. As the 3rd Duke himself explained to visiting Caithness farmers at his Kildonan works, 'the great object of course, is to increase the stock which these hills will bear, and which is necessarily limited at present from the want of winter keep'.[4]

---

[1] PP XXXVIII–XXXIX, 1895, *Royal Commission (Highlands and Islands, 1892), Report and Evidence* [hereafter *Deer Forest Commission*], Donald McLean, 600.

[2] Staffordshire County Record Office [hereafter SCRO], Sutherland Estates Papers, D593, K/1/8/10, Loch to Mackenzie, 8 Mar. 1869.

[3] C. G. Roberts, 'Sutherland Reclamation', *Journal of the Royal Agricultural Society of England*, 2nd series, 15 (1879), 398.

[4] *Northern Ensign*, 12 Sep. 1878. The cost of wintering was a recurring complaint and when

Land reclamation had been undertaken elsewhere in England, lowland Scotland and in other Highland counties, but the Sutherland works were on the largest scale ever attempted in Britain, in terms of both acreage and financial investment. The 1860s and 1870s saw other development projects in the Highlands, mainly in road, railway and harbour building, but nothing to match the scale of the Sutherland reclamations.[5] There were two main areas of reclamation; the first, known as the Lairg works, were in the central eastern part of the county on the north banks of Loch Shin and ran between 1870 and 1878. They encompassed approximately 1,500 acres and swallowed the bulk of the duke's financial investment. The second works, running from 1877 to 1884, were in the strath of Kildonan and though they were more modest in financial terms, they covered a vast 44,000 acres. These were the two main fields of activity, but there were two other, much smaller, areas reclaimed in Assynt and Tongue.[6] By far the most significant of the two was the creation of a model farm at Clashmore in Assynt: significant because the reclamation of land for this farm necessitated the removal of a number of crofters, the results of which are dealt with in Chapter six. Connected to these reclamation works, and set up to complement them, were various industrial works centred mainly at Brora on the east coast, including a coal mine, brickworks and lime kilns. They were set up on the basis that it would be cheaper in the long run for the estate to produce its own tools and fuel for the works, rather than having to import them.[7] The huge scale of these projects was reflected in the money spent; the total cost was eventually calculated at £210,000, roughly breaking down into £20,000 per year over twelve years out of an annual rental roll of £69,000.[8]

It is striking when looking at the scale of vision and expense of these reclamation works, especially in a purely Highland context, that they are rarely mentioned in modern histories of the region.[9] Yet they were significant outwith their Sutherland context. The 1870s were a decade of deepening

low prices did not offset these costs, as in 1868, sheep farmers could be in serious financial trouble; W. Orr, *Deer Forests, Landlords and Crofters: the Western Highlands in Victorian and Edwardian times* (Edinburgh, 1982), 16; R. Perren, 'The Effects of the Agricultural Depression on the English estates of the Dukes of Sutherland, 1870–1900', unpublished Ph.D. thesis (University of Nottingham, 1967), 19–20.

5 T. M. Devine, *The Great Highland Famine: hunger, emigration and the Scottish Highlands in the Nineteenth century* (Edinburgh, 1988), 274.

6 *Highlander*, 16 Sep. 1876; Ribigill farm, near Tongue, was the other site of reclamation.

7 Perren, 'Agricultural Depression', 25–6.

8 National Library of Scotland [hereafter NLS], Sutherland Estates Papers, Acc. 10225, Reclamations, 5, 'Abstract of expenditure on reclamation of land, buildings and farming to 31 Dec. 1886'; Acc. 12173, 99, Rental Abstracts (1872).

9 For example, in J. Hunter, *The Making of the Crofting Community* (Edinburgh, 1976); I. M. M. MacPhail, *The Crofters' War* (Stornoway, 1989); E. A. Cameron, *Land for the People? The Scottish Highlands and the British Government c.1880–1925* (East Linton, 1996); R. H. Campbell, 'Too much on the Highlands? A Plea for change', *Scottish Economic and Social History*, 14 (1994), 61–3.

mistrust and antagonism towards Highland landownership, criticised for
its allegedly high-handed and profit-driven management, but the 3rd Duke
of Sutherland, through the reclamations, was identified as an exception
to this negative rule.[10] He was variously complimented for his 'energy and
generosity', and described as a 'true nobleman, and far above the vulgarity
of those owners of property who in the spirit of mere dealers in land who
never venture on Improvements unless they are sure of a speedy return
in the base form of pounds, shillings and pence'.[11] This praise is doubly
astonishing when viewed in the unforgiving light of the family's public
reputation as the greatest clearance landlords in the Highlands.[12] The
travails of the Sutherland clearances were fixed in the popular memory,
backed by many publications; some recording eyewitness accounts, others
deconstructing the ethos of the political economy that made the clearances
possible.[13] How far the reclamations went in repairing this poor familial
reputation will be examined in this chapter. Firstly, the practical and financial framework of the reclamations will be outlined, including the extent
of their success. Secondly, there will be an examination of the wider issues
generated by the reclamations, including the personal reputation of the
3rd Duke and general attitudes to land in the Highlands, both as a source
of income and simply as a landscape. Lastly, there will be an assessment
of the political ramifications of the works through the burgeoning land
reform debate, the Crofters War and the investigations and interventions
of government from the 1880s.

The reclamations throw into sharp relief the strengths and weaknesses of
the Sutherland estate management and form an essential context for both
the crofting agitation in the coming decades and the 3rd Duke's investment
activities in other parts of the Empire. Although a unique event in terms of
scale and expense, the reclamations were by no means singular in terms of
style or direction of management. This can be seen in three ways. Firstly,
the personal influence and interests of the 3rd Duke were paramount;
this style of directorship can be seen in every aspect of his career, from
the development of Strathpeffer Spa in Cromartie to his plans for railway
building in the Middle East and Turkey.[14] Secondly, much of the work for
the reclamations was contracted out. For example, when in 1878 the duke

---

[10] *Times,* 7 Sep. 1872; 14 Sep. 1872.

[11] *Scotsman,* 17 Sep. 1872; 24 Aug. 1874, letter to the editor from J. S. Blackie.

[12] E. Richards, *The Leviathan of Wealth: the Sutherland fortune in the Industrial Revolution*
(London, 1973), 253–4, 275–8.

[13] See, for example, K. Marx, 'Sutherland and Slavery, or the duchess at home', *People's Paper*
(London, 1853); D. Macleod, *Gloomy Memories in the Highlands of Scotland* (Toronto, 1857);
A. Mackenzie, *A History of the Highland Clearances* (Inverness, 1883).

[14] E. Richards and M. Clough, *Highland Life: Cromartie, 1650–1950* (Aberdeen, 1989), 257,
269; D. Cannadine, *Aspects of Aristocracy: grandeur and decline in modern Britain* (London,
1994), 60; J. Forbes Munro, *Maritime Enterprise and Empire: Sir William Mackinnon and his
business network, 1823–1893* (Suffolk, 2003), 215–21, 287–90.

appointed an official commissioner for the works, it was George Greig, an agent for Fowler and Sons, the steam plough manufacturer based in Leeds, who was chosen; an outsider, in relation both to the existing estate management and the county. This decision was typical of the estate management's policy, and was perhaps inevitable due to the vast size of the estate. Thirdly, and most importantly, the reclamations can be contextualised within the estate management's central aim when dealing with its acres in Sutherland: to make them economically self-sufficient.[15] This had been the professed aim of the estate since the early nineteenth century and explains the willingness of the family to divert large revenues from its other assets in order to fund huge capital expenditures in Sutherland, firstly on the creation of sheep farms and roads up to the 1850s, then on railways in the 1860s and finally on the reclamations in the 1870s. No equivalent expenditure was lavished on the estate after the end of the reclamations in the early 1880s, for the simple reason that the policy had clearly failed. Despite all the plans, funds and hopes the estate had pinned on these various measures over the course of seventy years or so, the Sutherland family's Highland estates were still not economically profitable.

Practical patriotism

The Sutherland reclamations were the largest works of their type ever attempted in the Highlands, and necessarily with such a vast project, the motivations behind them were complex. For the estate, the central motive was financial. An increase in the arable acreage of the estate, it was deemed, would bring in increased rents from the sheep farmers, who already made up over one-third of the overall rental roll.[16] The preliminary report made by William Mackenzie and Kenneth Murray into the potential for land reclamation in Sutherland hammered this point home:

> The rental of these [farms] we have no hesitation in stating, with good management and a little expense could be doubled, with more than treble the number of respectable tenants . . . We see no reason why a single sheep from this extensive tract of land should be sent out for wintering . . . We could not help thinking that what we saw was the Garden of Sutherlandshire although in a state of nature. We are satisfied that these places are not bringing the third of the rental they are capable of producing.[17]

[15] J. Loch, *An Account of the Improvement on the Estates of the Marquis of Stafford* (London, 1820), 60, 168; E. Richards, *Patrick Sellar and the Highland Clearances: homicide, eviction and the price of progress* (Edinburgh, 1999), 8; Perren, 'Agricultural Depression', 19–20.

[16] NLS, Acc. 12173, 16, Dunrobin accounts (1865); 38, Tongue accounts (1865); 61, Scourie accounts (1865).

[17] SCRO, D593, K/1/8/10, Report by Mackenzie and Murray to Loch, 29 Jun. 1869; it was later said of Kenneth Murray that 'he became a great favourite [of the 3rd Duke's] for

This desire to put the estate on a sound economic footing was part of a long-standing drive on the part of the management to make the estate self-sufficient. By portraying land on the estate as 'waste', with untapped profit potential, Mackenzie and Murray were appealing to the duke's business sense, and to his personal enthusiasm for the latest steam technology. Although secondary to the financial motives of the estate, the duke's interest in modern scientific methods of cultivation did affect the direction of the reclamations.[18] He spent huge amounts buying and modifying steam ploughs, sometimes to his own design; sums that some observers, not least his own commissioner, thought extravagant. This was because the engines, although powerful and time-saving, were not cheap to run and did not save on labour costs; up to one hundred men were needed on each site to clear the plough's path and get it out of frequent difficulties.[19] The engines often broke down, wasting time and requiring expensive repairs, and were also costly to run, one observer claiming, 'they needed a coalmine in front of them and a river of water behind them in the field where they were at work'.[20] It is possible that the duke first became aware of the steam plough in Egypt, when an employee of Fowler and Sons of Leeds gave a demonstration of its prowess on the banks of the Nile in 1863. The duke, 'fired by wonderful visions of what might now be done with the aid of steam', regarded Sutherland as a likely object to benefit from this technology.[21] He invested in eight Fowler steam plough sets, seven traction engines, and personally modified the design to cope with the rocky Sutherlandshire ground.[22] In 1873, the duke was elected a Fellow of the Society for the Promotion of Scientific Industry for these efforts.[23]

These were the two main motives behind the works, but as time passed and it became clear to the estate that the reclamations were a financial and agricultural failure, other motives were flagged up. The duke was seen as undertaking the works at great financial loss for reasons of 'patriotism', dutifully investing in his heritable estates and British agriculture, which by the late 1870s was ailing. The way some reports in the press presented it, the duke had never expected a financial return, only a moral one: 'the Duke of Sutherland has been actuated by public spirit and patriotism, in the highest and purest sense of the word, much more than by commercial considerations'.[24] There is no evidence of this being an original motive for

---

some years . . . not always for harmony in Sutherlandshire', J. Mitchell, *Reminiscences of my Life in the Highlands*, vol. II (1884; Newton Abbot, 1971), 218. On his death, the 3rd Duke built a monument to Murray on the banks of Loch Shin, which is still standing.

[18] Mitchell, *Reminiscences of my Life in the Highlands*, 101–2.

[19] G. E. Mingay, *Land and Society in England, 1750–1980* (London 1994), 195–6.

[20] H. Bonnett, *The Saga of the Steam Plough* (Newton Abbot, 1965), 78.

[21] Bonnett, *Steam Plough*, 54; Mitchell, *Reminiscences of my Life in the Highlands*, 8.

[22] Each plough set cost roughly £1,000; Bonnett, *Steam Plough*, 54.

[23] SCRO, D593, P/27/8/7, Certificate of election of the duke to vice-president.

[24] *John O'Groat Journal*, 13 Aug. 1874; Mitchell, *Reminiscences of my Life in the Highlands*, 101, 105.

the reclamations, but the estate did effectively use this positive comment when it appeared, as will be demonstrated later.

Why this praise was taken up so wholeheartedly by the agricultural and general press, and why so little criticism was made of the works, can be largely explained by the contemporary agricultural context. From the 1850s, despite the doom-mongering of those opposed to the abolition of the Corn Laws, British agriculture had prospered and continued to do so up to the late 1860s, undergoing a period of development known as 'high farming'. The idea behind 'high farming' was to use modern, scientific techniques and equipment, such as steam ploughing, to increase yields. It demanded large capital investment in mechanisation in return for heavy crops.[25] This type of farming was more common in England and lowland Scotland than the Highlands, mainly due to the lack of good-quality land in the Highlands, as well as a deficit of capital of many Highland landowners and their tenants due to the periodic atrophy of the Highland economy in 1846–50, 1862–5 and 1868–9.[26] The vast wealth of the Sutherland family, however, meant that those financial restraints did not apply and, moreover, doubts about the quality of the land, its high altitude and the generally adverse climatic conditions were confidently swept to one side.[27]

The 1860s and 1870s were generally good times for sheep farmers, as they benefited from high sheep and wool prices.[28] For instance, wool prices in 1869 were £1.2.0 and peaked in 1872 at £1.14.0. Similarly, cheviot sheep were selling at between 45 and 56 shillings in 1872.[29] The late 1860s must have seemed like an excellent time to invest, firstly in the fortunes of the Sutherland sheep-farming fraternity, to make the most of favourable markets; and secondly, in the long-term value of the land itself, the family's most stable asset. Indeed, in one letter, Loch's impatience for action shines through, when he claimed that 'these changes and improvements have been in my head for many years past'.[30] As one distinguished visitor put it:

The theory of these improvements is excellent. It is simply to combine with extensive sheep ranges a cultivatable area sufficient to raise winter

[25] G. E. Mingay, *Land and Society in England 1750–1980* London, 1994), 197–9; R. Perren, *Agriculture in Depression, 1870–1914* (Cambridge, 1995), 4–5.

[26] Devine, *Great Highland Famine*, 83–7.

[27] Devine, *Great Highland Famine*, 89–90; D. Spring, 'The role of the Aristocracy in the Nineteenth century', *Victorian Studies*, 4 (1960), 59; D. Cannadine, 'Aristocratic Indebtedness in the nineteenth century: the case re-opened', *Economic History Review*, 2nd ser., 30 (1977), 628, 642.

[28] Orr, *Deer Forests*, 13–15; Hunter, *Making of the Crofting Community*, 107–8; T. M. Devine, *Clanship to Crofters' War: the social transformation of the Scottish Highlands* (Manchester, 1994), 222.

[29] Orr, *Deer Forests*, 157–9.

[30] SCRO, D593, K/1/8/10, Loch to Murray, 12 Jul. 1869.

food for the stock which might be largely increased if keep for them in winter could be provided.[31]

It was not to be, however; just as the reclamations were on the cusp of completion, the bottom fell out of the market for sheep and wool and high hopes of profit for farmer or landowner had to be slashed. There was a sharp fall in prices and a downward turn in agricultural markets in the late 1870s, from which there would be little sustained recovery for the next two decades.[32] Potential tenants of the newly reclaimed farms were made wary by these adverse market conditions. As it became clear that it was proving impossible to attract large tenants to take the farms, the estate management pressed forward on a new front; that some of the reclaimed land would go to small tenants. There were some vague ideas of this in the planning stages of the works, when Loch mooted whether it would be possible if the land 'might not usefully be erected into small independent farms of 40 or 50 acres each for the purpose of encouraging a class of tenantry intermediate between the small tenants and the Great Farmers, which is an object much to be desired for many reasons'.[33] This objective serves to demonstrate two wider points about the estate. Firstly, that it was sensitive to criticism of Highland landownership for having encouraged the growth of large lucrative sheep farms at the expense of a 'middle' class which would have benefited Highland society more widely. Secondly, the estate had the resources and will required to attempt social as well as economic engineering projects. Just as it had created huge sheep farms fifty years earlier, it could also choose to transform them and absorb the possible financial loss that change would entail.

It must be borne in mind that at no point was the estate going to give large acres of reclaimed land to the smallest tenants, the crofters. Indeed, only eight crofters were eventually placed on the reclaimed land, despite J. S. Blackie's optimistic hopes of 'a due allotment of small crofters' being given back the land in the county where 'a mania of large farms raged most virulently'.[34] The duke, in a speech to some visitors to the reclamations, laid out the objectives:

> I shall propose to divide Bannockburn [Kildonan] into five small farms of 100 acres each, with a good large outrun, so that a farmer coming

---

[31] SCRO, D593, V/6/79, *Report on the Sutherland Reclamations by the President and Secretary of the Scottish Chamber of Agriculture*, July 1878.

[32] Orr, *Deer Forests*, 12, 16–17.

[33] SCRO, D593, K/1/8/10, Loch to Mackenzie, 8 Mar. 1869; this was a recurring theme in the thinking of both George Loch and, ironically, his father James. A similar idea was debated on the MacLeod estate, Skye; Dunvegan Castle, MacLeod of MacLeod MSS, 1406/24, Alex. Macdonald to MacLeod, 17 Aug. 1883.

[34] *Scotsman*, 24 Aug. 1874, letter to the editor from J. S. Blackie. Blackie was a vocal champion of the Highland crofters and respected academic: S. Wallace, *John Stuart Blackie: Scottish scholar and patriot* (Edinburgh, 2006), 269–70, 282–3; NLS, Blackie Papers, MS 2639, 3rd Duke to Blackie, 14 Feb. 1892.

there, and working with his family, might get along comfortably with a small capital of £500 or £600. I trust to see a prosperous and thriving people started up there.[35]

There is no mention here of the crofters, despite the re-population rhetoric; obviously, they did not have £500 of capital to invest. This soon became clear to interested observers, and by 1880 some criticism in the press, especially the more radical titles, started to appear:

> We have been very ready to give the present Duke of Sutherland credit for all the good he has been trying to do. Nay we have, as it turns out, given him credit for what he has not done at all; we refer to the anticipation entertained that there was to be a large proportion of peasant farmers to be established on the reclaimed lands at Shiness, when all we have are just seven.[36]

The press was slow to criticise the mechanics and purpose of the reclamations because the land reform movement was not yet urgently forcing criticism of the landowning classes, as it would in the 1880s. Also, in the context of growing and serious rural unrest in Ireland, the 3rd Duke's expenditure on the reclamations was seen in a positive light; that a modern landowner should behave in a munificent way towards his tenants, to prevent unrest and answer the case against landlordism as a system.[37] Indeed, land reclamation had been held up as a solution to the chronic poverty of the Highlands since the famine years. The noted doctor and social commentator William P. Alison suggested that the able-bodied poor should be set to work on reclaiming waste land, which, he argued, would reduce pressure on poor rates, increase the value of landed estates and improve Britain's 'national strength and power'.[38] The Sutherland reclamations failed to achieve that, however.

The only benefits for crofters were from day-to-day labouring on the works, but this was of short-term use only. Employment on the works also clashed inconveniently with the busy times in the crofting and fishing year. One critic expressed the situation in these terms:

> While the works are in progress they do a *temporary* good to a great many by giving them employment; but when the farm is cropped all this is at an end . . . What are the few shepherds and farm labourers

---

[35] *Northern Ensign*, 12 Sep. 1878.

[36] *Highland News*, 14 May 1880.

[37] A. G. Newby, *Ireland, Radicalism and the Scottish Highlands, c.1870–1912* (Edinburgh, 2007), 2–3, 31.

[38] W. P. Alison, *Observations of the reclamation of waste lands and their cultivation by croft husbandry, considered with a view to the productive employment of destitute labourers, paupers and criminals* (Edinburgh, 1850), 19, 36, 45, 54; C. Hamlin, 'William Pulteney Alison, the Scottish Philosophy and the making of a political medicine', *Journal of the History of Medicine*, 61 (2005), 145, 150–3, 176–7.

employed on these farms compared to the number of families that could be supported in comfort?[39]

At one point it had not even been the estate's intention to use local labour. There was some discussion during the running of the Kildonan works over the potential benefits of importing convict labour to do the work for free. The commissioner for the reclamation works, George Greig, spoke in glowing terms of the possibilities of convict labour 'as a national economy', and 'as a practical undertaking which would give satisfactory returns'.[40] At least two-thirds of the total cost of the works was expended on labourers' wages, a fact oft-quoted by the estate in the 1880s and 1890s, but this expenditure would have been sidestepped if the practicalities of organising convict labour had been feasible.

Most of the work was contracted out to private individuals or companies under the overall management of the duke and Loch, and then Greig. But Loch grew increasingly concerned about the quality of the work done. He criticised one of the reclamation contractors, Mr MacLennan:

> It rather struck me that he was trying to please the Duke by appearing to regard the performances of the steam plough, and the work executed by it, as being more complete than they really were . . . unfortunately MacLennan has committed himself to an opinion that it would take £14 per acre to trench this ground by contract . . . in my belief it may be done for less.[41]

George Loch certainly was keen to see the duke invest in his land in order to increase the returns from the relatively unproductive Sutherland estates. Once the works had started in earnest, however, Loch became increasingly concerned, not to say frantic, over both their slow progress and their escalating cost. He expressed his fears in his daily correspondence with Joseph Peacock, the Dunrobin factor, constantly complaining about the expense, which exceeded the estimates from the very beginning: 'I am getting very anxious about all this outlay, it is getting very enormous – much larger than, I think, the Duke is aware of.'[42] These fears were repeated again and again, but Loch had little control over the duke when he took such an enthusiastic personal interest. Loch was worried about this lack of restraint; control of estate finances was his main mechanism of influence over subordinate factors, but he could not contend with the duke.[43] Loch had encouraged

[39] *Highlander*, 27 Oct. 1877.
[40] NLS, Acc. 10225, Reclamations, 27, Greig to Wright, 22 Oct. 1881. This was not an uncommon idea; R. Johnston, "Charity that heals": the Scottish Labour Colony Association and attitudes to the able-bodied unemployed in Glasgow, 1890–1914', *Scottish Historical Review*, 77 (1998), 83, 87–8.
[41] NLS, Acc. 10225, Policy Papers, 93, Loch to Peacock, 1 Dec. 1872.
[42] NLS, Acc. 10225, Policy Papers, 95, Loch to Peacock, 24 Nov. 1873.
[43] Perren, 'Agricultural Depression', 5; Mitchell, *Reminiscences of my Life in the Highlands*, 215.

the principle behind the reclamation works, but by no means supported the scale on which they were being carried out, fearing (rightly) that any financial return was being lost, as the estimates were repeatedly pegged higher and higher. By 1877, Loch was in despair over the new project being proposed in Kildonan, writing despondently to Peacock, 'it would have been better to have abandoned these works altogether'.[44]

All in all, the estate spent £210,870 between 1869 and 1886, reclaiming a total of 3,471 acres, a vast outlay and one without a comparable British rival during the period.[45] Where did this money come from? Some came from the revenues of the estate, roughly £69,000 per annum, pushing them firmly into the red. The duke also sold government stocks in the late 1870s and early 1880s to the value of £99,492 and raised a further £22,500 from the sale of pictures from Stafford House.[46] As a short-term measure, the duke, with the permission of his son, Lord Stafford, raised two loans of £100,000 each.[47] This caused great consternation in the rest of the family, who saw it as unnecessary expenditure that would deplete the family's future capital resources. They unsuccessfully took the duke to the Court of Session to try to prevent the raising of the second loan in 1890, but as the Judge ruled, 'the Duke and Marquis in succession [could] burden the estate at pleasure and from time to time'.[48] The family's worries turned out to be unnecessary, as the duke paid out all his outstanding debts a few months later, in October 1890.[49]

Some personal economising was also considered; for instance, the duke cut back the number of servants in his employ. This retrenchment should be put into perspective, however; the duke still felt secure enough to spend nearly £32,000 on yachting between 1884 and 1888.[50] This sum was nothing to consumption by the family on clothes, food and entertaining. Annual expenditure on this was well over £30,000 and did not include the duties and jointures that were also the duke's responsibility.[51] For

[44] NLS, Acc. 10225, Policy Papers, 102, Loch to Peacock, 20 Mar. 1877; McIver attributed Loch's illness and death in 1879 to his worries over the reclamations; E. McIver, *Memoirs of a Highland Gentleman: being the Reminiscences of Evander McIver of Scourie*, Rev. George Henderson (ed.) (Edinburgh, 1905), 118.

[45] NLS, Acc. 10225, Reclamations, 5, 'Abstract of expenditure on Reclamation of land, buildings and farming to 31 Dec. 1886.'

[46] E. Richards, 'An Anatomy of the Sutherland fortune: income, consumption, investments and returns, 1780–1880', *Business History*, 21 (1979), 66; J. Yorke, *Lancaster House: London's greatest town house* (London, 2001), 149, 154–5.

[47] Richards, 'An Anatomy', 66.

[48] *Inverness Courier*, 7 Jul. 1890.

[49] R. Perren, 'The Effect of the Agricultural Depression on the English Estates of the Dukes of Scotland, 1870–1900', unpublished Ph.D. thesis (University of Nottingham, 1967), 38.

[50] SCRO, D593, P/24/3/7, 'List of expenditure on yachting in the 1880s'; D. Cannadine, *The Decline and Fall of the British Aristocracy* (London, 1990), 372–3; Perren, 'English Estates', 43, 45.

[51] Richards, 'An Anatomy', 55.

instance, the 3rd Duke made over the Cromartie estate to his second son in the 1860s in order to provide him with a fitting income, and his mother's annuity took £4,000 per annum.[52] But despite the fact that it was possible for the estate to absorb these losses on a short-term basis, it did mean selling off valuable capital assets to do so, weakening the family fortune for future generations.[53]

Was the expenditure on the reclamations justified in a financial or agricultural sense? The agricultural aspect will be looked at first, as much of the initial media comment surrounding the reclamations highlighted the fact that although they were unlikely to be remunerative in the 3rd Duke's lifetime, the pecuniary sacrifice was for the wider benefit of British agriculture. It was only in 1878, once the Loch Shin works were being completed and new works at Kildonan being initiated, that a number of independent experts inspected the works and made some telling criticisms.

A party from the Scottish Chamber of Agriculture which visited and reported on the Lairg works in 1878 questioned the validity of the method of reclamation followed by the estate: 'it was doubted whether that system (which was different from any practised in the experience of the party) would be successful'.[54] These doubts were occasioned by concerns over the quality of the topsoil created by the ploughing, liming and fertilising processes; they feared that it was too shallow in depth and that any value it did hold would be 'dissolved' and disappear after the first cropping.[55] This report, however, was fairly generous compared to two others made at the same time. The first of these was a report by C. G. Roberts, a representative of the Royal Agricultural Society of England, in 1879, who criticised the lack of knowledgeable supervision of the work.[56] This problem stemmed from the fact that the works were very large; insufficient experienced staff had been employed and this had resulted in some operations, especially draining, having been poorly executed and unlikely to be durable. Roberts' criticism reached beyond the supervisory level and attacked the quality of the labourers also, claiming that 'many of those who first offered themselves for work proved anything but well-trained work men', and noting the native Sutherland men as being 'untrained to steady work'.[57] This point was repeated in another report, a private paper by one Mr Colin Mackenzie, whose relationship to the estate is not noted and who, among six points listing why the Loch Shin reclamations made a loss, listed 'the character of the people', specifying that 'partly, it may be from constitutional causes, partly from their having been kept too much in tutelage, aided like

[52] Richards, 'An Anatomy,' 51.
[53] Richards, 'An Anatomy', 65.
[54] SCRO, D593, V/6/79, *Report on the Sutherland Reclamations*, 1878.
[55] SCRO, D593, V/6/79, *Report on the Sutherland Reclamations*, 1878.
[56] Roberts, 'Sutherland Reclamation', 441.
[57] Roberts, 'Sutherland Reclamation', 467, 484.

children and healed like children, fall far behind the Ross-shire men in enterprise and energy'.[58]

It was not only the workforce and its supervisors which were at fault, however, but also the sites chosen for reclamation, which were at too high an altitude and in areas where the climate was not only unfavourable, but capable of destroying a year's work in a night.[59] But the most startling evidence of failure was only uncovered in the 1890s, when it became clear what a tiny fraction of the land reclaimed in the 1870s was still under cultivation.[60] Figures put together by the estate for the visit of the Deer Forest Commission in 1893 show that only 757 out of 3,471 acres, or less than one-third of the reclaimed land, was still being cultivated; a damning figure which clearly vindicates the criticisms and doubts of the visiting agricultural experts.[61] The litany of failure continues when the financial record is examined.[62] After spending £210,000, the estate had generated a rent increase of £800 per annum.[63] These depressing figures sunk even lower as the years passed and many of the acres reclaimed at vast expense were gradually abandoned. The reasons behind this failure were two-fold. The first was that the expenditure exceeded all sensible limits, especially at the Lairg site. As early as 1875, Loch was fretting that 'the position of the banking account is becoming very serious, as it did last year; even to a greater degree.'[64] Most comment on the reclamations from outside the estate also focused on this huge expenditure, and although approval was usually expressed at the duke's willingness to pay, there was some concern over 'whether they will remunerate the enterprising owner'.[65]

The second reason why no return was made was due to a wider slump in British agriculture from 1879. That year, prices for sheep and wool fell steeply, undermining the position of the sheep farmers for whom the estate had laid out such huge sums.[66] In 1870, the estate had taken the Shiness lands

[58] SCRO, D593, N/4/1/4, 'A few rough notes on the reclamation of wasteland in Sutherland and Ross-shire', by C. Mackenzie, 1879; it was not an uncommon view and was based on the idea that the noted generosity of the ducal family had made the Sutherland crofters lazy, dependent and weak.

[59] SCRO, D593, V/6/82, R. M. Brereton, *A Word on the Duke of Sutherland's Estate Management*, 1887 (privately printed pamphlet); N/4/1/4, Mackenzie, 'A few rough notes'; Roberts, 'Sutherland Reclamation', 436.

[60] NLS, Acc. 10225, Reclamations, 42, 'Statement as to the reclaimed farms and lands, Jan. 1893'.

[61] P. T. Wheeler, 'Landownership and the crofting system in Sutherland since 1800', *Agricultural History Review*, 14 (1966), 51.

[62] 5th Duke of Sutherland, *Looking Back: the autobiography of the Duke of Sutherland* (London, 1957), 33.

[63] NLS, Acc 10225, Reclamations, 5, 'Table: statement as to cost and rent of reclaimed farms, 1883'.

[64] NLS, Acc. 10225, Policy Papers, 98, Loch to Peacock, 9 Jun. 1875.

[65] SCRO, D593, V/6/79, *Report on the Sutherland Reclamations*, 1878.

[66] Orr, *Deer Forests*, 20; Perren, 'Agricultural Depression', 25; Mingay, *Land and Society*, 195–6.

in hand as farms fell out of lease, so that the reclamations could be carried on entirely by the landowner, cutting off their rental revenue. But just as the finished works were being advertised on the market, prices were dropping and tenants were unwilling to take on the new farms.[67] As one witness confirmed to the Napier Commission in 1883, 'it is a fact now, is it not, that these very large sheep farms are so difficult to let, that it is almost impossible to get tenants? – That is coming to be the case.'[68] The estate was forced to repeatedly advertise the farms and eventually take some in hand, along with the sheep stock, at great financial loss.[69] When questioned about the reclamations at Clashmore by the Deer Forest Commission, Evander McIver bluntly stated that 'it turned out a very unfortunate speculation, so much so that the Duke of Sutherland never got a farthing of rent for the whole thing'.[70]

Years before these admissions, it had been clear to the estate management that the estimated expenditure had been vastly exceeded and that returns for the estate were likely to be extremely low. In 1878, the duke admitted 'that I do not expect a large per centage on my outlay; but my boy will reap some benefit of it, and as the money would likely have gone at any rate, I do not consider this a bad way of spending it.'[71] This cavalier attitude could not disguise the fact that the works had turned out to be a white elephant. George Loch had issued warnings almost every month when he received the accounts, but had been unable to curb the duke.[72] As one newspaper observed, the possible good, both financial and social, of the works had been secondary to the duke's need to 'gratify his craze for steam tillage'.[73] The end result was summed up by Kemball in front of the Napier Commission: 'can you say what the returns have been in connection with this great expenditure? – I have calculated that on the reclamations it is nil.'[74] Not only had the estate failed to make any return on its massive investment, but it had also failed to set any great agricultural example, both in terms of scientific technique or financial economy. Roberts expressed the feelings of many observers:

> A suspicion that, after all, it was merely the expensive amusement of a
> wealthy proprietor, justified chiefly on the grounds that a nobleman

---

[67] Orr, *Deer Forests*, 15, 18.

[68] PP XXXII–XXXVI, 1884, *Evidence and Report of the Commissioners of Inquiry into the condition of the Crofters and Cottars in the Highlands and Islands of Scotland* [hereafter *Napier Commission Evidence*], Rev. John MacKay, Free Church minister, Strathnaver, 1642; *Deer Forest Commission Evidence*, Donald MacLean, 640.

[69] Interestingly, the reclaimed land near Loch Shin was later repeatedly offered to the Sutherland crofters (1884, 1894) and then to the state (1916): see Chapters three, four and five.

[70] *Deer Forest Commission Evidence*, 721; McIver, *Memoirs*, 119.

[71] *Northern Ensign*, 12 Sep. 1878.

[72] Perren, 'Agricultural Depression', 35–6.

[73] *Highland News*, 23 Jul. 1887.

[74] *Napier Commission Evidence*, Kemball, 2526.

might as well create farms out of moorland for his pleasure as keep an expensive stud of racers.[75]

'The Iron Duke': public relations

Lairg by J. S. Blackie [76]

> Along the bare slope of the broad brown brae,
> Beneath the cold grey-blue October sky,
> What thing is that which smokes and snorts away,
> Mingling strange shrillness with the peewit's cry?
> 'Tis the stout carriage of the Titan Steam
> Which the brave Duke hath marched into this land
> The savage moor from the wilderness to redeem
> By gracious force of Labour's fruitful hand.
> O! It brings marrow to the bones to see
> The right man sometimes in the right man's place
> Who knows his work and from weak wavering free
> Holds his sure course, and moves with measured pace;
> Even as this Duke subdues the angry mould
> Tames the harsh rock, and turns the clay to gold.

This sonnet by J. S. Blackie, the noted academic and crofter champion, highlights a number of key themes. Primarily, it expresses a romantic view of the Highland landscape, of 'broad brown brae' and the 'savage wilderness'; but juxtaposed against this is the moral challenge of taming and redeeming the landscape, as a Victorian imperialist might do to a foreign race. How does this redemption take place? By the power of the latest technology, 'Titan Steam'; but not this alone. For progress to take place there needed to be the 'right man', 'the brave Duke', to translate idea into action.

The Sutherland reclamations were unique in nineteenth-century British agriculture, in terms of the scale of both acreage and expenditure. They can be placed in a wider context, however, both in Sutherland and the rest of the Highlands, by placing them alongside the infamous Sutherland clearances of the early nineteenth century. There are two motives behind this comparison. The first is the many similarities that can be drawn between the reclamation works of the 1870s and the clearances of the early nineteenth century. Both were attempts by the estate to make Sutherland's acres self-sufficient and huge amounts of capital were sacrificed to try to achieve this – both failed.[77] Secondly, it would be the clearances that the

---

[75] Roberts, 'Sutherland Reclamation', 484; NLS, Blackie Papers, MS 2639, Alex. Mackenzie, editor of the *Scottish Highlander*, to Blackie, 12 Sep. 1892.

[76] *Scotsman*, 24 Aug. 1874, J. S. Blackie, 'Lairg'; Wallace, *John Stuart Blackie*, 286.

[77] Richards, 'An Anatomy', 66.

Sutherland estate was chiefly remembered for; not the reclamation works which generated a plethora of positive media comment in the 1870s. Why this might be so will be addressed below. The second part of this section will concentrate on wider issues generated by the reclamation works. These include the perceived role of the aristocracy through the person of the 3rd Duke: a three-fold image of the 'dutiful' aristocrat, the clan leader and the noble as businessman. There are two further contexts to examine beyond that of the individual: the popular romantic image of the Highlands and the relationship between nature, agriculture and profit. In addition, the estate's attempts to extract political capital from the reclamations via parliamentary debate and evidence to royal commissions will also be examined.

It can be argued that one of the central aims of the Sutherland family throughout the nineteenth century was to make the Sutherland estate economically self-sufficient.[78] There were two main attempts to achieve this, both necessitating vast amounts of capital expenditure and years of effort. In the early nineteenth century, William Young and, later, James Loch radically reformed the tenancy structure of the estate; to concentrate the population on the coasts, so providing them with employment in either fishing or home industries, and allowing the interior to be turned over to large-scale sheep farming.[79] As James Loch later wrote,

> It seemed as if it had been pointed out by Nature that the system for this remote district, in order that it might bear its suitable importance in contributing its share to the general stock of the country, was to convert the mountainous districts into sheep walks and to remove the inhabitants to the coasts.[80]

Just as with the reclamation works of the 1870s, the estate was expecting a financial return for its massive investment; in all, from 1811 to 1833 a total of £60,000 was expended and, additionally, between 1811 and 1820 no income was received from Sutherland at all.[81] The long-term aim behind the clearances was to build a stable and profitable economy in Sutherland, resulting in a greater rental income.[82] The policy failed in both these aims, and more significantly, the clearances caused suffering and distress among the small tenant population which would rebound upon the estate again and again in the future.

The Sutherland clearances had transformed the economic structure of the estate, but they had failed to make it financially self-sufficient. In the late 1860s, the estate decided that to make the land profitable, they would literally have to create it from scratch, through reclamation. The duke and

---

[78] Loch, *An Account*, 60, 168; Richards, *Leviathan of Wealth*, 229–30, 235, 288.
[79] Richards, *Leviathan of Wealth*, 175–7.
[80] Loch, *An Account*, 47–51, 72; A. Russel, 'The Highlands – Men, Sheep and Deer', *Edinburgh Review*, 106 (1857), 487, 490; Richards, *Leviathan of Wealth*, 164–5, 197–8, 224.
[81] Richards, *Leviathan of Wealth*, 216, 231.
[82] Richards, *Leviathan of Wealth*, 229–30, 232, 235.

his advisors believed that the steam plough could lead the way in conquering the bogs and wastes that dominated his northern estates and turn them into profitable fields. Such high hopes did the duke have of this result, he confidently declared in 1878 that 'I hope to deal with a good more of Sutherland in the same way.'[83] His ambition was to be thwarted. Just as with the clearances, the reclamations were a financial failure; the estate did not become self-sufficient and there were no returns, even for future generations.

The reclamations affected a very small section of the population directly; a few hundred of the small tenantry were employed at the works, but they were aimed at benefiting an elite caste of sheep farmers and once completed quickly slipped out of use and faded back into waste to be all but forgotten, except in the estate account books. This was the contrast: the clearances created a new and permanent framework of habitation and employment on the estate; in comparison, the brief and localised flurry of the reclamations did not stick in the public mind. The sheer volume of writing and media attention that surrounded the clearances also kept them firmly to the fore. Although there were clearances on many other Highland estates throughout the nineteenth century, those in Sutherland came to symbolise all that was cruel and unjust in the policy; this was compounded by the fact that their long-term results were coming under increasing legislative scrutiny in the 1880s. At the commencement of the reclamations, there was much hopeful media comment that the duke's aim was re-population, illustrating the popular abhorrence of the clearances:

> A great mistake was committed, we believe, when in the days of his [the 3rd Duke's] grandmother, the Countess and first Duchess of Sutherland, the greater part of Sutherlandshire was converted into large sheep farms . . . The present Duke seems to understand this, and to be resolved to bring back agriculture properly so-called, to the suitable portions of his wide estates, by extending its sphere by the reclamation of land.[84]

While the press and other observers believed that the reclamations were going to benefit a wide range of the population in Sutherland, they heartily approved of them, to the extent of turning a blind eye towards a small but significant clearance in Assynt, deemed necessary for reclamation there. The importance of the clearances to the image and reputation of the family demonstrates how much value they attached to trying to keep their name 'clean' of any accusations or criticisms. The estate management were just as, if not more, concerned with this than the ducal family itself.[85] As Kemball put it rather extraordinarily to the Napier Commission in 1883, 'I

[83] *Northern Ensign*, 12 Sep. 1878; *Times*, 23 Jul. 1874.
[84] *The Courant*, 6 Aug. 1874; *North British Agriculturist*, 5 Aug. 1874.
[85] Mitchell, *Reminiscences of my Life in the Highlands*, 216.

maintain that, even though the Duke can do no wrong, no wrong should either be done in his name or without his knowledge.'[86] This almost exactly duplicated James Loch's statement of intent at the beginning of his published *Account*, defending both his and the Sutherland family name.[87]

The duke as an individual was closely associated with the reclamations, mainly through his well-documented personal enthusiasm for the steam technology behind them. He was the main financial supporter of railway building in the county (the duke owned an engine, the *Dunrobin*, which he was fond of driving himself), and his assiduous attendance at the sites of reclamation and his modification of the steam plough design were also commented on.[88] He was evidently proud of his role in the works, and in a portrait painted of him around this time he had pages of notes with 'Lairg' written on them and a diagram of a steam plough painted in, resting at his feet.[89] Many newspaper columns were filled noting this unusual ducal activity from which three main caricatures can be drawn; the duke as the 'dutiful' aristocrat, as a traditional clan leader, and finally as a businessman.

By far the most important of these themes was the first; much praise was doled out, especially at the beginning of the works, for the duke's moral energy and financial enterprise in initiating the reclamations. Writers extolled the duke's evident commitment to his estates through vast expenditure as an example of the very best qualities of landownership, where the owner was resident, interested, knowledgeable and ready to invest for future generations not just of his own family, but of all the inhabitants on his estate.[90] This image was favourably compared to common perceptions of reckless privilege; spending on gambling, horses and other morally uncertain activities.[91] The 3rd Duke was portrayed as a moral example to his peers; what landownership *should* be:

> Let us suppose that he will die at last a poorer man, so far as money goes, than if he had let this great enterprise alone. So would he if he had given himself up to horse racing or to almost any one thing to which his compeers in so many cases devote themselves . . . most

---

[86] *Napier Commission Evidence*, Kemball, 2528.

[87] Loch, *An Account*, 6.

[88] Cannadine, *Decline and Fall*, 407; D. Stuart, *Dear Duchess: Millicent, Duchess of Sutherland 1867–1955* (London, 1982), 33; B. Thompson, *Imperial Vanities* (London, 2002), 109; E. Richards, 'Gower, George Granville Leveson-, 1st Duke of Sutherland', *Oxford Dictionary of National Biography* (Oxford, 2004); Mitchell, *Reminiscences of my Life in the Highlands*, 7, 102, 213.

[89] This painting, by R. Herdman, is currently on display on the main staircase of Dunrobin Castle.

[90] Praise for investment in agriculture by landowners was common at this time: Duke of Bedford, *A Great Agricultural Estate: being the on-going administration of Woburn and Thorney* (London, 1897), 9; Cannadine, *Aspects of Aristocracy*, 183; *Times*, 12 Sep. 1876.

[91] *Highlander*, 8 Jan. 1876.

heartily we wish him god speed. He will soon have imitators, we cannot but think. There does seem to be a dawning upon the minds of our nobility of the truth that truly noble lives are to be led, not for self and in miserable indulgence, but in those lofty enterprises which go to increase the numbers and to ensure the prosperity of man.[92]

The reclamation works were convenient for covering up the duke's deficiencies; not horses, but a decided lack of interest in politics, a traditional duty of the aristocracy. As one newspaper optimistically phrased it, 'the Duke of Sutherland . . . makes up for his silence in the arena of public life by a good deal of practical wisdom exhibited in other directions'.[93] *Punch* was predictably less generous, judging of the duke's political abilities that 'he is clearly the wrong man in the wrong place on any platform except that of a steam engine'.[94] Overall, however, the reclamations did the duke's reputation, which until then had been fairly lacklustre, the power of good.

Connected to this image was the increasingly old-fashioned concept of the duke as a traditional clan chief, responsible for and caring about the population on his land in a paternalistic sense, a surprising assessment of the duke's character when juxtaposed with the third and final image of the duke as shrewd businessman and entrepreneur. This last image is surely the more accurate; he invested his huge assets in a wide-ranging and exotic selection of investments, as his extensive business portfolio demonstrates. The duke was heavily involved in railway and canal building projects, both in Britain and abroad; unsurprising given his family's history, but for a landed peer to be dabbling in activities normally disparaged as 'plutocratic' was in the 1870s more unusual than it would later become.[95] On his landed estates, the duke was active in other projects of dubious rationality. On his wife's Cromartie estate, for example, he invested heavily from 1861 in developing a fashionable spa at Strathpeffer. A joint-stock company, to which he was the chief subscriber, was launched in 1876 to further develop buildings and facilities, and in 1885 the railway was diverted to make ease of travel greater.[96]

Not all members of the estate management approved of the duke sinking capital into risky speculation, however, preferring investment into that most stable and traditional avenue, land.[97] Until the advent of the Great Depression in 1879, the value of land rose steadily and was deemed the

---

[92] *Christian News*, 28 Sep. 1872.

[93] *Glasgow Herald*, 19 Sep. 1876.

[94] *Punch*, 26 Jan. 1878.

[95] Cannadine, *Decline and Fall*, 5, 444; Forbes Munro, *Maritime Enterprise and Empire*, 215–18; Richards and Clough, *Cromartie*, 273.

[96] Richards and Clough, *Cromartie*, 279; Cannadine, *Aspects of Aristocracy*, 58–60.

[97] Richards and Clough, *Cromartie*, 250; F. M. L. Thompson, 'English Landed Society in the twentieth century: II: New Poor and New Rich', *Transactions of the Royal Historical Society*, 6th ser., 1 (1991), 1, 12–13. This view was not universal: many clan leaders had, from the early eighteenth century, followed their commercial instincts outwith the sphere of land;

most safe, although admittedly not the most remunerative, of investments. Also, even though returns were relatively low compared to those available through other ventures, in the very long term the benefits of increasing the value of land would be reaped by future generations of the family. There was an additional social restraint, at least in the eyes of George Loch, who believed that aside from the risk of financial loss, business outside of land was 'simply not the function of a landlord'.[98] As with the land reclamation project, however, the duke ignored Loch on this point, as his investment portfolio testifies.

These diverse images were highlighted by the reclamation works at different times by the estate and popular media as the project progressed. When the works started the duke was praised on all three counts; as a successful investor, a clan chief caring for his tenants and a dutiful aristocrat. By the 1880s, however, when it was clear that the works were failing financially and agriculturally, the best that could be salvaged was that the duke was making personal financial sacrifices for the benefit of his tenants, but when it became clear that the new land was not going to be made available to crofters, the remaining picture of the duke was not a happy one. The rise and fall of the duke's public image goes some way to explaining why, during the period of the Crofters War, the crofting tenantry demonstrated little respect for the duke or his estate management, and it was the clearances, not the reclamations, which were the main historical discussion on the table.[99]

The Sutherland family and its foibles was not the only issue relative to the reclamations; attitudes towards land and nature in late-Victorian society were also thrown into relief. Since the early nineteenth century the Highlands had been seen as essentially Romantic in nature, a fashion which ranged from the sentiments expressed by the poems of 'Ossian' to the queen's purchase of the Balmoral estate.[100] This attitude contrasted with another, that is, land as a mechanism of profit: these two seemingly diametrically opposed views were held in apparent tandem by many, and were applied to the reclamations:

> While Her Majesty was staying at Dunrobin castle, she had the satisfaction not only of looking upon such wild uplands that give a charm of savageness to her own Highland home, but of knowing that the owner

Devine, *Clanship to Crofters' War*, 32–3; A. I. Macinnes, *Clanship, Commerce and the House of Stuart, 1603–1788* (East Linton, 1996), 210–11, 221–8.

[98] Richards and Clough, *Cromartie*, 273; J. A. Smith, 'Landownership and Social Change in late Nineteenth century Britain', *Economic History Review*, 2nd ser., 53 (2000), 768.

[99] *Highland News*, 23 Jul. 1887.

[100] P. Womack, *Improvement and Romance: constructing the myth of the Highlands* (London, 1989), 74–8; I. MacPhail, 'Land, Crofting and the Assynt Crofters Trust: a Postcolonial Geography' (unpublished Ph.D., University of Wales, Lampeter, 2002), 61–2; J. M. Mackenzie, *Empires of Nature and the Nature of Empires: imperialism, Scotland and the environment* (East Linton, 1997), 68–70.

of the immense estate which stretched away on every side had clearly
realised the responsibilities of his high position . . . the present Duke,
at least, is acting on a wholly different plan; for he is taking means to
increase the population by increasing the productive power of the
soil.[101]

Attitudes to the Highlands were a paradox, therefore; the wildness of
nature in the region was admired in its own right, but at the same time
there was an urge to 'conquer' that wildness, to improve it and turn it into
a profitable and commercial concern.[102] The duke was observed as having
'successfully inaugurated a raid on the wastes of the beautiful Highland
county of which he is almost the sole proprietor'.[103] The *Inverness Courier*
gave the duke the honorary title, 'Iron Duke', going on to claim that 'with
his titanic steam ploughs and other marvellous appliances for subduing
and transforming the stony waste and wilderness, the Duke conquers the
stubborn soil of the North as triumphantly as the first great Iron Duke
conquered the armies of France'.[104] It was through modern technology,
never seen or used by the native crofters, that the duke was to finally turn
Sutherland into a commercially successful estate.[105]

In this way the reclamation works were turned into an act of patriotism;
a self-sacrifice on the part of the duke for a huge range of beneficiaries,
including crofters, sheep farmers, Scottish and British agriculture and the
British nation at large. As it became clear to the Sutherland family and
estate that the reclamations were going to fail financially and agriculturally, they increasingly aligned themselves with these ideas, to make any
gains they could, including attempts to extract political capital from its
financial disaster through parliamentary debate and two royal commissions that visited the Highlands in the aftermath of the reclamations;
the Napier Commission in 1883 and the Deer Forest Commission in
1893.

The first comments of any real political significance concerning the
reclamations were made in the House of Commons in 1881 by the prime
minister, Gladstone. The Land Law (Ireland) Bill was the legislation under
discussion, specifically a hotly debated motion to allow the government
to fund and organise land reclamation on a large scale to improve rural
conditions. Gladstone was strenuously opposed to such a clause, calling
reclamation work in general 'the most doubtful, the most slippery and the

[101] SCRO, D593, P/24/7/5, newspaper cutting, no source or date; see also *Scotsman*, 17 Sep.
1872.
[102] T. C. Smout, 'The Highlands and the roots of Green Consciousness, 1750–1990', *Scottish
Natural Heritage, Occasional Paper*, 1, Nov. 1990, 24–5; Womack, *Improvement and Romance*,
61, 71–2.
[103] *Scotsman*, 17 Sep. 1872.
[104] *Inverness Courier*, 6 Aug. 1874.
[105] The view that crofters were unable to manage this themselves was almost universal among
landowners and government officials; Cameron, *Land for the People*, 88–90, 98–100.

most hopeless to be undertaken by anybody . . . even for private persons'.[106]
He continued, using the Sutherland reclamations as his template,

> The last considerable attempt at reclamation that I have heard of – in
> fact the only one that I have heard of late – is going on now in the
> hands of a landlord in the North of Scotland. It is universally acknowl-
> edged to be most creditable to the person who has it in hand; but I am
> sorry to say that every account that reaches me is to the effect that, in
> a pecuniary sense, the operation has been a mistake.[107]

Predictably, this generated several refutations, including one from George
Greig in a letter to the *Times*.[108] It could be argued, however, that the estate
actually benefited from these comments, even though they proclaimed the
works to have failed. That they had done so was obvious even to the most
sympathetic observer, but perhaps Gladstone's confirmation of this in a
political sphere was a kind of absolution for the estate. Had not Gladstone
himself declared that carrying out reclamation work successfully was 'hopeless', and that, moreover, a body as powerful as the British government
should not attempt to undertake it? Gladstone also gave personal credit to
the landowner, thereby boosting the popular image of the duke, even when
his project had failed.

Through Gladstone's comments the estate had received an unexpected
political bonus, but from 1883, the estate management would be far more
active in forging a positive picture out of a negative situation. The first
opportunity for this came with the visit of the Napier Commission in 1883,
which had been appointed to examine the grievances of the Highland
crofters and to make recommendations for possible reform. The estate,
through its factors and commissioner, Kemball, defended its record
towards the small tenants by pointing to the vast sums of expenditure
lavished on the estate, which since 1853 added up to almost £1 million.[109]
The estate included the sums spent on the reclamations with the rest of
the permanent improvements, making up one-quarter of the final figure
given. Some questions were raised about how much of this investment had
benefited crofters directly, but these made only a small dent in the impact
of the hard figures displayed by the estates' account books. Comment on
the reclamations themselves was fairly limited, as it was land law reform that
was the primary issue, but the estate factors were happy to emphasise that
the reclamations had failed.[110]

This failure was exposed even more energetically during the visit of the
Deer Forest Commission in 1893. This was because the Commission was

[106] *Hansard Parliamentary Debates*, 3rd ser., vol. 263 (1881), 662.
[107] *HPD*, 3rd ser., vol. 263 (1881), 662.
[108] *Daily Free Press*, 19 Jul. 1881; *Times*, 29 Jul. 1881, letter to the editor from George Greig.
[109] *Napier Commission Evidence*, Kemball, 2526.
[110] See *Napier Commission Evidence*, 1704–31, 1764–70, 2516–37; *Deer Forest Commission Evidence*,
599–618, 638–40; 697–754.

investigating the possibility of taking land under sheep and deer and allowing small tenants to reclaim and reside upon it. In order to try to prevent having to face future land reform and the possibility of handing land over to small tenants under legal compulsion, the estate argued vigorously that most land in Sutherland was simply unsuitable for cultivation. To back up these claims they pointed to the failure of the estate reclamations, asking if all the capital of the estate and imported scientific expertise could achieve so little, how could a crofter fare any better?

> There can be no better illustration of the absurdity of cultivation to any extent in high-lying and exposed situations than that afforded by the Duke of Sutherland's reclamations . . . there was expended the enormous sum of £184,454 [Lairg only] exclusive of the great loss on farming the land while on hand, and the result both as regards the land itself and return for the money expended has proved a failure in every sense of the word.[111]

The thrust behind the estate's exposure of its financial losses and blunders to public bodies was for a specific political purpose: to protect its future interests in relation to the land and crofters' rights to it.

This view was not without its detractors, however, who refused to see the estate's financial losses on the reclamations as any reason to refrain from criticism. Much of this came from other witnesses giving evidence to the visiting commissions, claiming that for all the fantastic figures bandied about by the estate, little or none of it directly benefited the crofters at all.[112] It was not only the results of the reclamations that were criticised; many witnesses also stated that they had not been carried out to a sufficiently high technical standard. One witness stated that, in his opinion, the land was only 'scraped', and that 'it was not trying to make the work good they were, but how many acres they would go over in one day'.[113]

The sheer waste of money the reclamations represented was heavily criticised by witnesses, but some went further, specifically rejecting the right of the estate to claim absolution for its treatment of the crofters in return for these failed investments: 'when he [the duke] squanders his money to no purpose, he can tell his Chief Commissioner to go before the world with the statement that the expenditure was for the benefit of the crofters'.[114] This criticism became more widespread after 1883, when the unofficial grace period for the reclamations had well and truly ended.

---

[111] *Deer Forest Commission Evidence*, MacLean, 600; Richards, 'An Anatomy', 68.
[112] *Napier Commission Evidence*, Angus Sutherland (the future MP for Sutherland), 2433.
[113] *Napier Commission Evidence*, James Sutherland, 656.
[114] *Highland News*, 23 Jul. 1887, editorial.

Conclusion

The Sutherland reclamations are largely ignored in histories of the Highlands, which seems surprising when the plethora of contemporary media comment and their important political applications are noted. It can be concluded that significant sections of Victorian society were interested in these works as a national example of an individual's capital being put to good use in a patriotic cause. Despite this, they are relatively unknown today, perhaps because of the lack of any visible sign of them; by the 1890s, they had receded to a third of their original size. This physical disappearance, however, should not undermine their significance in political and agricultural circles and as part of the wider debate on land in the Highlands. The reclamations were not the point at which the Sutherland family began their decline – politically, financially and territorially – but they were a turning point in how the estate regarded 'Improvement' in the future. The reclamations were the last large capital scheme seen in Sutherland; simply put, the estate was never again willing or able to tolerate such expensive failure.

The public image of the Sutherland family certainly benefited in the short term, however, if such champions of the crofters' cause as J. S. Blackie felt able to support the duke; the grandson of the very man who oversaw the notorious clearances of which he was such a vocal critic. Blackie wrote another sonnet, specifically honouring the duke, which goes a long way in illustrating the sort of sentiments the land reclamations generated about an otherwise uninspiring peer.

The Land Improver

> What man is he that walks the mountain-side,
> With lordly front and arm of brawny sway,
> Who ploughs his way in glory and in pride,
> Through tangled wood, rough dell and shaggy brae?
> I know him well; oft has he crossed my path
> On the green slope of some high-shouldered Ben
> Where with swift eye he scanned the fruitful strath,
> And mapped the brae for homes of happy men.
> As when a great commander lifts his mace
> And signs the way through danger with a crown,
> And mows down giant foes at every pace,
> And from the brow of Fortune plucks the frown,
> So he, most like a god, with conquering skill,
> Subdues the glen and moulds them to his will.[115]

---

[115] SCRO, D593, P/24/7/6, cutting from *Times* no date [1874?]; 'The Land Improver', from 'Highland Sketches No. 1' by J. S. Blackie.

This sonnet draws together the threads of the public image of the duke in the early years of the reclamations. 'Most like a god', the duke with his works was expected to turn his land from wasteful bog into productive soil; an Arcadia to replace the chronic poverty of the Highlands.

As we have seen, this did not happen; indeed, reclamation on the scale which the duke envisaged may have been impossible. There were voices, however, which claimed that reclamation on a smaller scale, undertaken by crofters, could work, pointing to the reclamation crofters had been forced to undertake in the aftermath of the clearances. Generally, however, the reclamations were indicted for being improperly and extravagantly done, and looking at the evidence, this was probably a fair criticism. They also did little to help improve relations between the estate and the small tenants in the long term, who received only a tiny portion of the new land, even when the farms remained unlet. Instead of improving relations with the crofting community from their state of unease and mistrust, the reclamations merely added to the list of grievances against the estate during the Crofters War.

CHAPTER THREE

'Agitation amounting to legalised coercion': The Sutherland Estate 1880–6[1]

Introduction

The Sutherland estate was still embroiled in its vast reclamation projects in the early 1880s, since 1879 under the more sceptical eye of the new commissioner, General Sir Arnold Burrowes Kemball.[2] He had little knowledge of Highland estates, or land management generally, but he could put his diplomatic and organisational training, as well as his imperial, military and business contacts, to good use.[3] He was extremely active on behalf of the 3rd Duke across his landed and business empire, attending to every administrative detail personally, recognising that a complete mastery of all the affairs of the estate was necessary for the defence of its reputation once the public and government eye was focused on the region.

By 1882, it was becoming clear to the estate as the reclaimed farms at Lairg were repeatedly advertised in the press that they would have to remain in estate hands for some time to come. This, as well as Kemball's stricter approach, meant a more cautious attitude towards expenditure crept into the management.[4] On the eve of the crofters' agitation in the Highlands, therefore, the Sutherland estate was in a phase of semi-retrenchment. This is not to say that there were any major cutbacks on day-to-day expenditure, but the estate had lost heavily by the reclamations and was reluctant to give any major concessions to the crofters, such as enlargement or the creation of new holdings.[5]

---

[1] National Library of Scotland [hereafter NLS], Sutherland Estates Papers, Acc. 10225, Crofters, ZN/a, Kemball to McIver, 3 Jul. 1884.

[2] *Times*, 22 Sep. 1908, obituary.

[3] E. McIver, *Memoirs of a Highland Gentleman: being the reminiscences of Evander McIver of Scourie*, Rev. G. Henderson (ed.) (Edinburgh, 1905), 120.

[4] E. Richards and M. Clough, *Cromartie: Highland life, 1650–1950* (Aberdeen, 1989), 257; NLS, Acc. 10225, Policy Papers, 141, Kemball to Crawford, 27 Jun. 1883. This was in contrast to the policy followed by the Ulbster estates in Caithness, which gave a blanket rent reduction for crofters of between 10 and 20%: Ulbster Estates MSS, Factor's Letterbook 1880–87, Logan to Sir Tollemache, 29 Mar. 1883.

[5] Richards and Clough, *Cromartie*, 364; R. Perren, 'The Effects of Agricultural Depression on the English estates of the Duke of Sutherland, 1870–1900', unpublished Ph.D. thesis (University of Nottingham, 1967), 29; NLS, Acc. 10225, Policy Papers, 141, Kemball to Crawford, 27 Jun. 1883.

Additionally, by the early 1880s, the 3rd Duke seems to have lost the brief flare of interest he had demonstrated in the estate as it became clear his reclamations were not the agricultural or scientific triumph for which he had hoped. Whereas in the mid-1870s he spent a relatively large amount of time in Sutherland, supervising the progress of the works and attending meetings with the managers in charge of them, by 1880 he was increasingly absent. It was common for him to spend only two to three weeks a year in Sutherland, a fact criticised by crofter supporters and even members of his own staff. McIver commented unfavourably on the duke's frequent absences from Britain during such a troubled period: 'I see the Duke was at the Panama Canal and wish he was at home once more at the helm of his own affairs!'[6] The duke spent a good three to five months of every year in the 1880s abroad, usually on his steam yacht with his mistress, Mrs Blair, in exotic parts of the world.[7]

The fact that the estate management was so concerned by the duke's habitual absence can be explained by the rapidly changing political context in the Highlands between 1882 and 1886. The Sutherland estate covered almost the whole of a crofting county; as a result, stresses and difficulties within landlord–tenant relations were on a large scale. This chapter will begin by examining crofters' conditions up to 1886, within a context of economic fluctuation and estate management policy and philosophy. After agitation by crofters across the Highlands blossomed from 1882, a royal commission under Lord Napier was established to take evidence on the crofters' grievances, the 'Highland Problem' generally and to make policy recommendations.[8] How the estate dealt with this unprecedented and unwelcome development will be examined, including its own proposed solution to the crofter question, the 'Duke's Memo' scheme. The formation of and reaction to this attempt to delay or prevent government intervention in the rights of property will be examined, as it is essentially the estate's official response to both crofter agitation and the Napier Commission. It was not a success, however, and, in addition to the increasing politicisation of the crofters, was not enough to prevent the passage of the 1886 Crofters Act or Kemball's resignation.

'The small tenants are vegetating as usual': the Sutherland crofters, 1870–86[9]

As we have seen in previous chapters, the estate management's view of its small tenants can be characterised by exasperation, and an embedded view

---

[6] NLS, Acc. 10225, Policy Papers, 215, McIver to Geo. Taylor, Stafford House secretary, 5 Mar. 1886.

[7] Staffordshire County Record Office [hereafter SCRO], Sutherland Estates Papers, D593, P/24/4/A.74–82, Diaries of the 3rd Duke, 1883–90; places visited included Egypt, Greece, America and the Caribbean.

[8] E. A. Cameron, *The Life and Times of Charles Fraser Mackintosh, Crofter MP* (Aberdeen, 2000), 117.

[9] NLS, Acc. 10225, Policy Papers, 58, Kemball to Duke, 13 Sep. 1881.

that the crofters were a social and economic burden, rather than a secure source of rental income. The factors bore the brunt of responsibility for the crofter and cottar population, and a significant portion of their time was taken up with crofter business. They were inundated with requests and petitions, ranging from complaints about neighbours' behaviour, including boundary disputes and arguments over rights such as peat cutting; requests for building materials for houses and fences; applications for crofts as they fell vacant; complaints about the behaviour of ground officers; and, most commonly, requests for rent reductions and land enlargements.[10] These requests were common to crofters all over the Highlands and they demonstrate that on the Sutherland estate the crofters were not far from the poverty line; rights to peat and the formation of clear boundaries as well as keeping large farmers' stock out of their fields demonstrate intense competition over limited resources.[11] In the Scourie and Tongue managements regular requests were made by the factors for seed corn and potatoes for the crofters, demonstrating that harvest failure remained common into the 1880s. One night of bad storms could flatten a township financially and make it dependent on aid reluctantly given by the estate.[12] Even in areas where conditions were slightly better, land hunger and insecurity were rampant among the small tenantry.[13]

How the estate management dealt with these requests came under scrutiny in 1883 through the Napier Commission, and the picture was not a favourable one. Additional land or rent reductions requested by crofters were always refused: as the majority only paid nominal rents, they could not negotiate for better treatment like the large tenants.[14] The continuing practice of enclosing crofters' grazings for the benefit of neighbouring sheep farms or shooting lets was one manifestation of this attitude; crofters were rarely consulted, and their rents were not usually reduced as compensation.[15] Examples of this were given at the hearings of the Napier Commission in 1883. One delegate blamed the overcrowding of his township on 'making way for extending sheep farms at two or three

[10] NLS, Acc. 10225, Crofters, G/b.

[11] This was common on other Highland estates, for instance on the Macdonald estates in Skye: Armadale Castle, Macdonald MSS, 2816, Kilmore tenants to Alexander Macdonald, factor, 10 Jun. 1884; 21 Jun. 1884; 23 Jun. 1884.

[12] These were echoes of the economic crises seen in 1862–5 and 1868–9 described in Chapter one; for example, NLS, Acc. 10225, Policy Papers, McIver to Kemball, 23 Nov. 1881; 28 Aug. 1882; 14 Dec. 1882. This was also the case in Cromartie: Richards and Clough, *Cromartie*, 259–61.

[13] J. Hunter, *The Making of the Crofting Community* (Edinburgh, 1976), 114–16; Perren, 'Agricultural Depression', 29.

[14] Hunter, *Making of the Crofting Community*, 117; Richards and Clough, *Cromartie*, 287; W. Orr, *Deer Forests, Landlords and Crofters: the Western Highlands in Victorian and Edwardian times* (Edinburgh, 1982), 18–20.

[15] This was common estate policy in the Highlands; I. M. M. MacPhail, *The Crofters' War* (Stornoway, 1989), 27.

different times, till at last they got their farm to their own mind and put all the people to the breadth of the seashore, where they are in danger of losing their stock and even their children over the rocks'.[16] Another witness described how the estate coerced crofters into signing papers supporting these enclosures: 'there was a threat that if they did not sign it they would be reported to the office as disloyal; and this frequently happens'.[17]

The perceived high-handedness of the estate management could also be seen in its response to other types of petitions: generally, they did not even acknowledge their receipt. As one witness said, 'the Duke has been appealed to at different times . . . but he invariably turned a deaf ear to their appeals'.[18] This problem cannot be blamed entirely on the local estate management; rather, it reflected a wider attitude towards the crofters, which was demonstrated by all estate personnel, including Kemball.[19] In a report to the duke in 1881 he spared a short paragraph on the crofters, irritated by their lack of prosperity: 'the small tenantry are vegetating as usual – it would be well if they could be persuaded to improve their dwellings and turn their holdings to better account, but they are not easily led'.[20] This attitude was part of a common contemporary stereotype of the 'lazy' Highlander, unwilling to make an effort to pull himself out of poverty, preferring instead to depend on demoralising handouts.[21]

The crofters, however, had more complex opinions about the estate management that controlled their lives. Most did not blame the duke for their treatment, identifying the factors as their enemies: 'they impute all the woes and cruelty, and repression they talk about to the Duke's officials. The Duke, in their opinion, can do no wrong.'[22] A cottar put the situation more bluntly: 'the Duke of Sutherland is a good proprietor, but his officials are tyrannical'.[23] There were some exceptions to this ideal of good feeling between tenant and proprietor. Some pointed out that, as the landowner, the duke was ultimately responsible for both the wellbeing of his tenantry

---

[16] PP XXXII–XXXVI, 1884, *Evidence and Report of the Commissioners of Inquiry into the condition of the Crofters and Cottars in the Highlands and Islands of Scotland* [hereafter *Napier Commission Evidence*], 1631, Peter MacKay, crofter.

[17] *Napier Commission Evidence*, 1667, Rev. Mr James Ross.

[18] *Napier Commission Evidence*, 1738, William Mackenzie, labourer.

[19] Richards and Clough, *Cromartie*, 287.

[20] NLS, Acc. 10225, Policy Papers, 58, Kemball to Duke, 13 Sep. 1881.

[21] Hunter, *Making of the Crofting Community*, 115; E. A. Cameron, *Land for the People? The British Government and the Scottish Highlands, c.1880–1925* (East Linton, 1996), 23; A. G. Newby, *Ireland, Radicalism and the Scottish Highlands, c.1870–1912* (Edinburgh, 2007), 95; P. Womack, *Improvement and Romance: constructing the myth of the Highlands* (Basingstoke, 1989), 74–8.

[22] *Napier Commission Evidence*, 2512, John MacKay, Hereford, a candidate for the Sutherland county seat in 1894; T. M. Devine, *Clanship to Crofters' War: the social transformation of the Scottish Highlands* (Manchester, 1993), 214.

[23] *Napier Commission Evidence*, 1645, Angus MacKay, crofters' son; Richards and Clough, *Cromartie*, 290.

and for the actions of his officials: 'it is the Duke! the Duke! the Duke! There is no room for enterprise or any independent spirit', shouted one witness.[24] Complaints about the duke's absenteeism were also made:

> All that we are allowed is to gaze with admiration on the retreating wheels of his carriage when he is going away. Last year was an exception. He spent three days here at that time, an unprecedented thing in the Tongue management.[25]

These were the exceptions to the rule, however; most crofters, at least up to the early 1880s, were loyal to the ducal family, and were completely attached to the basic principles of landlordism. There was no suggestion that there should not be a Duke of Sutherland; the crofters just wanted social and economic improvements and a change in the behaviour of the estate's employees.[26] There were many alleged instances of tyranny of factors towards the crofters and they built an overall picture of an autocratic management gone mad in the North:

> Factors find themselves placed in remote districts with enormous and almost absolute power over nearly every person there, and the more they exercise this power, the more the love of power increases, and impatience of all opposition increases; these men in these circumstances would be more than human if they did not sometimes commit excesses in the exercise of this power, and do things which it would be painful to bring to light, and which they can hardly see in their true colour unless set before the eyes of the public.[27]

Whatever the root cause, moral or historical, it was clear that the crofters regarded the factors and the ground officers as their opponents.[28] One witness's description encapsulates the position: 'the agents of His Grace are his hands, his eyes, his ears and his feet, and in their dealings with people they are constantly like a wall of ice between his Grace and his Grace's people'.[29]

The estate management was obviously aware of its unpopularity, as after

---

[24] *Napier Commission Evidence*, 1601, Rev. Mr James Cumming; for a fuller elucidation of Cumming's views on the land question, see NLS, Acc. 5931, Papers of Rev. James Cumming, 'Observations on our Land Laws', Mar. 1883.

[25] *Napier Commission Evidence*, 1651, Rev. Mr Donald MacKenzie. Landlord absenteeism was a controversial issue across the Highlands and Ireland; Dunvegan Castle, MacLeod of MacLeod MSS, 1377, Sir Stafford Northcote to MacLeod, 22 Jun. 1882; Newby, *Ireland, Radicalism and the Scottish Highlands*, 89–90.

[26] Newby, *Ireland, Radicalism and the Scottish Highlands*, 73, 89–90.

[27] *Napier Commission Evidence*, 1716, Rev. Mr N. N. MacKay; this would happen to McIver in 1886; Hunter, *Making of the Crofting Community*, 121; A. W. MacColl, *Land, Faith and the Crofting Community: Christianity and social criticism in the Highlands of Scotland, 1843–1893* (Edinburgh, 2006), 113.

[28] *Napier Commission Evidence*, 1645, Angus MacKay, crofter's son.

[29] *Napier Commission Evidence*, 1596, Rev. Mr James Cumming.

the 'Battle of the Braes' in Skye in early 1882 it was on the alert for trouble; there were, however, no major crofter protests on the Sutherland estate to match those occurring in the Hebrides.[30] This was not especially surprising, despite the fears of the estate staff. Sutherland crofters were not facing particularly high rents, eviction or the type of catastrophic economic conditions seen in 1880–1 in areas such as Skye or Lewis.[31] The most pressing conditions for active agitation were not present in 1882, therefore; this was a relief to the Sutherland factors, who had feared the worst when the news of the events in Skye broke.[32] In his report on the small rent collection in Scourie in 1882, McIver was pleased to have 'on the whole done better than was anticipated . . . when faced with the visage of lawlessness on Skye, His Grace has come to be well pleased that his tenants seem willing and anxious to pay'.[33] There was a relative quiet among the crofters, therefore, but the estate management, rightly so, still felt uneasy about the possibilities of protest to come.[34] This was a great fear of McIver's, who, although he had a large measure of control in Scourie, knew that if the crofters chose to rebel, there would be very little he could do. As a result, he was in favour of the authoritarian policies advocated by Sheriff Ivory in Skye:

> The agitation and excitement among the small tenants in Skye is soon to operate on the whole crofting population in the North of Scotland – and we may be prepared to feel its effects in various ways. 'Tis fortunate that the authorities in Inverness-shire acted with such prompt and decided measures – at some time then are agitators at work poisoning the minds of the poor ignorant people who are too ready and willing to listen to people professing to be their friends and holding out promises they cannot realise.[35]

McIver began to blame every dispute with crofters on these 'agitators', appalled at the new-found assertiveness of crofters' demands.[36] Throughout

---

[30] Armadale Castle, Macdonald MSS, 4675, correspondence between Alex. Macdonald and J. D. Brodie, solicitor, on crisis at the Braes, 6 Feb. 1882; 20 Apr. 1882; 25 Apr. 1882; 10 Jun. 1882; 8 Sep. 1882; 25 Sep. 1882, 20 Dec. 1882.

[31] Hunter, *Making of the Crofting Community*, 131; C. Whatley, 'An Uninflammable People?', in I. Donnachie and C. Whatley (eds), *The Manufacture of Scottish History* (Edinburgh, 1992); E. Richards, 'How Tame were the Highlanders during the Clearances?', *Scottish Studies*, 17 (1973).

[32] Hunter, *Making of the Crofting Community*, 149.

[33] NLS, Acc. 10225, Policy Papers, 214, McIver to Kemball, 14 Dec. 1882.

[34] This feeling was shared with the Cromartie estate staff; Richards and Clough, *Cromartie*, 301.

[35] NLS, Acc. 10225, Policy Papers, 214, McIver to Kemball, 3 May 1882; the Skye landlords certainly subscribed to this view; Highland Council Archive [hereafter HCA], Papers of Christie and Ferguson, solicitors, Kilmuir estate MSS, D1232e, W. Fraser to Alex. Macdonald, 10 Sep. 1882.

[36] E. Richards, *The Highland Clearances: people, landlords and rural turmoil* (Edinburgh, new edn 2008), 379–80; estate managements across the Highlands commonly blamed 'outside' agitators for disturbances; HCA, Kilmuir Estate MSS, D123/1v, D. Nicolson to Alex. Macdonald, 31 Dec. 1883; W. Fraser to Alex. Macdonald, 17 Jan. 1882.

1882, for instance, he battled with the Durness crofters, who were demanding grazing in Strath Dionard for their horses, which McIver had steadfastly refused them. His position on this issue reflected current opinion in management circles; horses were regarded as wasteful and factors could not understand why crofters needed them. The Durness crofters disagreed and on a number of occasions threatened to run their horses onto the grazings without authorisation, leading McIver to comment, 'I was afraid from the state of excitement in which they were said to be on this subject that they would act forcibly and illegally . . . there is no doubt but that the Durness tenants are now following the example of their brethren in Skye and other parts of the country.'[37]

The estate also found itself in the difficult position of having to defend and account for its treatment of crofters, both past and present, as criticisms were publicly made. Of course, due to its unenviable reputation as the pre-eminent clearance estate of the Highlands, the family and management had always been on the defensive in public, and subject to sporadic published attacks over the years.[38] But the Crofters War saw a positive bombardment of correspondence, public and private, criticising the estate for its actions in almost every sphere. Stafford House was even threatened with a bomb attack at this time, a note dropped through the door ominously warning that 'the house and property of all evicting landlords is condemned. Three weeks warning is hereby given to all of you to leave this house which is sentenced.'[39] Despite the fact that since the 1850s there had been no major clearances (except in the case of Clashmore), the bombers evidently believed that the estate had much to answer for.[40] The Crofters War saw an intense revival of interest in Highland history of the last century, and the Sutherland estate and ducal family starred as the top villain in these narratives. Attacks were made very publicly; at the hearings of the Napier Commission, which were widely reported in the press; speeches, meetings, and lively debates in the correspondence columns of newspapers all meant that the Sutherland estate's dirty laundry was well and truly hung out for all to see.[41]

---

[37] NLS, Acc. 10225, Policy Papers, 214, McIver to Kemball, 13 Jun. 1882. Grazing disputes were a common basis for agitation elsewhere in the Highlands: MacPhail, *Crofters' War*, 127.

[38] For example, K. Marx, 'Sutherland and Slavery, or the duchess at home', *People's Paper* (London, 1853); D. MacLeod, *Gloomy Memories in the Highlands of Scotland* (Toronto, 1857); A. Mackenzie, *A History of the Highland Clearances* (Inverness, 1883); Richards, *Highland Clearances*, 361.

[39] SCRO, D593, P/24/1/6, 'Note addressed to the servants', Stafford House, St James, 17 May 1882; the note does not seem to have been regarded in a serious light, but it did clearly link the more violent Irish agitation, particularly the Phoenix Park murders of May 1882, to that in Sutherland; Newby, *Ireland, Radicalism and the Scottish Highlands*, 54, 67.

[40] Richards, *Highland Clearances*, 363.

[41] Many Highland estates came in for this public criticism, though not to the same extent; Ulbster Estate MSS, Factor's Letterbook 1880–7, Logan to Sir Tollemache, 8 Jan. 1884; Richards, *Highland Clearances*, 362–4.

'It is as well to be prepared for the worst': preparation for the Napier Commission[42]

Between March 1883, when the appointment of the Napier Commission was announced, and May when it began taking evidence, the Sutherland estate was busy preparing for its arrival. Urged on by Kemball, all the factors began a large information-gathering exercise, partly to enable them to complete the forms sent out by the Commission which asked for details such as rents, population and acreages, and partly for the benefit of the estate itself.[43] Kemball understood the importance of using statistics and figures in any defence, and so collected additional information, such as how much had been spent *gratis* on the crofters, seeking to emphasise a more positive aspect of the estate management.

Another tactic was persuading the Napier Commission to visit the east coast of Sutherland in order to impress them with the better condition of the crofters there. Initially, the Commission had intended only to visit the west and north coasts of Sutherland, which would have led them to see some of the poorest townships in the county. Kemball could not prevent them from seeing these areas, but he could try to mitigate the damage by persuading them to visit the more prosperous east coast as well:

> The Duke of Sutherland infers from the tenor of your letters, asking for statistical information respecting the crofters and cottars on the west coast of Sutherland, that the Royal Commission propose to confine their operations to that quarter. His Grace, while hailing their advent there with much satisfaction, desires me to submit for their consideration, that their investigation would probably be incomplete if not extended to the east coast, where the condition of the small tenants is sufficiently prosperous to exclude them from the distress which has elsewhere overtaken the fishermen and crofters and cottars, owing, almost exclusively, to the effects of storms and bad weather, or to causes beyond their control, and beyond the control of the proprietor.[44]

This effort was rewarded, Lord Napier being happy to oblige.[45] The duke also offered the Commission a tour around the reclamations at Lairg during their visit, an offer Lord Napier was again happy to take up, 'and I don't suppose the most suspicious or scrupulous critic of our proceedings could take objection to a meeting on such a scene!'[46] Evidently, Kemball

---

[42] NLS, Acc. 10225, Factor's Correspondence, 357, Peacock to Kemball, 10 Nov. 1884.

[43] Richards and Clough, *Cromartie*, 302; other estates did the same; HCA, Kilmuir Estate MSS, D123/2f, W. Fraser to Alex. Macdonald, 24 Apr. 1883.

[44] SCRO, D593, K/1/8/20, Kemball to the Royal Commission, 18 May 1883.

[45] SCRO, D593, K/1/8/20, Lord Napier to Kemball, 24 May 1883.

[46] SCRO, D593, K/1/8/20, Lord Napier to Kemball, 3 Sep. 1883. William Gunn, factor on the Cromartie estate, also urged Kemball to 'doctor' the route the Napier Commission

and the duke wanted to use the reclamations as evidence of investment in the region, and they would make a central part of Kemball's statement to the Commission.

In fact, despite Kemball's worry that the Napier Commission might condemn the Sutherland estate before the public eye, it seems that some of its members, particularly Lord Napier, Sir Kenneth Mackenzie and its secretary, Malcolm MacNeill, were privately sympathetic. MacNeill was a civil servant with considerable experience in Highland matters, was fluent in Gaelic and would continue his interest in the region after 1883.[47] In a confidential letter to Kemball written once the Commission had started its work, MacNeill reported the evidence as being 'wholly on one side, but today the other side are telling their story, and it is very clear that, at least in recent times, there is little to charge against the Proprietors beyond acquiesance . . . in squatting and over crowding.'[48]

The crofters also prepared for the arrival of the Commission, as they and their supporters realised the value of such public exposure and the necessity for preparing an effective case for reform.[49] A number of well-known activists were working in Sutherland before the arrival of the Commission, including John Murdoch, formerly of the *Highlander* newspaper, and Alexander Mackenzie of the *Celtic Magazine*.[50] The Sutherland factors kept a close eye on all proceedings, reporting back to Kemball.[51] John Crawford, the Tongue factor, was very suspicious of these 'outsiders' and was concerned about the effect they might have on the tenantry: 'I regret to say that several of the agitators from Inverness and elsewhere have been with the Free Church minister of Farr and others prompting them and others who are prepared to listen to their revolutionary slanders.'[52] One of these agitators was certainly Angus Sutherland: a native of the county, leading light in the Glasgow Sutherlandshire Association and radical Liberal, Sutherland had grown up surrounded by the folklore of the clearances, and their perceived injustice stayed with him as a politician in

would take in Cromartie: National Archives of Scotland [hereafter NAS], GD 305, Cromartie Estate Papers, Estate Correspondence, 1882, Gunn to Kemball, 11 Jul. 1883.

[47] Newby, *Ireland, Radicalism and the Scottish Highlands*, 1, 135; Cameron, *Land for the People*, 67, 85; Hunter, *Making of the Crofting Community*, 142; Cameron, *Charles Fraser Mackintosh*, 117–19.

[48] SCRO, D593, K/1/8/20, MacNeill to Kemball, 23 May 1883.

[49] Hunter, *Making of the Crofting Community*, 144; Devine, *Clanship to Crofters' War*, 220; Newby, *Ireland, Radicalism and the Scottish Highlands*, 90.

[50] J. Hunter (ed.), *For the People's Cause: from the writings of John Murdoch* (Edinburgh, 1986); Devine, *Clanship to Crofters' War*, 225; I. M. M. MacPhail, 'The Napier Commission', *Transactions of the Gaelic Society of Inverness*, 48 (1972–4), 447–8; Newby, *Ireland, Radicalism and the Scottish Highlands*, 87–90, 101; Cameron, *Charles Fraser Mackintosh*, 122–5.

[51] SCRO, D593, K/1/8/20, McIver to Kemball, 29 Jun. 1883.

[52] NLS, Acc. 10225, Policy Papers, 177, Crawford to Kemball, 23 Jul. 1883. Similar concerns were expressed by other estates: Ulbster Estate MSS, Factor's Letterbook 1880–7, Logan to Sir Tollemache, 29 Jan. 1883, 15 May 1883.

later years. Despite being passionately opposed to the Sutherland estate's restructuring of the early nineteenth century, he might be regarded as a success story of that process.[53] Forced, or encouraged, by lack of opportunity, he left Sutherland to train as a teacher and worked in Edinburgh and Glasgow, becoming involved in radical groups in the latter, such as the Sutherlandshire Association, established in 1885, and Irish campaigning groups.[54] Sutherland was further raising his profile by his efforts preparing and encouraging crofter delegates in Sutherland for the Napier Commission, along with giving his own fiery statement.[55]

Agitators were not the only threat perceived by the estate; the Free Church clergy in Sutherland were also seen, rightly, as taking a lead in preparing the crofters for the arrival of the Commission.[56] Needless to say, the factors were not pleased, and some of their most violent denunciations were applied not to crofters, Skye men or the Irish, but to the Free Church clergy: 'the ministers as a rule are most likely to do harm than good by this interference . . . their representations are more likely to be coloured and incorrect, for the people will be sure to state very fully their complaints to them'.[57] All the factors believed that the Free Church clergy were set against them, at the cost of truth, neighbourliness and proper class loyalty.[58] The usually fair-minded Kemball was also angry about the clergy's behaviour, regarding it as damaging to relations between the duke and his tenantry, and he advised the factors to ignore their activities: 'it is not only in Assynt, but in Coigach, that the Free Church minister has exercised his baneful influence to set the tenants against the proprietor. Our best course would be to ignore his existence and intervention and deal directly with the parties concerned.'[59]

---

[53] NLS, Dep. 313, 1179, Loch to 2nd Duke, 13 Aug. 1850; NLS, Acc. 10225, Policy Papers, 178, Crawford to Kemball, 26 Nov. 1883.

[54] Newby, *Ireland, Radicalism and the Scottish Highlands*, 167; J. Hunter, 'The Politics of Highland land reform, 1873–1895', *Scottish Historical Review*, 53 (1974), 46–7.

[55] NLS, Acc. 10225, Factor's Correspondence, 357, Peacock to Kemball, 10 Nov. 1884; Gunn reported similar problems on the Cromartie estate: NAS, GD 305, Estate Correspondence, 1882, Gunn to Kemball, 31 May 1883, Gunn to duchess, 30 Jun. 1883; Newby, *Ireland, Radicalism and the Scottish Highlands*, 46–7; *Napier Commission Evidence*, 2421–49.

[56] MacColl, *Land, Faith and the Crofting Community*, 108, 111–13; A. MacColl, 'Religion and the Land Question: the Clerical Evidence to the Napier Commission', *Transactions of the Gaelic Society of Inverness*, 52 (2000–2), 383–4.

[57] NLS, Acc. 10225, Policy Papers, 214, McIver to Kemball, 20 Feb. 1883. The role of the Irish, real and imagined, in the Highlands at this time is addressed in Newby, *Ireland, Radicalism and the Scottish Highlands*, 83–110; see also A. G. Newby, '"Scotia Major and Scotia Minor": Ireland and the birth of the Scottish land agitation, 1878–1882', *Irish Economic and Social History*, 31 (2004), 23–6.

[58] NLS, Acc. 10225, Policy Papers, 177, Crawford to Kemball, 26 Jul. 1883. Similar meetings were also reported on the Cromartie estate: NAS, GD 305, Estate Correspondence, 1887, Alex. Ross, ground officer, to Gunn, 1 Sep. 1884; MacColl, *Land, Faith and the Crofting Community*, 111–13.

[59] NLS, Acc. 10225, Crofters, ZO/h, Kemball to McIver, 25 Feb. 1884.

The estate was able to identify who they felt were the worst clerical offenders. Without a doubt, Rev. Norman N. MacKay of Assynt parish came top of the list for sheer interference and dangerous radicalism.[60] The Free Church minister of Durness, Ross, also came under a barrage of criticism after giving evidence to the Commission.[61] Lastly, in the Dunrobin management, Peacock was concerned about the Free Church minister in Helmsdale, MacRae; Peacock referred to him as 'the resident agitator' and reported on his activities as chair of crofters' meetings, and the hospitality he offered to the visiting Angus Sutherland.[62] The estate management reacted strongly to the Free Church ministry's conversion to the crofters' cause because they were influential individuals in both remote crofting communities and the outside world; their evidence was listened to with respect by the Napier Commission, as it came from highly educated men with both experience of the wider world and significant moral and spiritual authority.[63] For these reasons, the clergy were a significant threat to the reputation of the estate, which perhaps explains why the factors denounced them so forcefully.

The Napier Commission

They [the crofters] are discontented, and sheep farmers are discontented, and what is to become of the county in these circumstances? – The Millennium. That will make us all right and I am looking forward to it.

Can you not suggest anything more practical than looking forward to the Millennium?[64]

The Napier Commission took evidence all over the county of Sutherland, including Bettyhill, Kinlochbervie, Lochinver, Helmsdale, Golspie and Bonar Bridge, and also heard evidence of relevance to Sutherland in Inverness, Glasgow and Edinburgh. In common with all crofter delegates in the Highlands, those in Sutherland complained of four basic problems; lack of security of tenure, high rents, no compensation for improvements and land hunger. Their other main complaint was that they suffered under the 'tyranny' of estate factors and ground officers.

Security of tenure was demanded by every crofter delegate to the Napier Commission in Sutherland. Lord Napier asked various witnesses if they had

---

[60] NLS, Acc. 10225, Policy Papers, 214, McIver to Kemball, 20 Feb. 1883; MacColl, *Land, Faith and the Crofting Community*, 113.

[61] NLS, Acc. 10225, Policy Papers, 214, McIver to Kemball, 9 Aug. 1883.

[62] NLS, Acc. 10225, Factor's Correspondence, 357, Peacock to Kemball, 10 Nov. 1884.

[63] Richards and Clough, *Cromartie*, 299, 332; MacColl, *Land, Faith and the Crofting Community*, 116–17.

[64] *Napier Commission Evidence*, 2791, Thomas Purves, sheep farmer, Sutherland, questioned by Charles Fraser Mackintosh; for more on the redoubtable Purves, see *Northern Ensign*, 6 Oct. 1881.

ever requested leases from the estate; most said they would be refused, as it was not customary, in common with many crofting communities across the Highlands.[65] Perhaps not so common was the belief in Sutherland that as the ducal family were historically major clearance landlords, they could be so again: 'the feeling rankles in the breast of the people that they may be turned out any day. They don't believe that the present Duke would do it, but they don't know about his successor, so that they have no encouragement to improve.'[66] These two issues of security of tenure and improvement of lots were frequently linked: two witnesses had suffered the loss of their improvements, proving that the case was not just a theoretical one.[67] Another common demand was for fair rents, although many delegates added that they did not believe the Sutherland crofters were rack-rented as badly as those in Skye or Lewis.[68]

Land hunger was another bitter complaint; they emphasised the smallness of their lots, their poor quality and how congested the townships were: 'our chief grievance is the small size of our holdings and the want of sufficient hill pasture. We want more land to cultivate at a reasonable rent.'[69] Due to overcrowding in townships, land had been seriously damaged by overuse and productivity was falling, contributing to the crofters' poverty: 'the present crofts, on account of being cropped every year since that time [the clearances], say for seventy years or thereabouts, fail to yield anything like what they did thirty or forty years ago'.[70] Their solution was for the estate to 'return' to them land which had been lost in the clearances and subsequent small-scale enclosures:

> The great need is more land . . . the Government ought to come forward with a large and liberal measure, to co-operate with proprietors in once more getting the crofters and cottars settled in a fair measure of contentment and comfort. This would pay much better than wars with wild tribes. Let the crofters be settled on the land of their forefathers.[71]

Leading crofter supporters demanded that the land laws in the Highlands be reformed to reverse the clearances, and stop favouring the great landowners.[72]

[65] Hunter, *Making of the Crofting Community*, 144; *Napier Commission Evidence*, John MacKay, for example.
[66] *Napier Commission Evidence*, 1647, Angus MacKay.
[67] *Napier Commission Evidence*, 1635, Peter MacKay.
[68] *Napier Commission Evidence*, 1725, Rev. N. MacKay. Accusations of rack-renting also dogged Gunn in Cromartie: NAS, GD 305, Estate Correspondence, 1882, Gunn to Kemball, 31 Oct. 1883.
[69] *Napier Commission Evidence*, 1611, Adam Gunn.
[70] *Napier Commission Evidence*, 1603, Donald MacLeod.
[71] *Napier Commission Evidence*, 1720, Rev. N. MacKay.
[72] *Napier Commission Evidence*, 3278, J. S. Blackie, Professor of Greek, University of Edinburgh.

A number of other interesting themes are evident in the Sutherland crofters' evidence, the first being that of the great clearances of 1807–21.[73] They were seen by the crofters as a defining historical moment and the root of their continuing poverty:

> We feel it is needless to enlarge upon the many evils which must of necessity have followed this sudden impoverishment of people who had hitherto been in comparative affluence. At one fell swoop progress was forever made impossible, and everlasting poverty made certain.[74]

The Sutherland clearances had long been a grievance to the crofters, but this had been effectively re-kindled from the 1870s by historical, cultural and, latterly, political writing, which found fertile ground in Sutherland.[75] Crofters had more practical concerns about the consequences of the clearances, however, consequences they were still living with and which formed the basis of their demands and grievances. They argued that the clearances had put a long-term and intolerable burden on the townships which families had been removed to, resulting in congestion and poverty for everyone.[76] As one witness said in evidence that was repeated all over the county: 'there are forty-two crofters in this township [Strathy]. Previous to the Sutherland Clearances there were only four . . . the immediate result of these Clearances was over crowding'.[77] One witness described the townships after the clearances as 'just crowded like my fingers'.[78] As well as being overcrowded, the people also complained about the quality of the land they or their fathers had been removed to:

> That we and our forefathers have been cruelly burnt like wasps out of Strathnaver, and forced down to the barren rocks of the sea-shore, where we had in many cases to carry earth on our backs to form a patch of land. And now, after we have improved the land, at our own expense, and built houses, our rents are raised at every opportunity.[79]

One witness claimed bluntly that 'it was like penal servitude to put people to cultivate such a place'.[80] This argument, that poverty and congestion were a direct result of the clearances, was at the centre of the political debate over Highland land reform and was universally accepted by the

---

[73] C. W. J. Withers, '"Give us land and plenty of it": the ideological basis to land and landscape in the Scottish Highlands', *Landscape History*, 12 (1990), 46–7; Richards, *Highland Clearances*, 382.

[74] *Napier Commission Evidence*, 2432, Angus Sutherland.

[75] For example, Mackenzie, *Highland Clearances*.

[76] Hunter, *Making of the Crofting Community*, 124–5; Richards, *Highland Clearances*, 229.

[77] *Napier Commission Evidence*, 1611, Adam Gunn.

[78] *Napier Commission Evidence*, 1616, Angus MacKay.

[79] *Napier Commission Evidence*, 1645, Angus MacKay.

[80] *Napier Commission Evidence*, 1677, Donald MacKay.

crofters, their champions, the government and even by some estate managers, though not in Sutherland.[81] This view would remain an orthodoxy
among the Sutherland crofters: every initiative undertaken by the estate
management to improve the condition of the crofters met with a negative reaction, as further chapters will show, and this was usually attributed
to the legacy of the clearances. However, once the state actively stepped
in from 1886, its schemes were also a comparative failure in Sutherland;
de-population continued, as did low standards of living and high levels of
rent arrears.[82] Long-standing assumptions about the relationship between
poverty and clearance therefore need to be treated with caution.

The crofters were not the only ones who had to live with the clearances, however; in much of the evidence given to the Napier Commission,
the name of Patrick Sellar was raised.[83] To the crofters he was a historic
enemy, and they habitually blamed him, not the ducal family, for the cruel-
ler aspects of the clearances.[84] Despite this, two men tried to defend his
name in the 1880s; his sons Thomas and Patrick.[85] Thomas went before
the Commission in Edinburgh to give a verbal defence and published a
book on the same subject.[86] Patrick had taken over the tenancy of his
father's farms in Sutherland after his death and he asked the estate for
help in forming this defence.[87] Sellar believed that his family and the
estate should work together, as their aims were both the same; curbing the
crofters' agitation or, as he put it, 'cleaning up some communistic ideas'.[88]
But Peacock refused to help.[89] He thought that the issue should be laid to
rest, firstly because he believed it to be in the irrelevant past, and secondly
because continuing debate on the clearances shone an unfavourable light
on the family name and estate:

> You are aware that I have no personal knowledge of the operations you
> refer to in 1812 and 1819 . . . The fact cannot be questioned that the
> tenants were removed from certain districts to make way for the intro-
> duction of Sheep Farming, by order of the proprietor. Do you think
> it can be of any great importance to lay before the Royal Commission
> the date of each particular transaction and the names of the respective

[81] Cameron, *Land for the People*, 20, 23; Richards, *Highland Clearances*, xvi.

[82] Richards, *Highland Clearances*, 388.

[83] E. Richards, *Patrick Sellar and the Highland Clearances: Homicide, Eviction and the Price of Progress* (Edinburgh, 1999), 365–7; MacPhail, 'The Napier Commission', 455.

[84] *Napier Commission Evidence*, 1618, Angus MacKay.

[85] They had taken similar action in the 1850s when their father's reputation had been attacked in the press; Richards, *Patrick Sellar*, 349, 362.

[86] *Napier Commission Evidence*, 3177, Thomas Sellar; T. Sellar, *The Sutherland Evictions of 1814* (London, 1883); Richards, *Patrick Sellar*, 366.

[87] NLS, Acc. 10225, Factor's Correspondence, 787, Sellar to Peacock, 2 Oct. 1883; Richards, *Patrick Sellar*, 247.

[88] NLS, Acc. 10225, Factor's Correspondence, 787, Sellar to Peacock, 1 Oct. 1883.

[89] Sellar, *Sutherland Evictions*, preface.

sheep farmers put in possession of the land? . . . to attempt to do more, will, I respectfully submit, only invite further discussion about matters in detail.[90]

Peacock took a practical view of the clearances, neither denying them nor discussing them. This was the general position of all the estate management on the clearances before the Commission.[91] Emigration was one possible solution to the crofters' problems put forward by delegates. One witness claimed that if he was a young man on the estate, he would rather emigrate than continue living under the Sutherland management.[92] Crofters and their supporters were, however, generally ambivalent about emigration.[93] That land hunger was at the root of emigration was generally asserted; but whether it was thought of as a good or bad thing varied more widely.[94] Some argued that even if they wished to, the crofters were too poor to emigrate without help.[95] There were few outright rejections of emigration as a solution to the crofters' problems by witnesses in Sutherland, but few advocated it either.[96]

There were no other practical solutions to the crofters' grievances offered to the Napier Commission in Sutherland, with the exception of those devised by Mr George Greig, the duke's reclamations commissioner since 1881. He made it very clear that he was not giving evidence in his capacity as an employee of the duke or representing him in any way, but had some personal ideas based on his experiences in Kildonan.[97] He suggested that land in the interior straths of Sutherland should be parcelled out to crofters, and to help them stock their expanded lands, the government should allow stock to be mortgaged.[98] His statement caused a furore among the rest of the estate management, as they feared that it would be interpreted as a promise of future estate policy.[99] Kemball was furious with Greig and denounced his suggestions as unworkable within the existing boundaries of property rights:

> Mr Greig cannot know what I have done or what I am doing under the Duke's authority to ameliorate the conditions of the crofters, in true

[90] NLS, Acc. 10225, Factor's Correspondence, 353, Peacock to Sellar, 1 Oct. 1883.
[91] This was in direct contrast with the more emotional approach of Angus Sutherland, who was asked by Lord Napier to tone down his evidence; Newby, *Ireland, Radicalism and the Scottish Highlands*, 90.
[92] *Napier Commission Evidence*, 2541, Donald Simpson.
[93] *Napier Commission Evidence*, 1605, William Mackenzie.
[94] *Napier Commission Evidence*, 1680, Donald MacKay.
[95] *Napier Commission Evidence*, 1755, Donald Munro.
[96] This was in contrast to the landlord lobby, which saw government-funded emigration as the only realistic solution to the 'Highland Problem'; see, for example, *Napier Commission Evidence*, Kemball, 2527; McIver, 1707.
[97] *Napier Commission Evidence*, 2472, George Greig.
[98] *Napier Commission Evidence*, 2463, George Greig.
[99] SCRO, D593, K/1/8/20, Kemball to unknown correspondent, 17 Jul. 1884.

sympathy for whom I yield nothing to him and on whose behalf I am as
well assured as he can be that His Grace means every practical and reasonable concession to be made. What I have not done . . . is to talk clap
trap about dotting the straths with crofts . . . Plausible generalities of
this kind referred to, the stock in trade of agitation, whose designs Mr
Greig professed to counteract, are directed only to give birth to hope
sure to be falsified, as being realisable only by careful action gradually
in the manner that I wish to realise them.[100]

This dispute highlights the divisions and occasional open hostility which
erupted within the estate management and the extent of Kemball's desire
to keep tight control over policy making and the public image of the
estate.

The estate management had its chance to defend itself against the accusations made against it by crofter delegates. All three factors gave evidence
to the Commission, as did Kemball himself. The first factor to meet the
Commission was Evander McIver, seventy-three-year-old veteran of the
famine and the clearances of the 1840s and 1850s. He stated the expenditure made by the estate on crofters since 1845; he then pointed out that
the crofters regularly broke estate rules by subdividing their crofts, failed
to improve their position by taking the step of separating crofting from
fishing, and suggested that half of the population of the Scourie management should emigrate to ensure the prosperity of the remainder.[101] He
also claimed that dissatisfaction on the part of poor people was inevitable,
'under every proprietor and factor, let them be kind and good and liberal
as they may, there will be some dissatisfied spirits'.[102] He also argued that
the large sheep farmers were of more benefit to the proprietor than crofters because 'it is always desirable for the landlord and the county that the
tenantry should be thriving and prosperous. There is nothing more trying
than a poor tenantry to the proprietor.'[103]

McIver was later recalled before the Commission to answer more specific charges made against him in later evidence concerning Clashmore
and severity towards widows.[104] There is a sense of resignation in his
second batch of evidence: 'they [the crofters] have so many misunder-
standings I am not at all surprised at it; they have so many misunder-
standings as to what is done by the landlord's agent.'[105] McIver refused

---

[100] SCRO, D593, K/1/8/20, Kemball to unknown correspondent, 17 Jul. 1884.

[101] McIver, in an echo of the Malthusian ideas popular in the 1840s and like many Highland factors, believed that a reduction of population would improve welfare levels: McIver, *Memoirs*, 213.

[102] *Napier Commission Evidence*, 1707, McIver.

[103] *Napier Commission Evidence*, 1710, McIver; McIver means a financial burden, but strongly implies an emotional one too.

[104] See Chapter six for allegations concerning Clashmore; the author could find no evidence to corroborate the other claims of 'factorial tyranny'.

[105] *Napier Commission Evidence*, 1763, McIver.

to be drawn on the question of the clearances; he eventually conceded that they were not intentionally cruel, but tried to avoid the question altogether: 'that is going back to a time before you or I was born, and it is a subject on which I have no knowledge whatever'.[106] Overall, McIver's evidence presented an interesting paradox displayed by many of the landlord lobby at this time: he criticised the principles of crofting as an economic system and felt that prosperity was impossible in any area dominated by it. But, on the other hand, he, along with his colleagues, was completely opposed to any measure of land reform, whether government or estate led.

Next in front of the Commission were Joseph Peacock, the Dunrobin factor, and Sir Arnold Kemball, who appeared together. It was Kemball who did most of the talking, starting with a long statement which included detailed statistical support for his arguments; these concerned estate expenditure on crofters and the overall revenue and expenditure of the estate. Kemball suggested emigration as a solution: 'it is surely a matter of congratulation rather than that the lots themselves should be divided [sic]'.[107] Like McIver, he refused to comment on the clearances: 'I don't enter into the question of the Clearances, whether they were right or wrong. They took place eighty years ago, and we have to deal with facts as they are.'[108] He ended his evidence with the assurance that the duke wanted to help his tenants, although only in the vaguest sense: 'the Duke, I know, wishes well to his people, and will do what is good to them, but I cannot pledge myself to anything'.[109] Overall, Kemball's evidence was clinical and factual, aimed at counteracting the emotionally charged but more vague evidence of the crofters and their supporters. He was careful not to commit the estate to future action in front of the Commission; his suggestions would come in the following year.

The last of the factors to give evidence was John Crawford, and his performance was quite different in tone and style to that given by his colleagues; indeed, he was nearly dismissed for his behaviour. Crawford was aggressive, sarcastic, dismissive, and made some disrespectful comments about a local Free Church minister.[110] There was a reckless lack of caution in his evidence, making accusations of official arrogance and tyranny easily believable. Crawford retired in 1885 under a cloud of displeasure

---

106 *Napier Commission Evidence*, 1708, McIver.
107 *Napier Commission Evidence*, 2527, Kemball: E. Richards, 'An anatomy of the Sutherland fortune: income, consumption, investments and returns, 1780–1880', *Business History*, 21 (1979), 63–4, 67.
108 *Napier Commission Evidence*, 2527, Kemball.
109 *Napier Commission Evidence*, 2533, Kemball.
110 *Napier Commission Evidence*, 2556, Crawford. It is worth noting that by 1883, Crawford was almost completely deaf and may have found the tense public setting of the Commission very strenuous and difficult. I am indebted to Mr Geoffrey Baggott for this information.

generated by this performance; Kemball made it clear to him that the duke would have dismissed him instantly, but for his own intervention.[111] Crawford, and his style of management, was no longer tenable; his style was arbitrary and his judgement questionable. He was let off with an honourable retirement, however, as a mark of respect for the decades of service he had provided.

The estate management did not present a united or effective front before the Napier Commission. No remedies were suggested for the crofters' grievances, and only a defensive description of contemporary estate policy was offered. As far as possible the management would not comment on historical issues such as the clearances, something which must have been deeply unsatisfactory to crofters who believed them to be the root of all their problems. Instead, the management tried to defend the estate by using statistical evidence of the type the crofters and their supporters were rarely able to produce and finished by commenting generally about the duke's generosity and liberality.[112] This rang slightly hollow and the evidence seemed remote, out of touch and overcautious. Most estate managers and landlords who gave evidence to the Commission had similar problems, however, indicating that the Sutherland estate was not alone in its struggle to meet the demands of governmental and public opinion. It also reflected the wider truth that the estate was not coping well with the challenges it had been confronted with since 1882. Difficult under any circumstances to keep such a large organisation united, in the face of such a contentious issue as land reform it proved virtually impossible for the Sutherland estate. Despite all the advantages the estate had on its side – influence with the Commission itself, statistical resources and time – its defence was still lacklustre.

After the Napier Commission had produced its Report in 1884, the Sutherland estate management, along with its crofters, waited for the results. Most expected legislation, but it became clear as the months passed that the government was not going to act.[113] This was partly caused by disagreement over the conclusions of the Report of the Commission, and also in part due to the government's wish for Highland landowners to work out their differences with the crofters without having to resort to legislative intervention.[114] The estate was active on the crofter question in 1884, however, and tried to produce an independent solution to the problem, in lieu of government help.[115]

---

[111] NLS, Acc. 10225, Policy Papers, 145, Kemball to Crawford, 5 Jan. 1885; he was replaced by John Box in mid-1885.

[112] The exception to this was Angus Sutherland, who utilised statistical material to match the estate's approach; Newby, *Ireland, Radicalism and the Scottish Highlands*, 90.

[113] Hunter, *Making of the Crofting Community*, 146.

[114] Cameron, *Charles Fraser Mackintosh*, 126, 133–5; Hunter, *Making of the Crofting Community*, 153.

[115] Cameron, *Land for the People*, 32–3.

The Duke's memorandum, 1884

Despite the title, this document was, predictably, penned by Kemball after extensive consultation with a number of knowledgeable advisors, including the three factors, Lord Napier and Sir Kenneth Mackenzie.[116] It sprang from a much longer and more detailed paper on the crofter question written by Kemball in August 1884, in which he laid down what he believed to be the solution for the 'Highland Problem'. He believed that a minority of irresponsible landowners had brought potentially adverse legislation down on their own heads: 'it is the abuse of their rights and privileges and the disregard of their obligations, by the jobbing sort of landowner, which alone justify legislation.'[117] Kemball concluded that good landowners had nothing to fear from legislation; indeed, it would serve to clarify their responsibilities.[118] He then went on to list a number of matters that should come within the remit of potential legislation, including rents, tenure, size of crofter holdings, leases and common pasture. These practicalities were dealt with in the first half of the paper; Kemball then addressed what he saw as the wider evils in crofting society.

The first of these were cottars. Kemball ruled that none of the benefits he intended for crofters should be given to cottars, and he insisted that they be treated as labourers, and 'their number must necessarily be limited by the demands for labour . . . but this discretion should be regulated by recognised sanitary rules in respect to the cottar's dwelling'.[119] He then turned his attention to the crofters and the vexed question of land hunger. He made one point clear straight away; that the estate would concede to the expansion of existing holdings, but not the creation of new holdings.[120] Kemball's firmness on this point would leave a lot of people uncatered for, and his solutions for this 'surplus' population were firstly, emigration, and secondly, the development of communications to benefit the fishing industry.[121] Like many in the landlord lobby, Kemball wished to put the responsibility for these two spheres on the shoulders of government, especially from a financial point of view: 'the resources of Highland landowners are not always adequate to the purpose, and the independent agencies at

---

[116] NLS, Acc. 10225, Crofters, ZN/a, 'Memorandum in reply to Petitions to His Grace The Duke of Sutherland, from various parishes in Sutherland, 1884'.

[117] NLS, Acc. 10225, Crofters, ZN/a, 'Paper as to Crofters', Kemball, 14 Aug. 1884; McIver, *Memoirs*, 75.

[118] Kemball was not alone in this view in the landowning community; Cameron, *Land for the People*, 28–30; Dunvegan Castle, MacLeod of MacLeod MSS, 1381, MacLeod to Cameron of Lochiel, 1 Dec. 1884.

[119] NLS, Acc. 10225, Crofters, ZN/a, 'Paper as to Crofters,' Kemball, 14 Aug. 1884.

[120] NLS, Acc. 10225, Crofters, ZN/a, 'Paper as to Crofters,' Kemball, 14 Aug. 1884.

[121] The Napier Commission also placed emigration at the heart of its Report; indeed, Sutherland was given special mention in this regard; PP XXXII–XXXVI, 1884, *Report of the Commission of Inquiry into the conditions of the crofters and cottars in the Highlands and Islands*, 105–12.

work to promote the same ends may be deemed worthy of recognition and support of the state'.[122]

In producing this paper, Kemball hoped to construct a defence against the crofting lobby by offering moderate reforms in order to stave off potentially more radical losses. He made this clear to McIver, who had sent in a sheet of comments on the paper, criticising all parts of it which offered concessions to crofters, much to Kemball's frustration:

> The negative answer given to every scheme for the amelioration of the condition of the crofters without alternative proposal to the same end is disappointing the expectations of those who entertain moderate and reasonable views of the situation, and justifying the proceedings of leaguers and sympathisers, who, by urging their protégés to lawlessness, seek to force the hand of Government: a Govt [sic] whose policy in Ireland is an [sic] earnest of their acquiescence in agitation amounting to legalised coercion . . . Moreover as I before warned you, the effect of continued inaction on our part must be to bring in outsiders, and deprive the Duke's responsible advisors of the control which is essential to a satisfactory issue. The Duke, and especially Lord Stafford, are prepared to make the necessary sacrifices.[123]

If McIver did not appreciate Kemball's efforts, there were others who did. Lord Napier and Sir Kenneth Mackenzie both viewed the situation as Kemball did; that unless moderate reforms were offered soon, Highland landowners would be forced to give up more by government at a later date.

Kemball turned this general paper into a much more specific Memorandum, which laid out an experimental scheme for the Sutherland crofters, addressing contentious issues such as leases, compensation for improvements and extension of holdings.[124] Land in Rogart (400 acres), Embo Muir (150 acres) plus all of the reclaimed lands at Shiness, near Lairg (1300 acres) were to be made available as crofts, to those crofters willing to relinquish the holdings they already had.[125] They would be allowed leases and their rent would be 'nominal' to begin with, but then 'fixed by arbitrators mutually appointed' once deemed fully reclaimed. The use of an outside arbitrator in fixing rents was now seen as a necessity. This offer of land was limited to crofters, however; cottars could not apply, because it 'would be not

[122] NLS, Acc. 10225, Crofters, ZN/a, 'Paper as to Crofters', Kemball, 14 Aug. 1884; this view was almost universal among Highland landowners; Cameron, *Land for the People*, 29; Hunter, *Making of the Crofting Community*, 178–9.

[123] NLS, Acc. 10225, Crofters, ZN/a, Kemball to McIver, 3 Jul. 1884; Hunter, *Making of the Crofting Community*, 153.

[124] NLS, Acc. 10225, Crofters, ZN/a, 'Memorandum'.

[125] Since the reclamations had been completed at Shiness in 1881, the estate had been unable to let it privately. Its appearance in the duke's Memo scheme would be followed by other offers in 1894 and via the Board of Agriculture for Scotland in 1916 (see Chapters four and five).

only to perpetuate the limitation of the land of Crofters in possession – or, in other words, the state of things which it is ought to remedy – it would be beyond the means and resources of any proprietor'.[126] The crofts given up would be doled out among those left behind, enlarging existing lots.

Kemball sought the advice of experts in the field of land reform while preparing the scheme; Lord Napier said that it reflected well upon the duke and fitted in with the suggestions made in his Report.[127] He had doubts that the provisions in the Memo could be applied across the Highlands, although that was not, of course, ever Kemball's intention. Napier pointed out that most Highland landowners did not have the Duke of Sutherland's vast financial resources, which had enabled him to propose to accept only nominal rents from crofters:

> I assure you I have no preference for compulsory measures and no desire to abridge the rights of property. But under the actual circumstances of the Islands, especially of Skye, I do not think that either expensive improvements would be carried out without some power of pressure on the proprietors, who are in some conspicuous cases so much embarrassed that voluntary effort on behalf of the crofter class can scarcely be expected from them.[128]

He did approve wholeheartedly of the duke's decision to allow rents to be fixed by arbitration, as an act both symbolic of offering the olive branch to the crofters and recognising their recent political empowerment.[129] Kemball's other advisors also approved of the scheme, regarding it as liberal and beneficial for the battered public image of landowners; indeed, their only criticisms stemmed from their belief that the duke was being too generous.[130] Only Sir Kenneth Mackenzie, possibly through his connections with the Highland Land Law Reform Association [hereafter HLLRA], warned that the crofters might not accept the terms offered in the Memo, commenting that 'probably today in Sutherland they will expect better terms.'[131] In this prediction, Mackenzie was correct.

After the duke's Memo was distributed among the crofters, they discussed

---

[126] NLS, Acc. 10225, Crofters, ZN/a, 'Memorandum'.

[127] SCRO, D593, K/1/8/20, Napier to Kemball, 9 Mar. 1885; Richards, *Highland Clearances*, 383; Cameron, *Charles Fraser Mackintosh*, 135.

[128] SCRO, D593, K/1/8/20, Napier to Kemball, 9 Mar. 1885. One of these 'embarrassed' landlords was surely Lord Macdonald of Skye, who by 1862 was in debt to the tune of £94,770.18.3 with a yearly rental of just £10,918.2.5 and no other sources of income. The situation became much worse in the 1880s with his crofting tenants on widespread rent strike. Of course, under these circumstances it would have been impossible for the Macdonald estate to attempt such schemes as the Duke of Sutherland was proposing; Armadale Castle, Macdonald MSS, 5167, 'Note of total rental, draft of debts, and burdens of the Macdonald estates, 1862'.

[129] SCRO, D593, K/1/8/20, Napier to Kemball, 9 Mar. 1885.

[130] SCRO, D593, K/1/8/20, Whitbread to Kemball, 26 Sep. 1884.

[131] SCRO, D593, K/1/8/20, Mackenzie to Kemball, 13 Sep. 1884; Cameron, *Land for the People*, 24–5.

its terms in meetings organised by the Sutherlandshire Association and the HLLRA, and their replies were, without exception, negative. The reason given for their refusal was the same in every case; the alleged poor quality of the land offered. The Rogart crofters, advised in meetings with John MacKay, Hereford, took the lead, publishing their answer to the duke's Memo in the *Scotsman*'s letters page, using the weapon of publicity to try to shame the estate management.[132] Although they admitted that any offer of reform was better than nothing, they expected something more in the post-Napier Commission Highlands.[133] They claimed that

> It would be impossible for the petitioners to name any part of the county of Sutherland more useless and less capable of improvement than the portions at Lairg and Embo . . . As is well known to His Grace, the lands offered at Shiness were originally, at enormous expense, intended and reclaimed for large farms . . . no tenant could be got for them, and consequently they are lying on the hands of the proprietor at considerable loss . . . As no other use can be made of them these farms are now offered on certain conditions to the petitioners.[134]

The crofters accused the estate of cynically trying to recoup its losses on the reclamations, while at the same time repairing its public image after the damaging attacks made on it during the Napier Commission.[135]

This rejection sent a clear message to the estate management; that the crofters would not settle for scraps offered by the duke and were prepared to wait for government schemes. All of Kemball's careful planning had backfired; he had hoped to make an impact on the land reform debate and set an example among the landowning community. Instead he had received a humiliating public rejection of his scheme, which in turn sparked a further heated debate, putting the Sutherland estate just where he did not want it – in the national newspapers.[136] Kemball tried to mitigate the damage, writing personally to the *Scotsman* defending the quality of the land offered and renewing the offer, but it was not taken up.[137] The estate had underestimated both the scale of the crofters' demands and their recent radicalisation; they would not be appeased by moderate reforms put forward by Kemball, just as Sir Kenneth Mackenzie had predicted.[138]

---

[132] John MacKay of Hereford was a Sutherland native and wealthy railway contractor, who was one of the leading lights of the crofters' movement in Sutherland; *Scotsman*, 15 Jan. 1885, letter to editor from MacKay.

[133] *Scotsman*, 29 Dec. 1884; Hunter, *Making of the Crofting Community*, 144.

[134] *Scotsman*, 29 Dec. 1884.

[135] *Scotsman*, 29 Dec. 1884.

[136] *Northern Ensign*, 25 Dec. 1884; *Scotsman*, 2 Jan. 1885, 8 Jan. 1885; NLS, Acc. 10225, Policy Papers, 24, Kemball to Peacock, 24 Nov. 1884.

[137] *Scotsman*, 2 Jan. 1885.

[138] *Scotsman*, 12 Jan. 1885; at this time 'monster meetings' demanding land and franchise reform were held at Portree and Bonar Bridge, which provide a context for the Sutherland crofters' actions; *Scotsman*, 15 Jun. 1885.

The failure of this scheme was the first indication to the Sutherland estate that the crofters wanted reform on their own terms, not scraps from the ducal table. The crofters were politically organised and had new advisors; the Napier Commission had radicalised them and they were prepared to wait for government legislation.[139] The comments made about the estate and the tone of the meetings held across Sutherland reported in the press show a new bold and irreverent attitude towards the once-feared 'Castle Government'. The estate, through the duke's Memo scheme, thought that by pre-empting government legislation it could block the necessity of government intervention on the estate: it was wrong.

Election year: 1885

> What tenderness! What pathos! What self-denial! What appeal! Crofters of Sutherlandshire, will you not respond to it? Weave around you the webs of officialdom, forge anew the links of your fetters, sell your liberties – do anything, but for Heaven's sake spare the feelings of a Marquis! Consider how your feelings were spared – your fathers', with their homesteads blazing to Heaven.[140]

The year 1885 promised to be one of great change for the Sutherland crofters; the first election after the reform of the franchise laws was due, and debate on the land question and demand for reform was increasing accordingly. The county seat was to be contested in Sutherland for the first time in over fifty years, and Lord Stafford, the sitting MP and future 4th Duke, was concerned: the electorate had increased by 880% in 1884, from 326 to 10,011, and clearly action would have to be taken if he wanted to keep his seat.[141] In 1885, Angus Sutherland stood as one of six 'Crofter' candidates for Highland seats, all backed by the Highland Land Law Reform Association and all single-issue campaigners who wanted to push through legislation to reform the land laws in the Highlands.[142] Despite being a member of this loose 'Crofters Party', Sutherland was significantly more radical than some of his fellow candidates, such as Charles Fraser Mackintosh and Donald Macfarlane.[143] Unlike his more

---

[139] MacPhail, *Crofters' War*, 85–6.

[140] *Northern Ensign*, 25 Mar. 1885, letter to the editor.

[141] F. W. S. Craig, *British Parliamentary Election Results, 1885–1918* (London, 1974), 527.

[142] One of these, Dr Roderick Macdonald, was busy in Ross-shire, to the consternation of the staff of the Cromartie estate; NAS, GD 305, Estate Correspondence, 1883, William Gunn to duchess, 1 Mar. 1884; I. M. M. MacPhail, 'The Highland Elections of 1884–86', *Transactions of the Gaelic Society of Inverness*, 50 (1976–8), 383; J. P. D. Dunbabin, 'Electoral reforms and their outcome in the UK, 1865–1900', in T. R. Gourvish and A. O'Day (eds), *Later Victorian Britain, 1867–1900* (London, 1988), 113, 122–4.

[143] D. Meek, 'The Catholic Knight of crofting: Sir Donald Horne McFarlane, MP for Argyll, 1885–86, 1892–95,' *Transactions of the Gaelic Society of Inverness*, lviii (1992–4); *Crofter*, 5, 1 Aug. 1885; Cameron, *Fraser Mackintosh* (Aberdeen, 2000).

conservative colleagues, Sutherland was a radical on other issues, aside from land: he was heavily involved in campaigns for Irish Home Rule and believed that land nationalisation was the solution to the land question.[144] Sutherland also faced a unique challenge in his campaign to become MP; his opponent, Lord Stafford, also set himself up as a 'Crofter' candidate, earning himself the popular soubriquet the 'Radical Marquis'. That left the Sutherland electors with two radical candidates to choose from, both competing in how 'advanced' they could become to secure the votes of the newly enfranchised crofters.

Lord Stafford began cultivating his image as a champion of the crofters in late 1884, but it was really in 1885 that this conversion came to the fore as his election campaign intensified.[145] Until 1884, Lord Stafford had not been a noted campaigner for the crofting tenantry on the estate he was one day to inherit, but the work of Angus Sutherland and the Sutherlandshire Association had raised expectations to such a degree that Stafford recognised he would have to radicalise in order to retain his seat.[146] Many greeted this change of heart with either suspicion or derision, including some of his politically active relatives, such as his uncle, the 8th Duke of Argyll. As Argyll complained to McIver, 'Lord Stafford has made the wildest and most ignorant promises and has done great harm.'[147] Argyll, as an active member of the landlord lobby on the crofter question, may have felt that Stafford had betrayed his own class: the 3rd Duke's opinion on his son's radicalism is not known.[148] Most of the suspicion and derision directed at Stafford came from the crofters, however, and supporters of Angus Sutherland, who accused him of cynically cashing in on crofters' issues to get re-elected. They also pointed out that he had done little to help the crofters in the eleven years he had already been their MP:

> I do not doubt the sincerity of the noble lord, especially since the landlords have made the wonderful discovery that the 'interests of the landlords and crofters are identical': but would not the exercise of this newborn zeal have appeared more graciously before the sword of

[144] Newby, *Ireland, Radicalism and the Scottish Highlands*, 49. Only one of his fellow 'Crofter' MPs, Dr G. B. Clark, who stood for and won the Caithness seat in 1885, matched Sutherland in radicalism.

[145] MacPhail, 'Highland Elections', 387; Cameron, *Fraser Mackintosh*, 155.

[146] Newby, *Ireland, Radicalism and the Scottish Highlands*, 165–6; D. Kemp, *The Sutherland Democracy* (Edinburgh, 1890), 14; A. Adonis, 'Aristocracy, agriculture and liberalism: the politics, finances and estates of the third Lord Carrington', *Historical Journal*, 31 (1988), 876–88.

[147] NLS, Acc. 10225, Policy Papers, 197, Argyll to McIver, 5 Oct. 1885.

[148] Argyll, 8th Duke of, 'A Corrected Picture of the Highlands', *Nineteenth Century*, 16 (1884); Argyll, 8th Duke of, 'On the Economic Condition of the Highlands of Scotland', *Journal of the Royal Statistical Society of London*, 26 (1883); Argyll, 8th Duke of, 'The Prophet of San Francisco', *Nineteenth Century*, 15 (1884); Hunter, 'Politics of Highland land reform', 53–4; E. H. Green, *The Crisis of Conservatism: the politics, economics and ideology of the British Conservative Party, 1880–1914* (London, 1995), 80–2.

avenging justice gleamed in the distance and compulsory laws loomed in the rear?[149]

Some believed that Stafford, coming from a social sphere and background far above that of the crofters, could never fully comprehend their needs and doubted whether he would actually deliver on any of the radical promises he made.[150]

Stafford spent weeks visiting various townships in Sutherland, meeting his crofter constituents on an individual basis and listening to their grievances.[151] He was keen to correct as many of these as possible in order to win support, and forwarded applications to the factors and Kemball to sort out. This added a huge burden to their workload, though the individual requests were small; in a common demand, Donald MacKay of Clerkhill wrote to Stafford, 'I intend to vote for you at the General Election. I have great need that some Reduction will be taken off my rent if you please and repeat my circumstances to Sir Arnold Campbell [i.e. Kemball] and to take this to consideration.'[152] Most crofters were referred to their factor by Stafford and wrote to them directly demanding that his promises be fulfilled: 'when his Lordship the Marquis of Stafford called on me about a fortnight after I stated my Grievance to him so he wished me to apply to you the first time you came here and that he had not the least doubt but I would get satisfaction [sic]'.[153]

However effective this was in securing votes for Stafford, it caused trouble in the management, with Kemball eventually losing his temper: 'the enclosed letter from Donald McLeod to Lord Stafford will show you the difficulty I must encounter in dealing with no less than 145 similar cases brought to my notice'.[154] McIver, appalled at the crofter's assertiveness, also feared Stafford's policy could have ugly long-term side effects: 'Lord Stafford has laid himself open to receive complaints from querulous parties and I fear that all the rules laid down are likely to be broken, and the present dissatisfaction and management of crofters will become difficult if not impossible.'[155] Stafford was also careful to publicly distance himself from the estate management, while using his influence within it to rectify the minor grievances of the crofters. He recognised McIver's unpopularity, for instance, and so refused his offers of accompaniment through Assynt: 'his Lordship declined considering I suppose that it was as well that I should

---

[149] *Northern Ensign*, 25 Mar. 1885, letter to the editor from 'A Scorner of Flunkyism'.

[150] *Scotsman*, 16 Apr. 1885, report of a crofters' meeting at Lairg; *Scottish Highlander*, 31 Jul. 1885; 7 Aug. 1885.

[151] This type of electioneering was common on other landed estates; M. Cragoe, *An Anglican Aristocracy: the moral economy of the landed estate in Carmarthenshire, 1832–1895* (Oxford, 1996), 150, 155, 158, 161–2.

[152] NLS, Acc. 10225, Crofters, G/b, Donald MacKay to Lord Stafford, 29 Nov. 1885.

[153] NLS, Acc. 10225, Crofters, G/a, Hugh Frazer to Box, 5 Nov. 1885.

[154] NLS, Acc. 10225, Policy Papers, 145, Kemball to Crawford, 5 Jan. 1885.

[155] NLS, Acc. 10225, Policy Papers, 215, McIver to Kemball, 13 Oct. 1885.

not accompany him, in case it might be spoken of as undue influence!'[156] It is clear the estate management used its position to aid Lord Stafford's campaign through practical help to the crofters, but equally, it worked hard to avoid any accusations of actual corruption. With an enlarged electorate and secret ballot it was impossible for the estate to intimidate or influence crofters directly, but it is likely that the social hold the estate had over the crofters contributed to Stafford's eventual victory.[157]

Naturally, the estate management were pleased with the win.[158] Kemball believed that it could mark the start of a new era of improved relations between landlord and tenant, and commanded his factors to keep the peace with the crofters no matter which way they had voted:

> The return of Lord Stafford to Parliament with a majority of 643 may be regarded as proof of the confidence acquired by the constituency of Sutherland in the sincerity of his Lordship's desire to improve the relations existing between Proprietor and Tenant . . . In order that these results may be fully confirmed it is of primary importance that all traces of the recent contest in the sense of adverse partisanship should be entirely obliterated. I beg therefore that you will enjoin the Ground Officers in your District to repudiate any concern whatever in the votes recorded by individuals and to discourage any sort of inquisitional or discriminatory action, on the part of would-be advocates of Lord Stafford's cause to discredit their opponents.[159]

This command casts a shadow over the behaviour of the estate; that such a document had to be issued at all raises questions about the management's integrity, although no instances of preferential treatment to crofters who supported Stafford have come to light, or any punishment of crofters who did not.[160] Stafford's victory was short-lived, however; after the fall of Gladstone's Liberal government in 1886, there was another election and this time Stafford resigned his seat rather than stand again. What his personal motives for this decision were, after such an active fight only a year before, are unknown. One possibility may have been that he was strongly opposed to Irish Home Rule and therefore in conflict with his party leader.[161] Perhaps his defeat was too probable to risk standing and he wished

---

[156] NLS, Acc. 10225, Policy Papers, 215, McIver to Kemball, 26 Jun. 1885.

[157] A similar conclusion can be drawn from the actions of the Cromartie estate staff: NAS, GD 305, 1886, Estate Correspondence, Alex. Ross to J. Rae, Inverpolly, 30 Nov. 1885; Cannadine, *Decline and Fall,* 142–6.

[158] Stafford won with a majority of 643; Craig, *British Parliamentary Election Results, 1885–1918,* 562.

[159] NLS, Acc. 10225, Policy Papers, 146, Kemball to Box, 30 Nov. 1885.

[160] The debate over the role of landlord coercion in elections has been examined in Cragoe, *Anglican Aristocracy,* 171–8, and essentially matches the situation found in Sutherland.

[161] NLS, Papers of J. S. Blackie, MS 2636, ff.227, Lord Stafford to J. S. Blackie, 5 Jun. 1885; W. C. Lubenow, *Parliamentary Politics and the Home Rule Crisis: the British House of Commons in 1886* (Oxford, 1988), 257, 260–3; Green, *Crisis of Conservatism,* 85, 87.

to end his parliamentary career more honourably than being beaten by a crofter's son.[162]

The political story of Sutherland was not just in national politics, but just as much, if not more so, in local politics, another arena that illustrates the waning of the estate's power. Traditionally, the estate management had used local political positions to exert control in Sutherland, seeing their seats on Parochial and School Boards as an automatic privilege. By 1885, this was no longer the case; crofter agitation had changed the issues driving politics in the Highlands and the crofters were more organised and politicised than ever before.[163] In mid-April there were elections for the Parochial and School Boards in Assynt, and McIver reported that there was a contest for these seats for the first time in forty years:

> There was a very striking proof of the efforts of agitation among the crofters. There was never any interest taken by the electors in Assynt in the constitution of the Parochial Board since 1845, when the Poor Law was introduced. There are four elected members and on Wednesday a crowd of men and women appeared and for the first time there was voting for various people all connected with the Established Church to be thrown out and four members of the Free Church were appointed. In a like manner since 1872 there has been no contest for election of members of the School Board. There are now eleven candidates for seven seats and I was told a strenuous effort is to be made to have no one connected with the Established Church on the School Board.[164]

There was also a clear change in every-day estate management in Sutherland from 1885. The factors and Kemball were already, in advance of any legislation, treating crofters' complaints and grievances very differently than they had in previous years: crofter expectations were high and the management found that it could no longer act with impunity. Kemball had to constantly remind McIver that all estate policy and actions now had to be carried out with reference to 'grievance mongers', as the public eye was firmly fixed upon them and acted almost as strictly as legislation.[165]

The biggest concession granted to the crofters before the passage of the Crofters Act was a blanket rent reduction of 50%.[166] It matched an earlier remission given to the sheep farming tenants, who after much lobbying had

[162] MacPhail, 'Highland Elections', 388; Cannadine, *Decline and Fall*, 191–2; Newby, *Ireland, Radicalism and the Scottish Highlands*, 166–7.

[163] Richards and Clough, *Cromartie*, 308, 339.

[164] NLS, Acc. 10225, Policy Papers, 215, McIver to Kemball, 24 Apr. 1885; MacColl, *Land, Faith and the Crofting Community*, 108, 113.

[165] NLS, Acc. 10225, Policy Papers, 195, Kemball to McIver, 27 Feb. 1884.

[166] NLS, Acc. 10225, Policy Papers, 146, Kemball to Box, 7 Dec. 1885; crofters on other estates were also offered rent reductions; HCA, Kilmuir Estate MSS, D123/2f, W. Fraser to Alex. Macdonald, 21 Jan. 1883.

been granted a 50% reduction in their rents by the estate.[167] Kemball had his eye on the positive effect on the estate's image the reduction could have and thought it might do something to heal the rift between the crofters and the management: 'I incline to think a deduction to the small tenants is desirable, not for its amount, but to show that the Duke feels for them as well as for the larger tenants.'[168] It may also have stemmed from the realisation that in some areas, crofters were refusing to pay their rents in protest, and reducing them all round might encourage more payers.[169] Deeply rooted attitudes among the factors had changed little, however: witness the outrage expressed when the crofters did not display the properly thankful behaviour for this rent reduction:

> I am sorry to say the spirit evinced by many of the Tenants in Assynt and the unthankful manner in which the abatement was received by not a few there was very striking, and to me it was distressing to witness the change which has come over the people of that parish. Their minds are diseased – in fact agitation and the recent canvass and election has quite demoralised them.[170]

And it was not only in the poorer western parishes that such attitudes could be observed. John Box in Tongue complained to McIver that 'it is very disheartening, after the unselfish manner in which the deliberations connected with the rent abatements were conducted, to find so much dissatisfaction and grumbling'.[171] Conflict between the expectations of the crofters and those of the factors would not come to an end in 1886.

Conclusion: the Crofters Holdings (Scotland) Act 1886

The style and direction of the Sutherland estate management changed beyond recognition between 1880 and 1886. The main impetus for this had not been direct crofter agitation, which was rare on the estate, but rather new and hostile public interest in Highland landlordism. The press, the public, through urban Gaelic groups, and finally the government, had turned an unsympathetic eye onto Highland estates and the Sutherland estate management had to face up to changing attitudes towards their

---

[167] Sheep farmers elsewhere in the Highlands also lobbied for similar rent reductions; Armadale Castle, Macdonald MSS, 4695, farm tenants to Alex. Macdonald, 18 Aug. 1885; Orr, *Deer Forests*, 19–20.

[168] NLS, Acc. 10225, Policy Papers, 215, Kemball to McIver, 6 Nov. 1885.

[169] NLS, Acc. 10225, Policy Papers, 215, McIver to Kemball, 28 Dec. 1885. A rent reduction of 50% was granted to the Cromartie crofters; NAS, GD 305, Estate Correspondence, 1886, Alex. Ross to Gunn, 2 Jan. 1885.

[170] NLS, Acc. 10225, Policy Papers, 215, McIver to Kemball, 28 Dec. 1885.

[171] NLS, Acc. 10225, Factor's Correspondence, 1475, Box to McIver, 9 Mar. 1886. This theme of crofter 'ingratitude' was common elsewhere: Richards and Clough, *Cromartie*, 300–1, 304.

policies, past and present.[172] Some staff never fully accepted these changes: Crawford and Peacock both retired within two years of the Napier Commission and McIver faced a hard struggle until his own retirement in 1895.[173]

The new movement for land reform, crofters' political rights and the changing way the rights of property were being viewed produced a fractured response from the estate management. The three factors could see no reason why the status quo should change; they were veterans of the Highland Famine and in their opinion, by the 1880s, in spite of a recent economic downturn, the crofters had never had it so good. They felt that their new and aggressive demands were a disgraceful liberty taken against the generosity of the duke. This attitude was in opposition to that of the upper management, including Kemball and Lord Stafford, who realised that changes had to be made, but both failed to convince the factors of this or provide solutions radical enough to meet the crofters' demands.

It says much about the extent of change that by early 1886 all parties on the Sutherland estate, from the factors to the crofters, were looking forward to the passage of legislation.[174] The failure of the duke's Memo scheme and continuing agitation made the estate more open to government leadership on the issue: 'it is greatly to be wished that legislation on the crofter question may end in a law which will inform landlords and tenants what their rights are and then the wild unreasonable expectations now afloat in the minds of the crofters may vanish and give way to common sense, when landlords can deal more easily with them'.[175] Kemball saw little to fear in the Crofters Act for the Sutherland estate in terms of rents and compensation for improvements: 'fair rents and compensation for improvements are already institutions in Sutherland. There is no harm in their being obliged to check the abuse of proprietary rights.'[176] He did foresee crofter dissatisfaction with the lack of generous provision for enlargement of holdings, which concerned him.[177]

Kemball was not to oversee the working of the Crofters Act in Sutherland, however, as he handed in his resignation just as it was passed. McIver wrote immediately on hearing the news: 'we are on the eve of economic changes, in relation to all the rights of landlord property, and these will demand

[172] Hunter, *Making of the Crofting Community*, 141, 145, 160.

[173] McIver, *Memoirs*, 74–83; Joseph Peacock retired to London in 1885, where he continued to undertake accountancy work for the estate. He was replaced by Donald MacLean, a political moderate.

[174] Cameron, *Land for the People*, 31; Richards and Clough, *Cromartie*, 307; E. A. Cameron, 'The Political Influence of Highland Landowners: a reassessment', *Northern Scotland*, 14 (1994), 31; NLS, Acc. 10225, Factor's Correspondence, 358, Peacock to McIver, 11 Mar. 1885.

[175] NLS, Acc. 10225, Policy Papers, 215, McIver to Kemball, 10 Mar. 1886; Cameron, *Land for the People*, 38.

[176] NLS, Acc. 10225, Policy Papers, 146, Kemball to Crawford, 26 May 1885.

[177] NLS, Acc. 10225, Policy Papers, 146, Kemball to Crawford, 26 May 1885.

much prudent consideration and caution on the part of Proprietors, and those acting for them. Therefore I feel that your resignation is at present no small misfortune over the estates of the Duke.'[178] How justified those fears were will be examined in the next chapter.

[178] NLS, Acc. 10225, Policy Papers, 215, McIver to Kemball, 11 May 1886.

CHAPTER FOUR

'Gladstone has much to answer for': The Sutherland Estate, 1886–96[1]

Introduction

In June 1886, Sir Arnold Kemball retired from the commissionership of the Sutherland estates and was replaced by R. M. Brereton, a thirty-eight-year-old engineer from Norfolk.[2] It is unclear how he came to be chosen as, like Kemball, he had no experience in land management and the post was, until 1882 at least, one of the most prestigious jobs in the British land market.[3] Like Kemball, he was an extremely active and at times demanding commissioner, who insisted on closely balanced books, being fully informed and determined to keep a strong grip on the reins of the Sutherland estate.[4] This was sound policy: the vast size of the estate, the almost continuous absence of the 3rd Duke from business in the 1880s and the introduction of the 1886 Crofters Act all warranted tight control.

Brereton soon ran into problems with his colleagues in the estate management, stemming from his proposed policies on crofters. Brereton believed that the spirit as well as the letter of the 1886 Act should be promoted by the estate, accepting that some degree of land reform was inevitable and in many cases desirable. He argued that this should be tempered by a policy of 'firmness' towards crofters who broke the law when agitating for reform. These views were met with hostility by some of the factors, notably McIver, and quickly led to serious tension. The relationship between the commissioner and the factors had always been one of much potential friction; although the factors tended to look back with nostalgia on the reigns of Kemball and George Loch, there had undoubtedly been disagreements and resentment in those relationships.[5] This was taken to new depths with Brereton, until working relationships could no longer be maintained.[6]

---

[1] National Library of Scotland [hereafter NLS], Sutherland Estates Papers, Acc. 10225, Factor's Correspondence, 1960, McIver to William Gunn, Cromartie factor, 28 May 1890.
[2] NLS, Acc. 10225, Policy Papers, 216, McIver to Kemball, 12 Jun. 1886; E. Richards and M. Clough, *Cromartie: Highland life, 1650–1950* (Aberdeen, 1989), 330–4.
[3] Richards and Clough, *Cromartie*, 335.
[4] NLS, Acc. 10225, Policy Papers, 181, Brereton to Box, 15 Mar. 1887.
[5] Richards and Clough, *Cromartie*, 334–5.
[6] NLS, Acc. 10225, Policy Papers, 198, Brereton to McIver, 9 Apr. 1887; Richards and Clough, *Cromartie*, 334.

The demands of post-1886 Highland estate management required a flex-
ible and harmonious staff, and this the Sutherland estate certainly did not
have. In June 1888, Brereton announced to the factors that he was stepping
down.[7] The 'retirement' was certainly forced and acrimonious; he refused
to co-operate with a smooth transfer of power, showing open and at times
vindictive hostility to his former colleagues, especially McIver.[8]

After Brereton's departure, Lord Stafford advised the duke to abandon
the principle of the commissionership and replace it with a committee: 'it
is to be observed that times are changed and instead of the old system in
Sutherland we require a more businesslike and routine system. This has
come about chiefly on account of crofter legislation, which has interfered
with the old relations between Landlord and tenant.'[9] Lord Stafford
added that the post of commissioner was inherently flawed, arguing that
'if you go on in the old system you are entirely dependent on the man
who manages for you – if he fails there is general confusion.'[10] The duke
agreed to this new arrangement, but confusion reigned among the factors
as to whom they should consult on matters of policy and the experiment
was short-lived.[11] The duke and Lord Stafford fell out irreconcilably in late
1889 over the duke's recent remarriage, the committee was dissolved and
the duke took the estate management into his own hands.[12]

In September 1892, the 3rd Duke died suddenly at Trentham of a per-
forated ulcer in the stomach; he left behind him a mixed reputation.[13]
Even in death the 3rd Duke was able to create discord, in this case over his
will. After his second marriage to his long-term mistress Mrs Mary Caroline
Blair in 1888, he had changed his will no fewer than ten times, eventually leaving nearly all of his personal fortune of £1.2 million and the vast
Sutherland estates either directly in her hands or under her control for her
lifetime, with the added clause that 'her late husband merely wishing that
she would prefer his heirs if they in her estimation treated her in a manner
becoming to her position as the Duke's widow and their step mother.'[14]
This sparked a sensational public wrangle and a complete breakdown of
familial discipline. The legal case with which Lord Stafford, now the 4th
Duke in title only, pursued her was only resolved in late 1894 in an out-of-
court settlement, in which he received back the estates in return for paying
the dowager duchess a huge cash sum, perhaps as much as £750,000, plus

---

[7] NLS, Acc. 10225, Policy Papers, 200, Brereton to McIver, 19 Jun. 1888.
[8] NLS, Acc. 10225, Policy Papers, 200, Wright to McIver, 6 Jun. 1888.
[9] Staffordshire County Record Office [hereafter SCRO], Sutherland Estates Papers, D593,
   P/24/3/2, note by Lord Stafford, undated [1888].
[10] SCRO, D593, P/24/3/2, Stafford to duke, 23 Jun. 1889.
[11] NLS, Acc. 10225, Policy Papers, 217, McIver to Stafford, 31 Mar. 1890.
[12] NLS, Acc. 10853, 34, Wright to MacLean, 18 Jan. 1890.
[13] *Scottish Highlander*, 29 Sep. 1892; *Times*, 24 Sep. 1892; *Scotsman*, 26 Sep. 1892; Richards and
   Clough, *Cromartie*, 378.
[14] D. Stuart, *Dear Duchess: Millicent Duchess of Sutherland, 1867–1955* (London, 1982), 44.

an annuity of £4,000.[15] The case was a disaster for the estate: a large chunk of its capital had been lost in a painful court battle in the full glare of a gleeful and scandal-hungry public.[16] Additionally, the estate management had been thrown into a general confusion between 1892 and 1894, with no rents being collected on the Sutherland estate for those years, in order to prevent them going to the dowager.[17]

This was just one of many conflicts within the Sutherland estate management between 1886 and 1896, years which can be characterised as among the most troubled in its history, undergoing frequent and damaging personnel changes at a turbulent time in wider Highland politics and society. The 1886 Crofters Act had not, as expected, led to peace in Sutherland; unrest continued, especially on the west coast, as the crofters protested that their demands for more land, rather than less rent, had not been met. The management also had to deal with the sittings of the Crofters Commission in the county, a huge organisational and administrative burden. Unfortunately for the management, the arrival of the Commission did not signal the end of their toil; many of the Commission's decisions concerning rents, land enlargements and the rents for those enlargements were, unusually in the Highlands, unpopular with the Sutherland crofters, who frequently refused to abide by them.[18] A royal commission on the Highlands and Islands [hereafter the Deer Forest Commission] followed in the early 1890s, which required the estate to rally once more and organise a defence of its income from the hated deer forests. Parallel to this government activity, in 1894 the 4th Duke set up his own 'Crofters Purchase' scheme, offering crofters the opportunity to buy their lots and become landowners in their own right. All these changes and challenges, combined with the fracturing of the Sutherland management at all levels, contributed to difficult working circumstances for the Sutherland factors. They felt constantly under attack from both government initiatives and the crofters, and were not being effectively supported by a united or harmonious upper management.

The estate finances were a further source of worry to the staff and, increasingly, the ducal family.[19] The 4th Duke embarked on a long period

---

[15] Stuart, *Dear Duchess*, 45; E. Richards, 'Gower, George Granville William Sutherland Leveson-,' *Oxford Dictionary of National Biography* (Oxford, 2004).

[16] J. Yorke, *Lancaster House: London's greatest town house* (London, 2001), 91, 155–9; Richards and Clough, *Cromartie*, 378.

[17] NLS, Acc. 10225, Policy Papers, 153, Wright to Box, 17 Nov. 1892; Bodleian Library, Harcourt Papers, 221, 4th Duke to Harcourt, 16 Oct. 1892.

[18] E. A. Cameron, *Land for the People? The British Government and the Scottish Highlands, c.1880–1925* (East Linton, 1996), 49; Hunter points to the 'reverence' with which the Crofters Commission was regarded generally, although he acknowledges its inability to tackle land hunger; J. Hunter, *The Making of the Crofting Community* (Edinburgh, 1976), 179–80.

[19] NLS, Acc. 10225, Policy Papers, 207, Wright to McIver, 1 Jan. 1894. For other cases of weakening familial and financial discipline; D. Spring, 'The role of the aristocracy in the nineteenth century', *Victorian Studies*, 4 (1960), 61–2.

of financial retrenchment after 1894, which had a significant impact on the Sutherland estates: 'we must economise all round for a year or two . . . I am economising in England too – I hope in a year or two we will be alright again.'[20] The management was supportive of this policy, having long been concerned about the Sutherland finances: 'I confess it makes me very anxious when I see the way he is expending money and I fear that in a few years he will find himself with a seriously reduced income . . . The household expenses are much greater than ever in the past and there is every appearance of them increasing rather than diminishing.'[21] The 4th Duke would struggle to control his domestic expenditure, and by the final years of the century he would be forced to make major land sales to shore up his finances.[22]

The estate was not in dire straits yet, as Donald MacLean, the Dunrobin factor, reported in 1892.[23] Rental income was noted as satisfactory, especially from shootings, farms and hotels. MacLean was also positive about income from fishings and plantations on the estate, assuring the duke that expenditure was economical and that the estate was functioning efficiently.[24] On a less positive note, MacLean highlighted the growing arrears of crofters' rents, which stood at over £1,500 in 1892.[25] Crofters aside, this report shows that despite all of the difficulties the estate had faced from 1886 – financial, managerial and organisational – for the most part it had maintained its financial equilibrium, propped up by sporting, hotel and farming rents.

Frequent and turbulent upheavals in the management of the estate undoubtedly had a major impact on how effective it was in carrying out its duties.[26] Policy decisions were delayed by absence, disagreement and division during one of the most challenging periods for Highland estates in the nineteenth century. This background can go some way to explaining the often inconsistent actions of the estate in the decade, as management turnovers meant a change in policy direction on a regular basis, not least in its approach to the new Crofters Commission.

---

[20] NLS, Acc. 10225, Policy Papers, 106, duke to MacLean, 8 Nov. 1897.

[21] NLS, Acc. 10225, Policy Papers, 207, Wright to McIver, 21 Oct. 1894; D. Cannadine, *The Decline and Fall of the British Aristocracy* (London, 1990), 93–5.

[22] E. McIver, *Memoirs of a Highland Gentleman: being the reminiscences of Evander McIver of Scourie*, G. Henderson (ed.) (Edinburgh, 1905), 123. The 4th Duke sold 100,000 acres in Tongue in 1899, the Stittenham estates in Yorkshire in 1912 and 50,000 acres of Assynt in 1913; see Chapter five for further details.

[23] MacLean wrote this report as an introduction for the 4th Duke to his vast inheritance; NLS, Acc. 10225, Policy Papers, 106, MacLean to duke, 4 Oct. 1892.

[24] NLS, Acc. 10225, Policy Papers, 106, MacLean to duke, 4 Oct. 1892.

[25] NLS, Acc. 10225, Policy Papers, 106, MacLean to duke, 4 Oct. 1892.

[26] Richards and Clough, *Cromartie*, 335–6.

**'Take the bull by the horns': the workings of the Crofters Act in
Sutherland, 1886–96**[27]

The 1886 Crofters Act legislated for a land court, the Crofters Commission,
to travel around the Highlands setting fair rents, cancelling arrears and
considering enlargements of crofters' holdings.[28] The Commission was the
physical incarnation of government interference on Highland estates and
the Sutherland estate management regarded it with mixed feelings. On
one side, the factors were keen for the Commission to come to their districts as soon as possible, to resolve the numerous grazing disputes and rent
strikes that were damaging estate finances.[29] They feared that a heavy level
of arrears would develop, only to be later cancelled by the Commissioners:
'it would be well if the Commission could be prevailed to visit Sutherland
soon, because if there is any long delay after the applications are sent in <u>we
shall get no rents</u> during that time, however long it may be'.[30] In the mean-
time, Brereton ordered a review of crofters' rents, allowing reductions so as
to make a good impression on the Crofters Commission.[31]

Even the 3rd Duke took an interest and made it clear that the
Commission should be dealt with as actively as possible; he wanted every
individual case to be judged on its merits, and opposed if need be, to make
it clear to the crofters that the estate was not going to just roll over:

> Applications will be recklessly made by the Crofters in every direction,
> if the belief gained currency that the office of the Commission was
> not to regulate rents impartially, but to reduce them whenever the
> silence of the Proprietor, in respect of his own rights, could be inter-
> preted to justify a doubtful claim: in other words whenever the Crofter
> should rely on the main chance of getting something without risking
> anything.[32]

---

[27] NLS, Acc. 10225, Policy Papers, 198, Brereton to McIver, 28 Mar. 1887.

[28] Hunter, *Making of the Crofting Community*, 169–70; I. M. M. MacPhail, *The Crofters' War*
    (Stornoway, 1989), 173–4; T. M. Devine, *Clanship to Crofters' War: the social transformation of
    the Scottish Highlands* (Manchester, 1994), 231–2.

[29] Cameron, *Land for the People*, 43; E. A. Cameron, 'The political influence of Highland
    landlords: A reassessment', *Northern Scotland*, 14 (1994), 31.

[30] NLS, Acc. 10225, Factor's Correspondence, 1480, Box to Brereton, 12 Dec. 1887. Other
    Highland estates also lobbied for the Crofters Commission to resolve disputes; Armadale
    Castle, Macdonald MSS, Alex. Macdonald to Lord Lothian, 12 Oct. 1888; Sheriff Brand to
    Alex. Macdonald, 27 Oct. 1888.

[31] NLS, Acc. 10225, Factor's Correspondence, 365, MacLean to Brereton, 10 Nov. 1886.
    The same task was undertaken by William Gunn on the Cromartie estate, but was more
    urgent, rents there being 'from 30% to 50% higher' than in Sutherland: National Archives
    of Scotland [hereafter NAS], Cromartie Estate Papers, GD 305, Estate Correspondence,
    1889, William Gunn to Brereton, 16 Nov. 1886. The Ulbster estate also reduced crofters'
    rents: Ulbster Estate MSS, Thurso, Factor's Letterbook 1880–7, Logan to Sir Tollemache,
    10 Jan. 1887.

[32] NLS, Acc. 10225, Policy Papers, 180, Brereton to Box, 10 Dec. 1886.

After the Commission's first sittings in the Dunrobin management in 1886, the estate realised it would not arbitrarily lower rents or automatically work in the crofters' favour. Indeed, MacLean was concerned for some of the crofters whose rents had been raised by the Commission: 'I am afraid that some of the increases will tell hardly on widows and old woman tenants who perhaps do not get the full benefit of the pasture.'[33] This view was not shared by McIver, unsurprisingly, who advised his old friend William Gunn, factor on the Cromartie estate, that he considered 'Mr McIntyre [one of the Crofter Commissioners] strongly in favour of the crofters and desirous to give much to them', and that it was 'of much importance to humour the Commission and assessors and not to appear too anxious or too keen – to restrain feeling – and to keep cool'.[34]

The Sutherland estate was the first place the Commissioners visited after their appointment; it had not influenced the Commission in this decision, despite the seemingly unlikely starting point.[35] There are several possible reasons why the Commission started its work in a quiet area of Sutherland. Firstly, it may have been keen to show the crofters that agitation such as that seen in Assynt, Skye and Lewis would not command its itinerary.[36] Secondly, the Commission may have simply wished to start its work in a relatively straightforward area to lay out the basics of its working practice, before tackling more troublesome regions, where agitation formed an additional challenge.[37]

One of the advantages Brereton saw in the Crofters Commission was that it could stop continuing agitation, especially in McIver's west coast management: 'I am sure we shall not be able of ourselves to allay this miser-able spirit of agitation amongst so large a crofting community as you have in Assynt. We had better therefore at once take "the bull by the horns," and appeal to the Commissioners to fix fair rents and to deal with the question of arrears.'[38] As MacLean pointed out for his Dunrobin manage-ment, 'the arrears are largest in that parish [Rogart] and there is I think more disaffection there than in any other; yet I believe the rents overall will be increased in it by the Commission.'[39] The curious paradox of the judgement of the Commission being desired by the crofters combined with the likelihood of it giving out unpopular or disadvantageous decisions was recognised with puzzlement by the estate management. In December 1886, the Commission left Sutherland to deal with other areas of the Highlands,

---

[33] NLS, Acc. 10225, Factor's Correspondence, 365, MacLean to Brereton, 31 Dec. 1886; NLS, Blackie Papers, MS2636 ff. 315, John MacKay, Hereford to Blackie, 20 Nov. 1886.

[34] NLS, Acc. 10225, Factor's Correspondence, 1960, McIver to Gunn, 30 May 1890.

[35] Cameron, *Land for the People*, 42; E. A. Cameron, 'Politics, Ideology and the Highland land issue, 1886–1920s', *Scottish Historical Review*, 72 (1993), 65.

[36] Cameron, *Land for the People*, 41.

[37] NLS, Acc. 10225, Factor's Correspondence, 365, MacLean to Brereton, 31 Dec. 1886.

[38] NLS, Acc. 10225, Policy Papers, 198, Brereton to McIver, 28 Mar. 1887.

[39] NLS, Acc. 10225, Factor's Correspondence, 382, MacLean to Jamieson, 2 Feb. 1891.

but it was not long before the estate was lobbying to have it back as soon as possible, especially to the districts where agitation was continuing.[40] It did not return until 1890, a decision that seems to have been influenced by the fact that a major bout of agitation in Assynt had been effectively resolved by mid-1888, making a visit less imperative when agitation was continuing in Lewis and Skye.[41] Sutherland was not a priority for the Commissioners, as agitation was rare and it was well understood that crofters were, on the whole, fairly rented by the estate and that their demands revolved around arrears and extension of holdings.

Despite this, McIver still viewed the Commission as a threat. By 1886, he had already been in post for forty-one years and he found it hard to come to terms with both the legislative changes affecting Highland landowner-ship and the upper management's approach to them. Typically, he viewed these changes as a personal betrayal by the crofters:

> It is to me a very trying disgusting business, and the change in feeling, manner and conduct of the people . . . is to one long among them almost intolerable. Socialism is speeding fast all over the Kingdom among all classes and we may expect that changes will occur which we at present cannot avert or keep back. Gladstone has much to answer for.[42]

As Brereton tried to explain to McIver, 'we must recognise the fact that "times have changed, old manners gone" and the Highland Chiefs are no longer as they were chiefs of the clan, in the olden sense'.[43] McIver refused to accept this view, which led to tension serious enough to alert Brereton:

> There are a number of old folks who may prefer to stick to the old order of things and management, but we have to deal more and more as years roll on with the younger [crofter] community whose thought and education are very different, and with whom the management has more or less lost touch.[44]

Brereton was beginning to see McIver's philosophy, management style and beliefs as a problem, rather than his experience as an asset.[45] For most of his colleagues, however, initial doubts about the Commission were soon dispelled, and along with many other Highland estates, the Sutherland

[40] Cameron, *Land for the People*, 44–6; NAS, Crofting files, AF67/ 9, Under-secretary for Scotland to Brand, Chair of the Crofters Commission, 14 June 1888; AF67/10, Duke of Sutherland to Lord Lothian, 3 Oct. 1888.
[41] Cameron, *Land for the People*, 56; NAS, AF67/10, Brand to Lothian, 13 Nov. 1888; see Chapter six for details of this agitation.
[42] NLS, Acc. 10225, Factor's Correspondence, 1960, McIver to William Gunn, 28 May 1890. Factorial bitterness of this type was very common; Richards and Clough, *Cromartie*, 298, 300–1; Cameron, *Land for the People*, 50.
[43] NLS, Acc. 10225, Policy Papers, 198, Brereton to McIver, 26 Feb. 1887.
[44] NLS, Acc. 10225, Policy Papers, 181, Brereton to Box, 26 Feb. 1886.
[45] Richards and Clough, *Cromartie*, 337–8.

estate lobbied hard in the first years of the Commission to get it to visit Sutherland as soon and as often as possible. It also applied on behalf of all the crofters on the estate to have their rents fixed and arrears examined.[46] The duke mellowed somewhat towards the Crofters Commission after 1886. He generally took a conciliatory stance towards the crofters, especially when faced with sustained and determined agitation such as that in Assynt, and was happy to co-operate with the Commission on the question of extension of crofters' grounds:

> The Duke . . . feels that every effort should be made to meet the wants of the Crofters generally in such a way as to remove, if possible, all excuse for discontent and especially that we should carry the Commission with us . . . The Duke sincerely hopes that . . . will not only be considered liberal but that they will really have the effect of rendering great and permanent improvement in the condition of the crofters.[47]

The duke was consistently willing to grant concessions demanded by the crofters to avoid any agitation, particularly if the legal authorities or government, in the form of marines and gunboats, became involved. This aversion was due to the family's deep and long-standing social and political sensitivity towards their reputation as great clearance landlords. The 3rd Duke wished to avoid violent scenes in his lifetime, and so in the teeth of factorial opposition, ordered that the crofters should as far as possible be granted their requests.[48]

Box and MacLean were in agreement, but McIver refused to back down: 'I think there are many objections to the Duke's appealing to the Commissioners to fix fair rents for the whole of his crofter holdings. My opinion is that the Duke desires the pecuniary benefit from the crofters.'[49] McIver was wrong in his assumption: the duke and Lord Stafford were willing to make financial sacrifices to avoid public criticism and crofter agitation.[50] McIver need not have worried, however, as the results of the work of the Crofters Commission show.

In two out of the three Sutherland managements, rents were actually

---

[46] NLS, Acc. 10225, Policy Papers, 181, Brereton to Box, 26 Feb. 1887. The Ulbster and Macdonald estates also did this: Ulbster Estate MSS, Factor's Letterbook 1880–7, Logan to Sir Tollemache, 15 Jan. 1887; Armadale Castle, Macdonald MSS, 4725, 1, 'Notice to Crofter tenants', 8 Dec. 1886; Cameron, *Land for the People*, 44.

[47] Acc. 10225, Policy Papers, 203, Wright to McIver, 29 May 1890.

[48] *Scottish Highlander*, 2 Jun. 1887.

[49] NLS, Acc. 10225, Policy Papers, 216, McIver to Brereton, 1 Mar. 1887. McIver was frustrated by this lack of proprietorial resolution: Richards and Clough, *Cromartie*, 302, 306–7.

[50] Other landowners were less sanguine; MacLeod of MacLeod wrote that he was 'quite annoyed' by the decisions of the Crofters Commission on his estate and opined that 'the Highlands will never recover from the demoralisation'; Dunvegan Castle, MacLeod of MacLeod MSS, 1390, 2, MacLeod to Crofters Commission, 6 Jul. 1889.

increased overall by the Commission: Dunrobin saw an increase of 12% and Tongue an increase of 0.25%. There was evidence of over-renting in the Scourie management, however, which saw a 5% reduction in rents. Large reductions were made in crofters' arrears across the estate, just as the factors had predicted; Dunrobin saw 23% of its arrears cancelled, Tongue 31% and Scourie 33%.[51] Arrears were high in Sutherland, partly due to rent strikes, but also because of the depressed crofting economy of the 1880s.[52] Overall on the Sutherland estate, rents were increased by 2.5% and 29% of arrears were cancelled. In order to put these figures into a wider context, rent reductions and arrears cancelled on the Skibo estate, owned by A. C. Sutherland, have also been examined. Skibo occupied a small pocket of Sutherland not owned by the duke and the differences in the figures are striking. Sixty-six applications were adjudicated on at Skibo: rents were decreased by an average of 39.9% and 63% of arrears were cancelled, clearly demonstrating the widely acknowledged fact that rents on the Sutherland estates were unusually low compared to the majority of Highland estates.[53] MacLean was right in his prediction that some of the crofters would be unhappy with the decisions the Commission had made.[54] In the wake of the Commission's sittings, the factors received petitions from crofters asking for their rents to be reduced, putting the management in a rather awkward position.[55] Although the estate refused to reduce individual rents that had been fixed by the Commission, they did periodically reduce crofters' rents wholesale across the estate. In 1887, for example, crofters' rents were reduced by 25% as a conciliatory gesture of goodwill to the crofters, in the hope that continuing agitation would cease.[56]

The other role of the Commission was to grant enlargements to crofters' holdings, and it was this issue that generated the most conflict in Sutherland. The crofters were keen to get additional land to relieve chronic congestion; in the Commission, they saw a fair and independent body that would be able to help them, although the reality would turn out to be much more complex than either the estate or the crofters had bargained for. Brereton and the duke accepted in early 1886 that giving land to the crofters, especially those in Assynt, was the only way to halt the agitation in that district: 'the authorities are wiging this matter [land extensions] upon my attention and it must be dealt with as soon as possible in order

[51] PP LXXX, 1888, *Report of the Crofters Commission*, Appendix A, 1–11; PP LX, 1889, *Report of the Crofters Commission*, Appendix A (5), 90–140; PP LXIX, 1894, *Report of the Crofters Commission*, Appendix A (4), 37–55.
[52] Cameron, *Land for the People*, 55.
[53] PP LXXX, 1888, *Report of the Crofters Commission*, Appendix A, 9–11; MacPhail, *Crofters' War*, 18, 176.
[54] Cameron, *Land for the People*, 49–50.
[55] NLS, Acc. 10225, Policy Papers, 152, Wright to Box, 4 Sep. 1891; *Scottish Highlander*, 17 Mar. 1887.
[56] NLS, Acc. 10225, Policy Papers, 181, Brereton to Box, 16 Oct. 1887.

to avoid a chronic state of discontent among the people'.[57] The duke was keen to avoid confrontation over land, although he did attempt to distinguish between giving concessions to 'law-abiding' crofters and those who agitated. He was willing in principle to allow land to be taken from large farms for the benefit of the crofters, provided they applied for it through the Commission and the Commission set the rent to be paid on it.[58]

The factors were in general agreement with this principle, except, inevitably, McIver. His opposition was partly based on his ideas about their agricultural abilities, but was mainly due to his view that crofters who had been acting illegally should not be granted their demands or they would continue to use agitation as a tool.[59] McIver simply refused to co-operate with Brereton in selecting potential townships which could benefit from extensions of land:

> I regret that I cannot select any tenants in the Stoer district and recommend them as deserving law-abiding tenants among whom the farms proposed to be divided should be cut up and distributed. There is such a universal feeling of rebellion to order and authority abroad in that district that it is impossible for anyone . . . to sit them down as tenants deserving an unusual favour from their landlord.[60]

Despite McIver's opposition, a number of enlargements, overseen by the Crofters Commission, were made in the Scourie management between 1888 and 1889. Enlargements were granted to the townships of Inverkirkaig, Strathan, Achmelvich, Clashtoll, Stoer, Clashmore, Culkein Achnacarnin, Clashnessie, Achnacarnin, Culkein Drumbeg, Drumbeg and Nedd, of nearly 6,500 acres in total.[61] In 1889, sixty crofters from Sangomore and Sangobeg, two of the poorest townships in Sutherland, were granted nearly 4,000 acres grazing, and the crofters of Oldshorebeg received the whole of Sandwood farm, nearly 2,000 acres.[62]

The greatest irony came in 1890, when the Tarbat crofters were granted the island of Handa as a grazing park, although it was part of a sheep farm already tenanted by none other than McIver: he assented to the decision, but grumbled: 'with regard to Handa it was the <u>cream</u> of my farm . . . The farm without it will be a poor affair . . . it will reduce my profits from £50 to £60 at the least yearly.'[63] The duke was aware of the political symbolism

---

[57] NLS, Acc. 10225, Policy Papers, 200, Brereton to McIver, 6 Jan. 1888.

[58] NLS, Acc. 10225, Policy Papers, 203, Wright to McIver, 29 May 1890. This was in contrast to some other high-profile Highland estates; Armadale Castle, Macdonald MSS, 3181, Lord Macdonald to Alex. Macdonald, 25 May 1886; Richards and Clough, *Cromartie*, 305–6.

[59] Richards and Clough, *Cromartie*, 307.

[60] NLS, Acc. 10225, Policy Papers, 216, McIver to Brereton, 12 Apr. 1888.

[61] NAS, AF67/14, Report by James Gordon on enlarged townships in Assynt, Feb. 1890.

[62] PP 1890–1 LXIII, *Report of the Crofters Commission*, 31 Dec. 1888–31 Dec. 1889, and PP 1896 LXVIII, *Report of the Crofters Commission*, 31 Dec. 1894–31 Dec. 1895.

[63] NLS, Acc. 10225, Policy Papers, 217, McIver to Wright, 21 Jun. 1890.

of this grant, and encouraged McIver to give up the land: 'where in this case <u>you</u> have a farm, the Duke feels that special care is required, seeing that your personal interests are concerned that your actions are watched with much jealousy'.[64] McIver was advised that he may have lost the best of his sheep farm, but he would be compensated by easier relations with the crofters: 'I think your action in regard to Handa will probably tend more than any other step to smooth your way in future and I feel convinced that what you have all round will knock the feet from under the southern agitators.'[65]

The granting of enlargements was only the beginning of the estate's problems, however; issues soon arose over their fencing. In most cases, the Commission had ordered that the landlord should provide the materials for fences, and that the crofters should build them before the date of entry. In many cases, the crofters refused to carry out this obligation, delaying indefinitely their date of entry onto the land. In some cases the crofters started pasturing their stock on the land regardless, to the fury of the tenant farmers onto whose land the animals inevitably strayed.[66] As McIver reported to Wright:

> I found when collecting the Assynt rents that the crofters to whom the Commission had assigned land were as a rule dissatisfied and full of complaints. The land assigned to the Inverkirkaig and Strathan tenants has not been taken possession of and as yet they have declined to erect the fence as prescribed by the Commissioners . . . A number of the tenants of Achmelvich who asked for pasture and to which the Commissioners arranged what they had asked for now repudiate it and say they don't want it and will never pay for it . . . I mention all this that the Duke may see how little these ungrateful troublesome people value his generosity and kindness – the more they get, the more discontented and troublesome they are.[67]

The issue of fencing was a serious practical problem, and the estate's Edinburgh lawyer wrote to the Scottish Office on the subject.[68] The estate was also concerned by the numbers of crofters who had received land enlargements, but had then pulled out of agreements and were refusing to pay their share of the new rents.[69] The Commission returned to Sutherland in 1891 to sort out the problem, and much to the satisfaction of the estate,

---

[64] NLS, Acc. 10225, Policy Papers, 203, Wright to McIver, 29 May 1890.

[65] He is perhaps referring to Angus Sutherland; NLS, Acc. 10225, Policy Papers, 203, Wright to McIver, 13 Jun. 1890; McIver, *Memoirs*, 217.

[66] Enforcing the decisions of the Crofters Commission was a widespread problem: Cameron, *Land for the People*, 57–8; Dunvegan Castle, MacLeod of MacLeod MSS, 1390, 14, Harlosh tenants to MacLeod, 17 May 1894.

[67] NLS, Acc. 10225, Policy Papers, 217, McIver to Wright, 13 Dec. 1889.

[68] NAS, AF/67/14, Jamieson to Lord Lothian, 18 Feb. 1891; minute by Mr Dunbar, 18 Feb. 1891.

[69] NLS, Acc. 10225, Policy Papers, 217, McIver to Stafford, 1 Mar. 1889.

No decisions were amended . . . The Commissioners are very much annoyed and incensed by the conduct of the parties who did not erect the fences as ordered, and they laid down strongest rules and fixed dates for the completion of these fences intimating that if they did not complete the work on these dates they would reconsider the former assignation of land and deprive them of the land altogether . . . I think this visit of the Commission will do good in Assynt, Sheriff Brand was very decided with the crofters.[70]

The estate was bitter over what it saw as the ungrateful behaviour of the crofters, but for them, the situation was not so clear cut. There were disagreements as to how the new grazing land was to be divided and maintained; often these disagreements had not been resolved before the land had been granted, resulting in a complete breakdown of earlier pacts. Many crofters also lacked the capital to stock their extended grazings and so derived no benefit from them, despite having to pay extra rent, and many complained that they had been bullied into signing up for the new land by their better-off neighbours.[71]

The estate meanwhile had to balance concessions to the crofters with its responsibilities for their large tenant sheep farmers, whose acres were being reduced for the benefit of the crofters. Most tenants did not complain about the Commission's decisions and negotiated a reduction in their rents from the estate easily enough.[72] This was not always the case, however; certainly not when it came to Mr Dudgeon, the tenant of Crackaig sheep farm near Helmsdale in the Dunrobin management. In 1888, forty-three Helmsdale crofters had applied for land within Crackaig and the estate had to come to terms with the Crofters Commission, Dudgeon and the crofters.[73] At first Dudgeon accepted a blanket rent reduction of £80 to compensate for the loss of ground, but soon made additional demands for improvements to his farm steading and offices, testing how far the estate would go to conciliate him.[74] MacLean was angry, but wary about losing Dudgeon, as there were already several sheep farms in hand across the county: 'I am afraid these [crofters'] applications will drive Mr Dudgeon away. He is very restless and annoyed about them, especially as there is no intimation from the Commission when they can be dealt with.'[75] That said, MacLean was still furious with Dudgeon's behaviour and the effect it was having on the crofters and

[70] NLS, Acc. 10225, Policy Papers, 217, McIver to Wright, 17 Jul. 1891.
[71] NLS, Acc. 10225, Policy Papers, 217, McIver to Stafford, 1 Mar. 1889; Crofters, G/a, Strath Halladale crofters to Box, 15 May 1886.
[72] For example, NLS, Acc. 10225, Policy Papers, 216, McIver to MacBrayne, tenant of Clashmore farm, 7 Dec. 1888.
[73] NLS, Acc. 10225, Factor's Correspondence, 371, MacLean to duke, 29 Jun. 1888.
[74] NLS, Acc. 10225, Factor's Correspondence, 373, MacLean to Stafford, 15 Nov. 1888.
[75] NLS, Acc. 10225, Factor's Correspondence, 374, MacLean to Stafford, 15 Feb. 1889.

the estate's relations with them.[76] Eventually, MacLean decided to call Dudgeon's bluff and accepted his notice on Crackaig farm, at which step Dudgeon backed down and agreed to 'give no further trouble'.[77] The case of Crackaig farm eloquently illustrates the difficulties the estate faced in balancing its duties towards its large and small tenants, especially when both groups were unhappy with the decisions of the Crofters Commission.[78]

Dealing with the activities of the Crofters Commission was a huge challenge for the estate, especially against a background of almost continuous conflict within the management itself. The factors were split on crucial issues such as enlargement of crofters' holdings, McIver having to be dragged kicking and screaming along a more conciliatory path. The sheer size of the estate also meant vast amounts of work for the factors in administrative preparation – covering nearly 1,500 applications. The estate had little to worry about over the crofters' rents; it was the issue of land that the Sutherland crofters were most concerned about, and the Crofters Act did not go far enough, even with the co-operation of the estate, to meet those demands: the result was continuing agitation in Sutherland.

'Some real prospect of disturbance': agitation, 1886–96[79]

Contrary to the hopes of the estate, crofter agitation continued after the passage of the Crofters Act and into the early 1890s. Most of this agitation occurred in the Scourie management; there were threats of action in the east and north, but they were rarely carried out. The fora for discussion and debate among the crofters, including the possibility of agitation and land raids, were public meetings, mainly under the auspices of the Sutherlandshire Association.[80] For example, action was threatened by the Bettyhill crofters in late 1887 on the Reay forest, on the Glencanisp deer forest by the Inverkirkaig crofters in early 1888 and on the Druinrurinie forest by the Knockan and Elphin tenants in February 1889.[81] None of these threatened raids was carried out, but they caused great alarm among the estate management. Even the threat of a

[76] NLS, Acc. 10225, Factor's Correspondence, 374, MacLean to Stafford, 25 Feb. 1889.

[77] NLS, Acc. 10225, Factor's Correspondence, 374, MacLean to Stafford, 9 Mar. 1889.

[78] For the rest of the Crackaig case, including trespass by the crofters and two cases taken to the Court of Session: NLS, Acc. 10225, Factor's Correspondence, 376, MacLean to Tait, 3 Jul. 1889, 4 Jul. 1889, 25 Jul. 1889, 26 Jul. 1889; 377, MacLean to duke, 11 Dec. 1889, 24 Dec. 1889; 378, MacLean to Wright, 29 Jan. 1890: 381, MacLean to Jamieson, 20 Oct. 1890, MacLean to Tait, 18 Nov. 1890; 382, MacLean to Wright, 2 Mar. 1891, MacLean to Jamieson, 24 Mar. 1891; 1490, Box to MacLean, 5 Mar. 1891; Acc. 10853, 35, Wright to MacLean, 4 Mar. 1891; *Scottish Highlander*, 19 Dec. 1889, 15 May 1890.

[79] NLS, Acc. 10225, Factor's Correspondence, 1481, Box to Brereton, 2 Feb. 1888.

[80] NLS, Acc. 10225, Policy Papers, 181, Brereton to Box, 22 Dec. 1887; A. G. Newby, *Ireland, Radicalism and the Scottish Highlands, c.1870–1912* (Edinburgh, 2007), 126, 136.

[81] NLS, Acc. 10225, Policy Papers, 198, Brereton to McIver, 24 Dec. 1887.

raid could be damaging to the estate, as it could conceivably frighten off a shooting tenant; this was, perhaps, the crofters' intention.[82] There was also almost continuous low-level agitation; trespass by crofters and their stock on sheep farms, illegal peat cutting, and pulling down fences and dykes being the most common offences.[83] Generally, the worst agitation was confined to the north and west coasts; there was much less on the east coast, with the one exception of the Muie crofters and their raid on the Blairich farm in 1886.[84]

It is hardly surprising that the majority of the agitation was carried on in these districts; the Crofters Act had been ineffective in settling the vexed question of land hunger, and the decisions the Commission had made in favour of the crofters were often in dispute.[85] The poverty of the crofters was another key reason for their agitation:

> I regret to learn there is some real prospect of disturbance among these people [the Melness crofters]. It is certain that some of them are beginning to feel real want and this has emboldened them to threaten disturbance. I understand that they have had a meeting and memorialised the Home Secretary for immediate assistance and have stated that if this is not complied with, they will make a raid on the deer forests.[86]

The crofters attributed their poverty to congestion created by the clearances, something the Crofters Act had not resolved. Crofters frequently claimed that they had rights to the land they were raiding; historical or moral rights rooted in pre-clearance Sutherland.[87] But the very act of granting land to the crofters was to some in the estate management an intolerable admission of failure on their part; failure of the rhetoric and policy of clearance that had been so forcefully put into reality in Sutherland in the early nineteenth century. This was combined with wider contemporary fears of socialism and communism, ideas which the factors felt had infected the Sutherland crofters: 'there are a number of young fellows about Bettyhill who go away for summer work in the States [USA]

---

[82] I. J. M. Robertson, 'The Historical Geography of Social Protest in Highland Scotland, 1914–c.1939', unpublished Ph.D. thesis (University of Bristol, 1995), 58.

[83] NLS, Acc. 10225, Policy Papers, 217, McIver to Wright, 16 Nov. 1889; Robertson, 'Historical Geography', 58.

[84] *Scottish Highlander*, 13 May 1886, 3 Jun. 1886, 10 Jun. 1886.

[85] NLS, Acc. 10225, Crofters, G/a, petition from crofters of Strathy West to Box, 7 Dec. 1886; McIver, *Memoirs*, 76.

[86] NLS, Acc. 10225, Factor's Correspondence, 1481, Box to Brereton, 2 Feb. 1888; the raid on Park deer forest, Lewis, in 1888 was similarly justified as providing food for 'starving families'; Hunter, *Making of the Crofting Community*, 172.

[87] NLS, Acc. 10225, Lawyer's Correspondence, 219, Tait to McIver, 6 Dec. 1889; C. W. J. Withers, '"Give us land and plenty of it": the ideological basis to land and landscape in the Scottish Highlands,' *Landscape History*, 12 (1990), 46–7; Robertson, 'Historical Geography', 23–4.

and return in winter bringing with them all sorts of democratic, even communistic views. I am a bit anxious about these fellows.'[88]

The estate's reaction to this agitation was mixed. When crofters threatened or carried out land raids, the estate's immediate response was to install watchers, so that trespassers could be identified and interdicts served.[89] The estate also tried to set an example by refusing to give land grants to those who broke the law, as

> It would never do that the crofters on the estate should be able to conclude that if they wished to get a certain piece of ground the way to do so was to become non-payers of rent – lawless, rebellious, take violent possession of what they coveted and in short accomplish their purpose by taking the law into their own hands.[90]

The estate, therefore, faced a perplexing problem; it was willing to grant land to the crofters through the Crofters Commission, but also wished to clamp down on agitation by attempting to grant land only to those who were not involved in any illegal activities, and prosecuting those who were.[91] In reality, the estate, partly by having its hand forced by the Crofters Commission, granted land extensions to both crofters who agitated and those who stayed within the law, despite their professed aim of differentiating between them.

A further indicator of the decline of the estate's influence can be seen in the first County Council elections in Sutherland, held in 1890.[92] All of the estate factors stood for election, as well as James Gordon, the Assynt subfactor, to ensure that the duke's interests would be represented on the new Council, although some had misgivings.[93] McIver was against the Council on principle, for being 'too much one-sided on democratic terms in this county . . . I shall do my best to get in for Eddrachillis but it is doubtful I fear . . . The people are full of the wildest ideas of the many benefits the County Council could confer upon them.'[94] McIver also complained bitterly that the crofters could no longer be trusted to vote the way they pledged, 'such is the effect of the secrecy of the ballot on unprincipled people! It leaves one in uncertainty what the result may be.'[95]

---

[88] NLS, Acc. 10225, Factor's Correspondence, 1484, Box to Wright, 13 Feb. 1889; the 8th Duke of Argyll was also concerned about 'Socialistic agitation'; Newby, *Ireland, Radicalism and the Scottish Highlands*, 105.

[89] NLS, Acc. 10225, Policy Papers, 201, Wright to McIver, 6 Feb. 1889.

[90] NLS, Acc. 10225, Factor's Correspondence, 1963, McIver to Gordon, 8 Dec. 1887.

[91] NLS, Acc. 10225, Factor's Correspondence, 1493, Box to Crofters Commission, 19 Mar. 1892.

[92] NLS, Acc. 10225, Policy Papers, 217, McIver to Wright, 26 Nov. 1889.

[93] J. P. D. Dunbabin, 'Expectations of the new County Councils and their realisation', *Historical Journal*, 8 (1965), 353–5.

[94] NLS, Acc. 10225, Policy Papers, 217, McIver to Wright, 26 Dec. 1889; A. Adonis, *Making Aristocracy Work: the peerage and the political system in Britain, 1884–1914* (Oxford, 1993), 189–90.

[95] NLS, Acc. 10225, Policy Papers, 217, McIver to Wright, 21 Jan. 1890.

The factors were not too shocked when the results came in, as their predictions had for the most part come true; out of the nineteen seats of the Sutherland County Council, seventeen, as McIver put it, 'have been gained by radicals and land leaguers'.[96] Only Donald MacLean gained a seat, a disaster for the interests of the estate, prompting much bitter reflection among the staff, from McIver most of all: 'we are well out of such a Council! formed of Radicals, Land Leaguers and troublesome Clericals! But the revelation to me is the duplicity of so many I have known for years is truly most disappointing and trying to us in the future!'[97] The factors were not satisfied with the winning candidates either, variously regarding the new councillors as ill trained, hypocritical and foolish. Box claimed the Farr councillor could barely read or write, and McIver crowed that they would never be able to fulfil the promises they had made to the crofters on their election.[98]

The Sutherland factors evidently felt deeply threatened by the County Council. Having to stand for election in a new and hostile political climate must have been daunting after decades of taking local seats as an unchallenged privilege.[99] Their ascendancy over the School and Poor Boards had been overthrown in the early 1880s and MacLean's fate on the Council did not help to dispel this feeling of gloom.[100] In late 1892, he pleaded with the duke to be allowed to step down. He believed his presence there, unsupported by anyone else with the same interests, was 'little else for me than an absolute waste of time; and, so far as I can learn, there is little likelihood of the new council being differently constituted.'[101] The Duke agreed and the Sutherland County Council lost its only member connected to the estate that covered most of its jurisdiction.

The shock of this loss of local influence hit the factors hard, none more so than McIver; most of his career had been spent in a political climate where estate interests, with no secret ballot, had reigned supreme. Although McIver's views were the most extreme, most of the other factors agreed with him to some extent. This may account for some of the extraordinarily bitter language that came from them, even from moderates like John Box. They blamed their failure on the work of local land leaguers, prominent merchants, ministers and school teachers. Some of their rage at

---

[96] NLS, Acc. 10225, Policy Papers, 217, McIver to Wright, 7 Feb. 1890; Newby, *Ireland, Radicalism and the Scottish Highlands*, 166; Cannadine, *Decline and Fall*, 160; J. Hunter, 'The Politics of Highland Land reform, 1873–1895', *Scottish Historical Review*, 53 (1974), 61.

[97] NLS, Acc. 10225, Factor's Correspondence, 1963, McIver to Gordon, 7 Feb. 1890.

[98] NLS, Acc. 10225, Factor's Correspondence, 1487, Box to MacLean, 8 Feb. 1890. The result in Caithness was very different, where it was noted that 'the Conservative or Moderate party have had their hand considerably strengthened', Ulbster Estate MSS, Factor's Letterbook 1880–7, Logan to Sir Tollemache, 14 Dec. 1892.

[99] Richards and Clough, *Cromartie*, 341; Newby, *Ireland, Radicalism and the Scottish Highlands*, 166.

[100] NLS, Acc. 10225, Factor's Correspondence, 1972, Gordon to McIver, 8 Mar. 1888.

[101] NLS, Acc. 10225, Policy Papers, 106, MacLean to duke, 15 Nov. 1892.

this group stemmed from a sense of betrayal and fear; after all, they were of the same class and education, but for reasons that the factors were unable to fathom, they had chosen to support the crofters. It could be argued that it was 1890, rather than 1886, which was the real political watershed in Sutherland. These elections truly demonstrated to the estate management that its political influence had been broken; that the county seat remained in the hands of a prominent land agitator only served to reinforce this defeat.

The Crofters Purchase Scheme, 1894

It was desired to create a class of <u>Crofter</u> proprietors, and that one of the essential features of the scheme should be the prevention of the sub-division of crofts and consequent overcrowding in each township. The reason seemed obvious, because if freedom of bequest and aliena-tion were permitted that would lead to overcrowding, the cry for more land, and the extension of the crofter class.[102]

One of the first acts of the 4th Duke, once his father's will had been settled with the dowager duchess, was to set up a scheme to allow croft-ers to purchase their holdings from the estate on generous terms. The duke's view was that it would be better for the long-term financial and political heath of the estate and, unlike most Highland landlords, he had the financial resources to attempt it.[103] Most Highland landowners were receptive to the principle of land purchase by crofters, or by the state on the crofters' behalf. They preferred land being taken off their hands completely for a fair price, rather than having the responsibility of the crofters and government interference on their estates.[104] As MacLean wrote on behalf of the duke, 'he prefers to dispose absolutely of his whole interest in the croft and so be rid of all future responsibility in connection with it'.[105] The terms of the 4th Duke's scheme were posted across the Dunrobin management, which was selected as a trial area, and advertised that crofters could buy their lots, including their section of common grazing, at a value based on the fair rents fixed by the Crofters Commission, and pay back the amount to the estate in monthly instal-ments over thirty years.[106]

---

[102] NLS, Acc. 10225, Crofters, ZQ/i, Messrs Macpherson and MacKay to Macaulay, 24 Sep. 1894.

[103] Other landowners shared the same vision, but lacked the resources to attempt it unaided by government; PP XXXVIII–XXXIX, 1895, *Royal Commission (Highlands and Islands, 1892), Report and Evidence* [hereafter *Deer Forest Commission Evidence*], Cameron of Lochiel, 1273; MacLeod of MacLeod, 131, 133; Cameron, 'Political Influence', 34–5.

[104] Cameron, *Land for the People*, 83.

[105] NLS, Acc. 10225, Factor's Correspondence, 396, MacLean to Messrs Macpherson and MacKay, 19 Sep. 1894.

[106] NLS, Acc. 10225, Crofters, J/b, Crofters Purchase Scheme: General terms, Apr. 1895.

Contemporary land purchase legislation in Ireland certainly influenced the content of the scheme in Sutherland.[107] In 1894, MacLean was granted an interview, on behalf of the duke, with Frederick Wrench of the Irish Land Commission to review the workings of the Irish Purchase Acts to see what could be applied to the scheme in Sutherland.[108] These links show the willingness of the estate, later followed by other Highland proprietors, to turn to land purchase as a way to deal with their crofter tenants. George Malcolm, secretary of the Highland Property Association, highlighted this when he wrote to the Sutherland estate requesting details of the scheme: 'land purchase would be the best escape for many Highland proprietors from the worries and losses of the Crofting tenancies, but now that that crofters are in possession of fixity of tenure, their leaders are preaching down purchase of their holdings'.[109] The Sutherland estate would soon come to realise the power of this opposition.

The three estate factors were consulted and all had reservations, theoretical and practical. McIver, although welcoming the scheme in principle, regarded the practical difficulties in launching it, especially with reference to his poverty-stricken management, as insurmountable. His concern was that no crofter would purchase his holding for the simple reason that they were almost all too small to support a family.[110] Box, in the Tongue management, agreed with McIver; he also highlighted the problem of common grazings and predicted that whole townships would have to purchase together: 'it would seem almost essential that all the tenants in a township and common grazing should come forward and purchase . . . this is far from likely; these people will combine for nothing else than politics – they distrust each other too much.'[111] This was not Box's main concern, however; he argued that the 1886 Crofters Act had been a point of no return ideologically and that the scheme would be unable to overcome this obstacle:

The greatest barrier to the successful carrying out of the proposal appears to me to lie in the direction of future legislation. The crofters have, during the last few years, found themselves raised to a position of important political power; they have been petted by the leading members in both Tory and Liberal governments; they have had several Royal Commissions of enquiry into their condition and wants; and they have had special legislation in their favour. In fact they have been treated in a manner that no other class of the community has ever experienced. They have elected their own members for nearly every

[107] Cameron, *Land for the People*, 83.
[108] NLS, Acc. 10225, Crofters, ZC/b, MacLean to Frederick Wrench, 3 Oct. 1894; B. Solow, *The Land Question and the Irish Economy, 1870–1903* (Massachusetts, 1971), 190–4.
[109] NLS, Acc. 10225, Crofters, ZC/b, Malcolm to MacLean, 21 Sep. 1894.
[110] NLS, Acc. 10225, Crofters, ZC/a, McIver to MacLean, 20 Oct. 1894.
[111] NLS, Acc. 10225, Factor's Correspondence, 1495, Box to duke, 7 Sep. 1894.

constituency in the Highlands . . . The crofters are not slow to realise
that future legislation will be in their favour; they expect great things
from the present Government [Gladstone's Liberal government],
greater freedom and benefits in every way – enlarged holdings, lower
rents, farms broken up and forests populated, with Government aid
for all outlays . . . I am strongly of the opinion that the power to purchase their holdings would not be responded to by the crofters; who
would still look with suspicion on any proposal that emanated from
the estate management; and who are certainly living in the hope of
much better times in the future, on much better terms than that of
purchase.[112]

This assessment not only gives a fair and accurate warning to the duke
of the likely success of the scheme, but also demonstrates a great understanding and balanced view of a situation complicated by many competing
interests. Indeed, the Congested Districts Board, established in 1897, would
face exactly these problems, demonstrating that land purchase, whether
estate or government led, would not be a quick-fix solution.[113] MacLean
added that in bad seasons, the purchasing crofters would be disadvan-
taged, as they would not be eligible to receive a reduction in their annuity
and could easily fall into arrears, with dire results for the scheme and the
purchasers.[114]

Despite the clear warnings from his factors, and their concern that the
poorer the holdings, the less desirable purchase would appear to the crofters, the duke was still keen to get the ball rolling: 'I am very anxious about
the subject of the Crofters Purchase Scheme. It is a very difficult matter but
I hope we may be able to work up a scheme. This crofter property especially
on the west coast is most undesirable and I attach a very great importance
to turning these people into proprietors even at a considerable sacrifice in
a pecuniary point of view.'[115]

In July 1894, the scheme was advertised.[116] Public opinion was generally
positive, and once again a duke of Sutherland was seen as a trailblazer for
crofter rights, righting the wrongs of his ancestors:

It [the scheme] is certainly a step in the right direction as bold as
it is undeniably liberal . . . It looks to me as if the present Duke has
resolved to wipe out, so far as that is now possible, the disgrace which
attaches to his family name . . . And by his new Crofters Purchase
Scheme he will now force the hands of other Highland landlords, and

[112] NLS, Acc. 10225, Factor's Correspondence, 1495, Box to duke, 7 Sep. 1894.
[113] See Chapter five for details on the workings of the Congested Districts Board in Sutherland; Cameron, *Land for the People*, 90, 94–6.
[114] NLS, Acc. 10225, Crofters, I/b, MacLean to George Taylor, 24 Mar. 1894.
[115] NLS, Acc. 10225, Policy Papers, 106, duke to MacLean, 18 Mar. 1894.
[116] NLS, Acc. 10225, Crofters, ZC/a, printed notice, 12 Sep. 1894.

at the same time probably lay the foundation of a system of peasant proprietary.[117]

That prediction was overconfident but the publicity did result in interest and offers of purchase from some surprising sources. One correspondent was Sir Kenneth Mackenzie, who had taken an interest in the estate and been an advisor since 1883. He saw that the scheme could set an important precedent: 'of course you understand that if the action of the Sutherland estate management is to be such as one gathers from the papers, it is likely to affect the relations of landlords and crofters everywhere'.[118] But his comments were not exclusively positive; he doubted whether the scheme would be a paying concern, 'considering the high price of other investments today', and saw a potential difficulty in the duke's reservation of sporting rights, which 'may to some extent prevent the new landowner from deserting altogether the agitator's camp. At least I should be afraid of it.'[119] The scheme also attracted the attention of the Deer Forest Commission, which was still collecting evidence in 1894 and requested the details for its own consideration.[120] But this early interest was not an accurate indication of the numbers of crofters likely to respond positively to the scheme; by December 1895, only seven crofters had come forward.[121] A further five purchase offers were made in 1896, bringing the total to twelve.[122]

This poor response to the scheme was not the estate's main worry, however; a more fundamental problem cropped up: the issue of valuation and tax assessment. On the crofts where an agreement of sale had been made, the County Assessor, to the fury of the estate, raised the value of the crofts from the figure based on the fair rents the Crofters Commission had set, which were of course very low, to a much higher amount, often two or three times above the Commission's figure.[123] This would mean that the purchasing crofters' share of the tax burden would be up to three times greater than that of their neighbours who remained crofters under the 1886 Act. MacLean recorded the duke's reaction: 'the Duke is much annoyed that these valuations for the purposes of taxation should be so much increased, as he feels, and it is certain, that the purchase scheme will be much affected thereby'.[124] The crofters, with the duke paying their expenses, took the case first to the Valuation Committee of Sutherland County Council and then to the Court of Session, but both appeals

[117] *Scottish Highlander*, 18 Oct. 1894.
[118] NLS, Acc. 10225, Crofters, ZC/b, Mackenzie to MacLean, 20 Sep. 1894.
[119] NLS, Acc. 10225, Crofters, ZC/b, Mackenzie to MacLean, 10 Oct. 1894.
[120] NLS, Acc. 10225, Crofters, ZC/b, Henry Munro (Deer Forest Commissioner) to MacLean, 17 Sep. 1894.
[121] NLS, Acc. 10225, Factor's Correspondence, 401, MacLean to Macaulay, 20 Dec. 1895.
[122] *Inverness Courier*, 21 Sep. 1896.
[123] NLS, Acc. 10225, Crofters, ZC/b, MacLean to Frederick Wrench, 3 Oct. 1894.
[124] NLS, Acc. 10225, Crofters, ZC/b, MacLean to Wrench, 3 Oct. 1896; MacLean to Crofter-Proprietors, 28 Aug. 1896.

were unsuccessful and the duke and estate had to admit defeat over the scheme.[125]

Although the purchases collapsed on a technicality, the scheme failed more generally. Only twelve crofters applied to purchase their holdings over the two years the scheme was in operation because they were better off as protected tenants under the 1886 Act, a truth that would haunt future attempts at land purchase by the government through the Congested Districts Act.[126] The effect of this failure on the 4th Duke was also significant, as he initiated no future schemes for the crofters; he co-operated with government legislation in the future, but the Crofters Purchase Scheme would be the last project initiated by the estate itself. It was the last in a long line of similar schemes, from the great clearances of the early nineteenth century, to the famine relief operation and assisted emigration of the 1840s and 1850s, to the duke's Memo scheme in 1884. The Crofters Purchase and the duke's Memo schemes had both tried to pre-empt government intervention in Highland landownership, and were an attempt by the estate to hang onto power which otherwise was slipping away from it. Both had failed due to resistance from the crofters: they knew where their interests lay, and that was with the protection of government, not through the paternalistic schemes of the estate.

'They appeared to me to desire to have the whole estate in their own hands': the Deer Forest Commission, 1892–5[127]

The Deer Forest Commission was appointed in 1892 by Gladstone's Liberal government to investigate a specific remit; what land in the Highlands could be removed from sheep runs and deer forests and given to the crofters to cultivate? Two notable commissioners in a Sutherland context were the county MP, Angus Sutherland, and his informal deputy and leading light in the Sutherlandshire Association, John MacLeod of Gartymore. The radical credentials of these two individuals raised hopes among the crofters that reform in their favour was possible.[128] The Sutherland estate factors shared this expectation, but did not view it in the same positive light. McIver declared himself amazed and disgusted by these choices, especially that of 'John MacLeod, Gartymore – a man of no reputation and who is not in a position socially to allow him to be a member of any Commission . . . the large majority of the members are prejudiced strongly against Deer forests and large farms.'[129]

The Sutherland factors were kept busy in the run-up to the Commission's

[125] *Inverness Courier,* 21 Sep. 1897.
[126] Cameron, *Land for the People,* 88, 101.
[127] NLS, Acc. 10225, Policy Papers, 217, McIver to Wright, 25 Oct. 1893.
[128] Newby, *Ireland, Radicalism and the Scottish Highlands,* 171–2.
[129] NLS, Acc. 10225, Policy Papers, 217, McIver to Wright, 30 Nov. 1892; Cameron, *Land for the People,* 77–8.

visit, preparing evidence and statements that would attempt to convince the Commission that firstly, there was little good-quality land to be had in deer forests, and secondly, if there was any it would be financially ruinous to the estate if it was removed and given to the crofters. They were not alone; estates all over the Highlands were busy constructing a defence of what was a major source of income for proprietors.[130] This was certainly the case in Sutherland, where shooting and fishing rents were, by the 1890s, the most lucrative and stable income the estate had. In 1893, the year of the visit of the Commission to Sutherland, McIver was urging the duke to afforest even more of Assynt, as the once-lucrative sheep farms fell into the estate's hands as profits from sheep farming plummeted.[131] The arrival of the Commission was seen as very threatening at this stage of the estate's conversion from sheep farms to deer forests. By 1892, 212,658 acres of land previously under sheep had been converted to deer forests, and this figure would rise through the 1890s.[132] Of course, the estate did not have a good reputation regarding its enormous sheep farms either: 634,301 acres were still under sheep, with Melness farm alone covering a staggering 81,000 acres.[133]

The factors were helped in their task with advice from the secretary of the Highland Property Association, George Malcolm, factor for Ellice of Invergarry.[134] Malcolm examined drafts of the factors' statements, and was in regular correspondence with them, Box especially.[135] Box became very anxious about the Deer Forest Commission, for the simple reason that Strathnaver was in his management and he dreaded the inevitable crofter evidence concerning the clearance of that emotive glen.[136] In return, the factors provided Malcolm with information on Sutherland deer forests and sheep farms for his own statement on behalf of the Highland Property Association.[137]

The evidence given to the Deer Forest Commission by the crofters and their delegates clearly articulated their demands and grievances in the wake of the 1886 Crofters Act, starting with their perceived historical and moral right to land that their forefathers had been cleared from decades before.[138] As one witness put it, 'the statement I am going to make has been written on my heart, as a descendant of those who were evicted', and they

[130] W. Orr, *Deer Forests, Landlords and Crofters: the Western Highlands in Victorian and Edwardian times* (Edinburgh, 1982), 91–2.

[131] SCRO, D593, K/1/3/81/a, McIver to Wright, 24 June 1893.

[132] *Deer Forest Commission Evidence*, George Malcolm, 1328.

[133] *Deer Forest Commission Evidence*, MacLean, 602; Box, 696; McIver, 715–16.

[134] NLS, Acc. 10225, Crofters, ZN/e, tabular information on Assynt for the Deer Forest Commission.

[135] NLS, Acc. 10225, Factor's Correspondence, 1497, Box to Wright, 13 May 1893; Cameron, 'Political Influence', 33.

[136] NLS, Acc. 10225, Factor's Correspondence, 1497, Box to Macaulay, 21 Aug. 1893.

[137] NLS, Acc. 10225, Factor's Correspondence, 1498, Box to McIver, 16 Sep. 1893.

[138] Withers, 'Give us land and plenty of it', 46–7.

highlighted the immorality of deer and sheep being prized over men.[139] They expressed willingness to move to land if they had to: 'we would be only too willing to return to Strathnaver tomorrow if we got the opportunity'.[140] Indeed, the demand for land was overwhelming; the crofters complained of congested townships, while thousands of acres were fenced off from them in game parks and sheep runs that used to be cultivated by their forefathers.[141]

This desire for land was made more urgent when the plight of the Sutherland cottars, and the burden they were to crofters, was highlighted: 'a great relief it would be to the poor crofters if there should be provided a place for the cottars, because the crofters are overcrowded with cottars. Each cottar, with a family, requires ground for peat; he requires grazing for perhaps a few sheep and a cow, and that is reducing the crofters to naught.'[142] When asked about land hunger, crofter delegates made it clear that such a desire was strong, but only 'if they can get it [land] on advantageous terms'.[143] By this, the crofters meant that a fair rent should be fixed for additional land by the Crofters Commission and that they should qualify for some scheme of government assistance to help them with building, fencing and stocking.[144] Most thought this should come in the form of low-interest government loans and that new townships would have to run their stock in a club farm system, to reduce the cost of fencing and make land grants more efficient.[145] These practical points were of much interest to the Commission, which feared that even if land had been held by crofters eighty years previously, it would now be unreclaimable. They quoted the failure of the 3rd Duke's land reclamations as evidence of this (as did the estate factors), but the crofters rejected that view: 'these reclamations having turned out a failure is no positive proof that the people could not live in comfort on the land held by their forefathers'.[146]

All three of the Sutherland factors gave evidence to the Commission, opposing the crofters' assertion that there was reclaimable land in the deer forests. They further argued that giving this land to the crofters would financially ruin the estate. For example, in the Dunrobin district, 70,200 acres were given over to deer forests, generating an annual income of £13,583.5.1, as compared to the 268,085 acres of sheep farms that

---

[139] *Deer Forest Commission Evidence*, William Matheson, crofter, 591.

[140] *Deer Forest Commission Evidence*, William MacLeod, crofter, 667. See Chapter five for details of the scheme that attempted to re-settle Strathnaver.

[141] *Deer Forest Commission Evidence*, William Macdonald, crofter, 584.

[142] *Deer Forest Commission Evidence*, Donald Morrison, crofter, 724; Hunter, *Making of the Crofting Community*, 180.

[143] *Deer Forest Commission Evidence*, William Macdonald, crofter, 585.

[144] *Deer Forest Commission Evidence*, Alexander Gunn, crofter, 597.

[145] *Deer Forest Commission Evidence*, William Macdonald, crofter, 586.

[146] *Deer Forest Commission Evidence*, John Sutherland, merchant, 620.

produced only £7,239.2.6.[147] Crofters' rents amounted to only £3,572 per annum, almost £10,000 a year less than income from shootings. This pattern was repeated in the other two districts.[148] MacLean also pointed out that by allowing the crofters to occupy the low-lying ground in deer forests, the whole value of the let would be wrecked: 'you at once seriously injure the remainder of the grazings and render immense tracts of land unlettable for either sheep or deer'.[149] Both Box and MacLean admitted that the solution to the crofters' problems was larger holdings, but refused to agree to the sacrifice of deer forests to that end.[150] Perhaps unsurprisingly, McIver had more fundamental concerns, telling the Commission flatly that, 'I don't think that any land is profitably occupied by crofters.'[151] McIver believed that by granting crofters land, the poverty that haunted them would simply be extended over a greater area; instead, he suggested emigration.[152] The statements made by the Sutherland factors were not significantly different to those given by other representatives of the landlord class across the Highlands and may indeed have been viewed as more reasonable than some, especially as the Crofters Purchase Scheme was underway. Overall, the estate's defence was well organised and uniform, presenting a united front difficult to achieve in such a huge and environmentally diverse estate. This surprising unity can be explained by the fact that the remit of the Commission was narrow, and all the staff could agree on defending the value of deer forests; finding a solution to the crofters' problems was a much more divisive issue.

The Deer Forest Commission reported in 1895 and its findings were mixed for both the estate and the crofters. On one hand, the Commission scheduled a total of 395,898 acres in Sutherland that could be given to crofters in various forms, a figure second only to the 549,598 acres scheduled in Inverness-shire.[153] This seemed to prove the crofters right, but there were significant qualifications; much of this acreage was in the eastern part of Sutherland, where demand for land was less than in the west. The Commission further pointed out that the poor soil and climate of the west and north coasts were significant barriers to successful cultivation.[154] It was also concerned that even the scheduled acres would not be enough to provide self-sustaining holdings.[155] As it stood, the Report of the

---

[147] *Deer Forest Commission Evidence*, MacLean, 599. For analysis on the decline of sheep farming, see P. T. Wheeler, 'Landownership and the crofting system in Sutherland since 1800', *Agricultural History Review*, 14 (1966), 47; Orr, *Deer Forests*, 23.

[148] *Deer Forest Commission Evidence*, Box, 696: McIver, 709.

[149] *Deer Forest Commission Evidence*, MacLean, 600; Box, 696.

[150] *Deer Forest Commission Evidence*, Box, 698; MacLean, 601.

[151] *Deer Forest Commission Evidence*, McIver, 718–19.

[152] *Deer Forest Commission Evidence*, McIver, 721.

[153] PP 1895, *Report of the Royal Commission (Highlands and Islands) 1892* [hereafter *Deer Forest Commission Report*], xxi.

[154] *Deer Forest Commission Report*, 11.

[155] *Deer Forest Commission Report*, 10.

Commission contained little to worry the estate and Gladstone's Liberal government fell before any legislation could be framed on the basis of its findings. The factors were concerned about the effect the Commission might have on crofter discipline, however. They were worried that expectations had been raised and that the estate would pay for the crofters' disappointment:

> The effect such an inquiry produces on the people – the feelings it ran and the passions it feeds are most injurious. It raises the convictions and wild desires of the crofters and sets them against their landlords . . . From first to last it was a reiteration of the cry for more land – for what they would like to take from others and get for themselves without reference to the possibility or impracticability of their being unable to possess or to stock or to get what they asked for and described as their wishes. They appeared to me to desire to have the whole estate in their own hands.[156]

These fears were needless; there was no upsurge in crofter agitation after 1895, and although the estate would face new legislation in 1897, it was introduced by a Conservative government and enshrined land purchase, not an extension of dual ownership.

Conclusion

The 1886 Crofters Act had been given a cautious welcome by the Sutherland estate management and its crofters. The crofters saw an independent body they could trust, working for their benefit, whereas the estate management hoped the Crofters Commission would resolve the issues behind the agitation blighting the west coast. Both parties were to be disappointed in these expectations. The crofters were unhappy with many of the decisions of the Crofters Commission regarding rents and enlargement of holdings, and the estate management was unhappy when the crofters subsequently refused to abide by them and turned back to petitioning the estate and agitating. The extent of the crofters' disillusionment with the 1886 Act was seen in front of the Deer Forest Commission, where the dominating cry was for more land: exactly as it had been in front of the Napier Commission in 1883.

The estate had attempted to seize the initiative on this question in 1894 with its Crofters Purchase Scheme, but it failed to convince the crofters of the benefits of landownership.[157] The crofters, who were protected by the privileges granted to them by the Crofters Act, preferred to wait and see what else the government would grant. Once again, the Sutherland estate had attempted to be a trailblazer in solving the 'Highland question', but

---

[156] NLS, Acc. 10225, Policy Papers, 217, McIver to Wright, 25 Oct. 1893.
[157] Cameron, *Land for the People*, 83.

failed due to a misjudgement of both the level of trust with which its small tenants regarded it and the ability of other estates to follow its example. Initial government intervention on the estate, through the Crofters Commission, was not an unqualified success, but the estate management (with the exception of McIver) gradually came to the conclusion that it was necessary to curb the hostility of the crofters and make relations with them workable. This process of government intervention in estate management, which began with the 1886 Act, was to be extended in 1897 with the Congested Districts (Scotland) Act and was the next challenge the estate would have to face.

CHAPTER FIVE

'Unstained were the diadems Cromarty wore': The Sutherland Estate, 1897–1920[1]

Introduction

In 1897, the Congested Districts (Scotland) Act was passed, establishing the Congested Districts Board [hereafter CDB], which was given an annual budget of £35,000 and a remit of land purchase for the benefit of crofters, as well as funds to invest in stockbreeding, the fishing industry, roads, marine works and bridges.[2] Land purchase was a popular policy among Highland landowners, as it lifted the burden of the crofting community from their shoulders permanently and was preferable to government interference in estates under the terms of the 1886 Crofters Act. The CDB was, therefore, enthusiastically greeted by the Sutherland estate despite the prominent presence of Angus Sutherland on it.[3] In 1897, as in 1886, there was a feeling of relief when some responsibility, not least financial, was removed from the estate management, as the government extended its remit in the Highlands.[4] Alleviating the crofters' grievances now rested, at least in part, with the government, although some crofter supporters were concerned that the CDB had no compulsory purchase powers.[5] If an estate chose to be unco-operative, there was little the CDB could do; this danger was most evident in Sutherland, where the duke owned almost the whole county. This would not be the problem the Board faced in Sutherland; rather, the duke was willing to sell land, but not in the right places for

---

[1] *Highland News*, 12 Jul. 1913.
[2] *Scottish Highlander*, 24 Jun. 1897; E. A. Cameron, *Land for the People? The British Government and the Scottish Highlands, c.1880–1925* (East Linton, 1996), 83–4; A. S. Mather, 'The Congested Districts Board for Scotland', in W. Ritchie, J. C. Stone and A. S. Mather (eds), *Essays for Professor R. E. H. Mellor* (Aberdeen, 1986), 198, 200, 201–2; E. A. Cameron, 'The Political Influence of Highland landlords: a reassessment', *Northern Scotland*, 14 (1994), 35; J. Hunter, *The Making of the Crofting Community* (Edinburgh, 1976), 184–5.
[3] A. G. Newby, *Ireland, Radicalism and the Scottish Highlands, c.1870–1912* (Edinburgh, 2007), 175.
[4] National Library of Scotland [hereafter NLS], Sutherland Estates Papers, Acc. 10225, Factor's Correspondence, 1511, Box to MacLean, 22 Feb. 1898. The 1897 Act, as the 1886 Act had been, was based on an Irish legislative model; D. MacKay, 'The Congested Districts Boards of Ireland and Scotland', *Northern Scotland*, 16 (1996), 147–8, 154–5; C. Breathnach, *Framing the West: images of rural Ireland, 1891–1920* (Dublin, 2007).
[5] Cameron, *Land for the People*, 84.

the right prices. A CDB scheme at Syre, in Strathnaver, and attempts to initiate a scheme at Melness were used, unsuccessfully, by the ducal family and estate management to garner some political popularity. This chapter will examine in detail the workings of the CDB in Sutherland, which were always controversial and, despite the best efforts of the Board, ultimately failed.

When in 1911 the CDB was replaced, the Small Landholders (Scotland) Act established the Board of Agriculture for Scotland [hereafter BoAS] and the Scottish Land Court, with the remit of extending land settlement schemes with a budget of £200,000 per annum.[6] The Act had virtually no impact on Sutherland until after the First World War, however; in 1916, the 5th Duke of Sutherland offered the farm of Shiness to the BoAS, but action was stalled due to war. When the plan was revived in 1919, Shiness had been sold by the duke, leaving the activities of the BoAS outwith the remit of this book.[7]

The changing financial and territorial structure of the estate in this period will also come under scrutiny. The 4th Duke began a radical re-structuring of the estate when he sold 120,000 acres between 1899 and 1901, and a further 50,000 acres shortly before his death in 1913.[8] It was his son, the 5th Duke, who oversaw the most significant break-up of the once territorially dominant estate, selling a further 445,000 acres in 1919. By 1920, therefore, the estate which had stood at 1.1 million acres just twenty years before had been reduced to a rump of around 385,000 acres.[9] This chapter will examine this process, looking at the motives behind and results of this radical change.[10]

Lastly, the social and economic position of the Sutherland crofters and cottars will be examined across this period of profound change. The remit of government agencies had been extended in 1897 to include land purchase and investment in the economic infrastructure of the croft-ing economy, but to what extent did the activities of the CDB address the basic demands of the crofters: more and better land and economic security? And did the attitudes of the estate management change towards them to match the broader legislative and economic changes in Highland society?

---

[6] Hunter, *Making of the Crofting Community*, 192; Cameron, *Land for the People*, 144; L. Leneman, *Fit for Heroes? Land Settlement in Scotland after World War One* (Aberdeen, 1989), 8.

[7] Leneman, *Fit for Heroes*, 53–70.

[8] NLS, Acc. 10225, Sales, 1, 'Disposition by 4th Duke of Sutherland in favour of W. E. Gilmour', 29 Mar. 1900; 'Disposition by 4th Duke of Sutherland in favour of Andrew Carnegie', 27 May 1899; 'Disposition by 4th Duke and Lord Stafford in favour of John William Stewart', 25 Apr. 1913.

[9] NLS, Acc. 10225, Sales, 7, 'Brochure of land divisions for sale (1914, 1919); Sales, 6, 'Note of sales made at auction, 1919'; *Times*, 4 Apr. 1914.

[10] D. Cannadine, *The Decline and Fall of the British Aristocracy* (London, 1990), 103–12.

'They are on the whole a very helpless, useless lot': the Sutherland crofters, 1897–1920[11]

By 1897, the Sutherland crofters had seen more than ten years of active government agency in the Highlands. The Crofters Commission had helped the crofters by setting fair rents but had been less successful in addressing the fundamental difficulty of land hunger. The creation of the CDB generated new hope, as for the first time government money was set aside for land purchase for crofters and investment in the economic infrastructure of the Highlands. The economic and social position of the majority of the Sutherland crofters clearly showed that this help was needed. Grinding poverty still characterised the lives of most crofters, leading to myriad social problems, and, for the estate, growing arrears of rent. The factors sent in regular reports to Stafford House on the state of the crofters, the same problems recurring time and again:

> I have been very much concerned about the appearance of the crofters' cattle. They are worse than I ever saw them and many must succumb before the growth of grass comes on . . . There is no doubt that this year the necessity for provender is urgent and the people who need it most are the very poorest . . . To add to the difficulties at present with us just now, there is a most complete epidemic of influenza all round . . . Some cases have proved fatal.[12]

Similar reports came in from the Sutherland factors well into the 1900s, proving that despite the best efforts of government, the Sutherland crofters still toiled under low standards of living. A clear indication of this can be seen in growing rent arrears, and in how the estate attempted to address the issue.[13] Crofters' arrears were a serious problem: in 1897, the Tongue management arrears stood at 64%, and in Scourie 70% of rents remained unpaid.[14] Of course, the rental income from crofters was relatively small compared with that from other sources such as farms and shootings; for example, in 1897, the Dunrobin management collected a total rental of £50,129.1.1, only £5,244.14.0 of which came from crofters' rents, £2,515.4.2 of which was unpaid. Shooting rents, by contrast, stood at £21,065.7.8 and there were no arrears.[15]

Despite this, the duke was happy to let the factors deal with the problem as they wished; his income did not depend on crofters' rents in the

---

[11] NLS, Acc. 10225, Factor's Correspondence, 1514, Box to duke, 6 Mar. 1899.
[12] NLS, Acc. 10225, Factor's Correspondence, 1511, Box to duke, 6 Apr. 1898.
[13] Rent arrears were a problem on many Highland estates, including the Cromartie and Macdonald estates too: National Archives of Scotland [hereafter NAS], GD 305, Cromartie Estate Papers, Estate Correspondence, 1900, Alex. Ross to William Gunn, 19 Feb. 1892; Armadale Castle, Macdonald MSS, 3533, Mary MacLennan to Alex. Macdonald, 6 Apr. 1895.
[14] NLS, Acc. 10225, Rentals, Abstracts for Dunrobin, Scourie and Tongue managements (1897).
[15] NLS, Acc. 10225, Rentals, Abstract for Dunrobin (1897).

north and the ducal family seems to have given up on the idea of making
Sutherland pay by the late 1890s.[16] The factors were frustrated by this attitude: 'the Duke won't take any legal action especially in the way of removal
and he becomes rather careless about the matter when it is mentioned
to him'.[17] McIver feared the crofters were taking advantage of the duke's
reputed liberality, a trait that he could no longer afford: 'many of them
[crofters] are under the impression that the Duke is a generous kind man
who will not press them or take steps against them – it will be necessary to
show these that payment of rent is a necessity and that His Grace cannot
permit such irregularity in payment of rents to go on.'[18]

The factors saw the non-payment of rents as a failure of discipline but
there was little they could do to combat the problem, which by this period
was due to poverty, rather than politics.[19] The management took legal
action where possible, usually by bringing the worst offenders to the Small
Debts Court, 'to avoid the inevitable consequences of such a bad example if
allowed to go on unchecked'.[20] The factors were acutely aware of the crofters' poverty; it only took a poor season for the fishings or cattle prices for
no rents to be forthcoming. These economic crises were repeated year after
year, yet no effective long-term strategy was developed by the management.
Indeed, perhaps this was impossible:

> There is no doubt that the people are very poor. Their resources have
> been much reduced by the very low price of sheep and by the almost
> total failure of the home fishings. The latter is a very serious business,
> and will I fear continue to have a very bad effect on this district. Still
> we cannot let these people go on getting yearly further into arrear as
> they would soon go beyond recovery and the example to their honest
> neighbours is so dangerous.[21]

Although the factors recognised the economic difficulties and poverty
of the crofters, they still labelled them 'dishonest' if they did not pay regularly.[22] Occasionally, the estate realised it was fighting a losing battle, and
cancelled the arrears of the very poorest.[23] There were also grants of seed
potatoes and oats in very difficult years, although the crofters were expected
to pay for these.[24] Continuing problems over crofter rents were linked to
land hunger and demographic trends which had been evident since the

---

[16] NLS, Acc. 10225, Sales, 1, 'Memorandum of meeting at Dunrobin Castle', 30 Apr. 1904.
[17] NLS, Acc. 10225, Factor's Correspondence, 429, MacLean to James Simpson, 7 Nov. 1902.
[18] Staffordshire County Record Office [hereafter SCRO], Sutherland Estates Papers, D593,
K/1/3/81/a, McIver to Wright, 11 Jul. 1893.
[19] NLS, Acc. 10225, Factor's Correspondence, 1508, Box to duke, 6 Jan. 1897.
[20] NLS, Acc. 10225, Factor's Correspondence, 1509, Box to Wright, 21 Jul. 1897.
[21] NLS, Acc. 10225, Factor's Correspondence, 1517, Box to duke, 6 Jan. 1900.
[22] NLS, Acc. 10225, Factor's Correspondence, 410, MacLean to duke, 27 Jan. 1898.
[23] NLS, Acc. 10225, Factor's Correspondence, 410, MacLean to James Simpson, 6 Jan. 1898.
[24] NLS, Acc. 10225, Factor's Correspondence, 449, MacLean to Taylor, 21 Dec. 1907.

1850s. Land hunger was prevalent, demonstrated by the crofters' obvious excitement when the CDB purchased Syre farm in Strathnaver in 1901.[25] Agitation had died down in Sutherland since the heady days of the 1880s, but the crofters' underlying desire for land was still smouldering; petitions were regularly sent in by crofting townships for extensions of grazings.[26]

Resources such as crofts and pasture were under dispute as crofters competed for space. This situation was well summarised in the long-running disagreement between the crofters of Knockan and Elphin in Assynt over their adjoining grazing. The pasture for the two townships had no fence to separate them; obviously, the stock of both townships wandered over the whole area, leading to friction. In 1898, the Elphin crofters took the Knockan crofters to the Sheriff Court for trespass of their stock, claiming £4.2/- for damages.[27] Thus a miserable irony arose: interdicting was a tactic frequently used by the estate against crofters whose stock had wandered onto sheep farms or deer forests. Now, land hunger was so acute that crofters were using it against each other. In retaliation, the Knockan tenants wrote to the Crofters Commission, asking it to amalgamate the two lots of pasture into one common, but this was rejected by the Elphin crofters in favour of building a fence between them, which was eventually done.[28] Land hunger was still a major factor for the crofters, therefore, even if it was expressed differently in the 1890s than in the 1880s.

Land was not the only question on the crofters' minds in the 1890s and 1900s: CDB investment in the economic infrastructure of Sutherland was a welcome boon. The Board poured money into amenities in the county, from harbours, piers and boatslips to roads, paths and bridges.[29] It also paid for improvements in stock in the form of bulls, rams and stallions loaned out to townships and, in an agreement with the Sutherland estate, many miles of new fencing was erected to protect and define crofters' ground.[30] Marine works were of especial import to the Sutherland crofters, many of whom spent more time fishing than farming. The Sutherland factors frequently pointed to failure in the fishings as the basis of the growing arrears in crofters' rents and could only watch as the fishings failed year after year, impacting heavily on payment of crofting rents.[31] The estate put

[25] NLS, Acc. 10225, Factor's Correspondence, 1514, Box to duke, 6 Feb. 1899.
[26] NLS, Acc. 10225, Crofters, A, Kinlochbervie crofters to MacLean, 21 Jun. 1907.
[27] NLS, Acc. 10225, Factor's Correspondence, 414, MacLean to Duke, 31 Jan. 1899.
[28] NLS, Acc. 10225, Factor's Correspondence, 417, MacLean to duke, 10 Nov. 1899.
[29] See, for instance, NAS, Congested Districts Board files, AF42/53, AF42/61, AF42/495, AF42/531, AF42/525 and AF42/3003.
[30] See, for instance, NAS, AF42/1082, AF42/1290, AF42/1474, AF42/1489, AF42/2301 and AF42/2423.
[31] NLS, Acc. 10225, Policy Papers, 108, MacLean to duke, 6 Aug. 1904: A. M. Tindley, 'Orkney and Shetland: Land Reform, Government Policy and Politics, c.1870–1914', unpublished M.Sc. thesis (University of Edinburgh, 2001), 16; PP 1904 XII, *Annual Report of the Fishery Board for Scotland*, 3; M. Gray, *The Fishing Industries of Scotland, 1790–1914: a study in regional adaption* (Oxford, 1978), 195, 211; J. R. Coull, *The Sea-Fisheries of Scotland:*

pressure on the CDB, proposing it fund boat loans and motor transport to markets.[32] There was little this type of investment could do to help in the face of falling fish numbers and the rise of steam trawlers, however, and the downward spiral of the fishing industry continued.

Crofters and fishermen were not the only groups struggling to make ends meet in these years. Sheep farmers, once the magnates of Sutherland society, were also floundering, low prices making their huge lets increasingly unviable.[33] An increasing number of requests for rent reductions were made as farmers fell into arrears, as reported by MacLean in 1898: 'I am sorry to say that a number of the farmers are very slow to pay. I am pressing them and trust they will soon pay up, but if they don't before the end of the year it may be necessary to take legal measures to compel them.'[34] There was some debate as to whether the sheep farmers would resort to crofters' tactics, by banding together to force the estate's hand:

Many thanks for the copy of the sheep farmers' petition. It is an extraordinary document and I am much surprised at seeing some of the names of those who signed it . . . There is, I think, no doubt that the greens [i.e. pasture] on sheep farms <u>are</u> getting worse year by year . . . If the farmers would do something to improve the greens by putting on basic slag it would be more to the point than making complaints of this sort. I am very glad the Duke has said he will only consider <u>individual</u> cases: it is a mistake in my opinion to treat with a lot of men collectively: they would form a sort of Trades Union in time.[35]

The sheep farmers' pre-eminent position was being usurped by the sporting tenants who paid well and promptly. The Sutherland estate did not have to worry about the rentals coming in from the deer forests, even if the moral principles behind them were under the spotlight.[36]

The estate management itself, after the convulsive changes of the 1880s and 1890s, remained relatively stable throughout this period. McIver retired in 1895, marking a watershed in the estate management. The 4th Duke, instead of appointing a replacement, simply did away with the Scourie management altogether, carving it up between the Tongue and Dunrobin managements.[37] There are a number of reasons why he may have

a *historical geography* (Edinburgh, 1996), 129–30; NAS, AF42/2633, Minute by Angus Sutherland, 11 Jul. 1905.
[32] NLS, Acc. 10225, Factor's Correspondence, 438, MacLean to CDB, 17 Feb. 1905; 440, MacLean to Sir Reginald MacLeod, Scottish Office, 8 Sep. 1905.
[33] W. Orr, *Deer Forests, Landlords and Crofters: the Western Highlands in Victorian and Edwardian times* (Edinburgh, 1982), 22–3.
[34] NLS, Acc. 10225, Factor's Correspondence, 413, MacLean to duke, 2 Oct. 1898.
[35] NLS, Acc. 10225, Crofters, A, Frank Sykes to MacLean, 8 Nov. 1905. For more on the idea of a sheep farmers' union, see *Northern Ensign*, 29 Sep. 1881.
[36] NLS, Acc. 10225, Factor's Correspondence, 442, MacLean to George Malcolm, 8 Mar. 1906.
[37] NLS, Acc. 10225, Factor's Correspondence, 1504, Box to McIver, 3 Sep. 1895.

decided to do this: perhaps he thought a new factor would easily become another hate figure for the crofters, or that with continued government intervention in the estate, intensive management was no longer needed. McIver's retirement heralded a new era for the estate, one that was not so closely rooted in the troubled past of the Highland Famine, clearances and the mentalities that accompanied them. In 1912, Donald MacLean retired after twenty-seven years' service; Colonel John Morrison, the Tongue factor since 1902, moved to Golspie to replace him.

Further changes affected the upper estate management. The 4th Duke had started to spend a lot of time abroad from around 1907, mainly in Canada, where he was undertaking major land purchases. During his early trips, he generally left the day-to-day running of the estates in MacLean's hands, but eventually more permanent steps had to be taken.[38] In 1911, the duke constituted a Board of Management, consisting of his son, Lord Stafford, and his personal secretaries Mr Humbert and Mr Prowse.[39] This Board of Management, like the one the 3rd Duke had instituted in 1889, had little opportunity to carry out its duties.[40] By mid-1913 the 4th Duke was dead and the Board was suspended while the 5th Duke took the reins of an estate very different in shape from that which his father had inherited in 1892. With the continued help of Prowse and Humbert, the 5th Duke took much of the running of the estate into his own hands, the duties for which were much reduced in 1919 when the estate was radically cut down in size.

'Is it Strathnaver no more?': Syre, 1899–1911[41]

Patrick P. Sellar, farmer grandson of the infamous factor and tenant sheep farmer, was, by the 1880s, having difficulty holding onto the vast enterprises left to him by his father.[42] In 1898, he was dead and his son was in no position to stay even at a reduced rent.[43] It was a watershed for both the Sellars and the Sutherland estate: for better or worse the Sellar family was intimately linked to the Sutherland clearances and, aside from the ducal house itself, was seen as their chief beneficiaries, tenanting wide acres in fertile areas such as Strathnaver ever since.[44] Box noted sombrely that 'he [Sellar] will have to leave the place with which the name of Sellar has been

[38] NLS, Acc. 10853, Policy Papers, 52, Alex. Simpson to MacLean, 28 Dec. 1907.
[39] NLS, Acc. 10225, Policy Papers, 170, duke to the Board of Management, 10 Apr. 1912.
[40] NLS, Acc. 10225, Policy Papers, 119, MacLean to duke, 20 May 1911.
[41] *Highland News*, 8 Jul. 1899.
[42] These included the farms of Morvich, Culmaily and the Strathnaver lets, which included Mudale and Syre; taken together they represented an annual rent of £2,206; NLS, Acc. 12173, 103, Dunrobin rentals (1876); 128, Tongue rentals (1876); E. Richards, *Patrick Sellar and the Highland Clearances: homicide, eviction and the price of progress* (Edinburgh, 1999), 362–3.
[43] NLS, Acc. 10225, Factor's Correspondence, 1512, Box to duke, 11 Jun. 1898.
[44] Richards, *Patrick Sellar*, 5, 120, 332–3, 361–2.

so long connected',[45] but there was little real sadness on the estate's part. The continuing presence of the family in the county had kept alive the clearances in a very immediate way.[46] The *Highland News* crowed over the departure of Sellar from Strathnaver:

> Among Highland Straths, Strathnaver holds the first place in respect of its extent, fertility as well as the ruthless manner in which its entire inhabitants were swept away in the first half of this century . . . Notwithstanding that Mr Patrick Sellar got possession of the immense lands of Strathnaver as well as the farms of Culmaily and Morvich, next year his descendants are to be quit of the county of Sutherland.[47]

The farm of Syre was now available to any incoming tenant, and for the newly constituted CDB and its hopeful crofter constituency, it was an opportunity for 'the estate management of Sutherland to do some-thing practical to repair the mischief caused by the Management [sic] or rather mismanagement of a century ago'.[48] The CDB, led by Sir Kenneth Mackenzie, opened negotiations with the duke: the estate offered Syre farm, a substantial holding of 500 acres arable and 11,500 acres pasture, and gave the CDB a twelve-month option on it.[49] The CDB had already set up other schemes in the Highlands, but Syre was the first opportunity to come up in Sutherland. Schemes on Skye – at Kilmuir and Glendale – Barra and Vatersay were under consideration or had already been pur-chased, with mixed results and ongoing controversy.[50]

The CDB now had to decide how exactly Syre should be disposed of. In 1898, Sir Arthur Orde, a landowner in North Uist, had set a precedent by working with the CDB to subdivide two farms on his estate, minimising the cost to the CDB and allowing the crofters to remain tenants.[51] Sir Arthur was roundly praised for his actions: the *Highland News* urged, 'let him [the duke] give the farm of Syre on the same terms as those on which, to his credit, Sir Arthur Orde gave his tenants'.[52] The CDB was keen to come to similar terms for Syre, the secretary hoping the CDB could 'induce the Duke to "Orde" Syre into adequate holdings'.[53] The duke refused to recon-sider his offer, however: the CDB could purchase Syre from him and then do what they pleased with it, but he would not subdivide the farm while

45 NLS, Acc. 10225, Factor's Correspondence, 1512, Box to duke, 11 Jun. 1898.

46 *Highland News*, 15 Dec. 1894; Richards, *Patrick Sellar*, 366.

47 *Highland News*, 4 Mar. 1899.

48 *Highland News*, 4 Mar. 1899.

49 NAS, AF42/325, Mackenzie to CDB, 15 Mar. 1899; NLS, Acc. 10225, Policy Papers, 159, Wright to Box, 6 Feb. 1899.

50 Cameron, *Land for the People*, 88–9, 92–3, 97, 102–13.

51 PP XXX, 1899, *First Report of the Congested Districts Board for Scotland*, 9; Cameron, *Land for the People*, 87–95.

52 *Highland News*, 1 Apr. 1899.

53 NAS, AF42/325, Minute by Sir R. MacGregor, 10 Feb. 1899.

still the landowner. Other Highland proprietors, such as Lady Gordon Cathcart, took a similar stance.[54] Sir Kenneth Mackenzie, an old correspondent of the estate, who had given advice on the 1884 Duke's Memo scheme and the 1894 Crofters Purchase Scheme, made a last-ditch attempt to convince the duke to divide Syre himself, with assistance from the CDB.[55] Despite an offer of generous assistance coming from a fellow landowner and trusted advisor, the duke would not budge:

> Private. The Duke will certainly not entertain the idea of breaking up the farms and dealing with them as Sir A. Orde has done but he will give every help to the CDB who have been appointed by the Govt. to deal with the subject, so far as he can do without materially reducing his revenue.[56]

The duke maintained this stance despite pressure applied by the CDB and the press.[57]

The duke had put over 100,000 acres of land in the Tongue management up for private sale in 1898, and was in no mood to grant land *gratis* to the government.[58] His factors were well aware of this and urged the duke to stick to his guns:

> For my own part, I do not see why you should sell any part of your estate below market value, whatever may be its purpose. Sir Kenneth talks of buying land in Ireland at 12 to 14 years' purchase. He certainly admits that Highland properties cannot be expected now at those prices, but in making up the valuations for the estate sale we have calculated such farms at 25 years' purchase.[59]

Despite this, the idea of land purchase was a popular one among Highland landlords at this time, and its appeal for the Sutherland estate had been long-standing, as its Crofters Purchase Scheme of 1894 demonstrated.[60] The idea of selling land to the CDB was even more appealing as then the government would take on the financial burden of setting up the

---

[54] Sir Kenneth also tried to persuade Lord Macdonald to voluntarily divide some of his land, but to no avail; Armadale Castle, Macdonald MSS, 5710, Mackintosh to Sir Kenneth Mackenzie, 7 Feb. 1898; Cameron, *Land for the People*, 91.

[55] NAS, AF42/325, Mackenzie to Wright, 18 Feb. 1899.

[56] NLS, Acc. 10853, Policy Papers, 44, Wright to MacLean, 5 Apr. 1899.

[57] For example, *Highland News*, 1 Apr. 1899, 8 Jul. 1899, 21 Oct. 1899 and 1 Dec. 1899.

[58] Land belonging to the duke had to be disentailed, with the permission of his heir and the Court of Session, in order to be sold; a costly legal process which in theory was put in place to protect the integrity of landed estates from unscrupulous holders who might wish to sell or contract debt against the interests of their estate; C. C. Cheshire and E. H. Burn (eds), *Modern Law of Real Property* (14th edn, London, 1988), 237–50; R. Campbell, 'On Land Tenure in Scotland and England', *Law Quarterly Review*, 2 (1885), 103–5; J. Habakkuk, *Marriage, Debt and the Estates System: English landownership, 1650–1950* (Oxford, 1994), 6.

[59] NLS, Acc. 10225, Factor's Correspondence, 1511, Box to duke, 28 Feb. 1898.

[60] Cameron, *Land for the People*, 83.

crofters on new lands, which would be hefty and perhaps irretrievable: 'I also think the CDB can never make their proposal . . . pay. I am sure that the cost of creating these new holdings will prevent their becoming in any way a commercial success unless a large proportion of the government money be expended.'[61]

Rumour of a scheme in Strathnaver quickly caught on in Sutherland, putting the CDB and estate under increasing pressure to make a deal, but there was an obstacle: the sale price of £10,546.10/-.[62] There was also the question of the farm stock, which the estate wanted to sell to the CDB, just as they would to any incoming tenant or purchaser. The CDB proposed to then sell the stock on to the crofter-purchasers, but, as resolutions from crofters' meetings in the area made clear, the potential applicants feared they could not afford this condition.[63] The CDB found itself between a rock and a hard place: on the one hand, they had to meet the duke's terms or they would lose the farm altogether, and on the other the terms meant that either the potential crofter-purchasers could not afford to take the land offered or they would have to accept a loss on the scheme.

The Scottish Secretary and Chair of the CDB, Lord Balfour of Burleigh, clarified the position: the CDB would almost certainly make a loss on Syre, and did not even regard it as an ideal subject for crofting, but these problems were worth tackling to avoid a savaging in the press and Parliament.[64] Despite this, negotiations for Syre collapsed in February 1900, just after the death of Sir Kenneth Mackenzie.[65] Lord Balfour put the failure down to 'perhaps a feeling that the price of the land was high . . . I am of opinion that the chief difficulty in the way is to be traced to the want of means on the part of the applicants and the consequent inability to stock the holdings.'[66] The Sutherland estate was concerned: 'the moment the CD Board gives up your offer and retires from the Strath we may expect strong and persistent appeals from the people for your Grace to undertake some scheme yourself by which the descendants of the people removed from the Strath long ago may be restored to it'.[67] The crofting press was furious, pinning the blame

[61] NLS, Acc. 10225, Factor's Correspondence, 1511, Box to duke, 28 Feb. 1898.

[62] NAS, AF42/341, Minute by Mr MacGregor, 3 Mar. 1899; NLS, Acc. 10225, Factor's Correspondence, 1514, Box to Lord Balfour of Burleigh, Secretary for Scotland, 27 Mar. 1899.

[63] NAS, AF42/462, Resolutions passed in regard to Syre by crofters of Farr, Skerray and Melness, 27 Oct. 1899.

[64] NAS, AF42/462, Minute by Lord Balfour, no date [between 14 Nov. and 5 Dec. 1899]. The 'stock at valuation' question concerned the value of sheep on a farm at a change of lease or sale, and whether that valuation should (as it usually did) include the acclimatisation value of that stock, a fairly subjective value that could wildly increase the amount to be paid; Orr, *Deer Forests*, 18.

[65] NAS, AF42/530, Memo by Lord Balfour, 23 Feb. 1900.

[66] NAS, AF42/530, Memo by Lord Balfour, 23 Feb. 1900.

[67] NLS, Acc. 10225, Factor's Correspondence, 1517, Box to duke, 9 Feb. 1900.

firmly on the estate.[68] Not all was lost, however; the duke granted the CDB another year to consider the Syre proposals.[69]

When the CDB re-opened negotiations with the duke in July 1900, Lord Balfour appealed to his better nature:

> From our previous correspondence and conversation I am led to believe that you take an interest in the success of the experiment proposed apart from its purely economic aspect and I am therefore emboldened to put the whole circumstances before you and ask whether you are open to reconsider the question of price. I do this with some reluctance and in grateful acknowledgement of the kind and generous way in which you have met the wishes of the Board and sympathised with our desire to test by practical experiment whether a class of small holdings can be established in the districts of the Highlands with which you are specially interested.[70]

This appeal fell on deaf ears: the duke refused to budge, insisting that the market price be paid for the land.[71] The duke laid out the situation to Lord Balfour:

> My view of the price to be paid is that the C.D.B. should pay the fair market price, and then, if the applicants or crofters cannot give as much, that the latter should have the land from the C.D.B. at such a price as they can afford. In other words the C.D.B. would be the losers, not the private owner. I cannot imagine that it was ever intended that a landowner should have to give up land at a price below its known value for an experiment of this sort, which in its present form will do nobody any good. In fact, if the crofters are to be moved and settled on new lands, the expense and responsibility must be taken by the Government, through the C.D.B. and the Crofters Commission, and I think that now this is perfectly understood.[72]

The duke utterly rejected the idea that he should lose by his transactions with the CDB: he believed that land purchase was the way to deal with crofters, but after the failure of his 1894 Crofters Purchase Scheme, he wanted the burden to be carried by government.

Faced with this inflexibility, the CDB was forced to accept the market price: in early 1901, the CDB finally purchased Syre from the duke for £10,546.10.[73] The secretary of the CDB, Sir Rob Roy MacGregor, wrote

---

[68] *Highland News*, 3 Mar. 1900.

[69] NLS, Acc. 10225, Factor's Correspondence, 1517, Box to duke, 8 Mar. 1900.

[70] NAS, AF42/633, Lord Balfour to duke, 27 Jul. 1900.

[71] NLS, Acc. 10225, Factor's Correspondence, 1518, Box to duke, 29 Aug. 1900.

[72] NAS, AF42/633, duke to Lord Balfour, 22 Sep. 1900.

[73] NAS, AF42/795, 'Conditions of Purchase for Syre', 20 Feb. 1901; AF42/862, 'Legal documents of Sale of Syre', 1901; the price represented 17 years' purchase and worked out at less than £1 per acre.

quietly in a minute, 'this is gratifying' – something of an understatement after three years of negotiations.[74] The next step for the CDB was to advertise for and select the crofter purchasers who would be planted in Strathnaver. During the negotiations, the CDB had made it clear that it wanted to create small farms worth £20 or £30 rent per annum, rather than tiny crofts, so that the purchasers could make their living entirely from the land.[75] This plan had obvious disadvantages, however; the larger the holdings, the more capital the applicants would need for the purchase annuity, stocking and buildings, but most of the applicants were poor cottars or crofters from the coasts, with very small means.[76] This was the fundamental problem the CDB had at Syre: it wanted to create a class of small farmers who would be able to support themselves on the land, but the crofters and cottars on the coasts did not have the means to match these expectations. The CDB needed the Syre experiment to be a success; after all, it was answerable to Parliament and the public in a way the Sutherland estate never was, and it needed crofters with some capital to guarantee a better chance of success. Ultimately, this was not possible; the CDB caved in and drew up twenty-nine lots of only 16 to 20 acres each, arguably condemning the scheme to failure from the very start.[77]

The crofter purchasers were given loans from £150 to £300 each from the CDB to build their houses and byres, which they would pay back to the CDB on top of their purchase annuity.[78] This was paid in twice-yearly instalments and worked out at between £30 and £130 per year, per settler, a huge increase for crofters who may have only paid a nominal rent for their old lots.[79] On top of these burdens, they were also liable for increased rates of tax: the total tax bill for Syre came in at £100 per annum, split between the settlers.[80] From these figures, it was clear that the Syre settlers were going to have to work very hard and hope for extremely favourable economic circumstances to be able to meet their obligations to the CDB.[81]

Difficulties at Syre began to emerge only months after the settlers officially took up residence in the strath in September 1901.[82] In November, the CDB received its first petition from the settlers, asking for the Board to double the period of payment of the purchase annuity, effectively halving the yearly payments. The settlers explained that 'we find that when all the

[74] NAS, AF42/795, Minute by MacGregor, 2 Mar. 1901.
[75] This was a basic objective of the CDB; NLS, Acc. 10225, Factor's Correspondence, 1515, Box to Wright, 24 May 1899.
[76] *Northern Times*, 15 Mar. 1900.
[77] NAS, AF42/912, 'List of holdings and applicants intended for each', 1901; Leneman, *Fit for Heroes*, 55.
[78] NAS, AF42/3791, 'Statement of indebtedness of Syre settlers in respect of annuities for purchase price and building loans', 31 Oct. 1906.
[79] NAS, AF42/3784, 'List of settlers with amounts due by them', 7 Mar. 1907. Most crofter rents on the Sutherland estate ranged from £1 to £4 per annum.
[80] NAS, AF42/3612, 'Syre rate collection', 6 Dec. 1906.
[81] *Highland News*, 3 Mar. 1900.
[82] *Highland News*, 7 Sep. 1901.

expenses are considered that the yearly burden is to be very heavy and that in the present state of agricultural depression the produce of the holdings can hardly warrant it . . . we have no source of income while getting the places into working order'.[83] The settlers, who had celebrated laying the foundation stone of the first building in the Strath only two months earlier, were now facing the shocking reality of their first bill from the CDB, at a time when their holdings were in complete disarray. Hardly anything was built, no crops had been put down and finding short-term alternative employment was impossible in a deserted strath miles from the populated coasts. The settlers asked for the first three years' annuity to be lifted to give them a fighting chance, but both this and the request for the payment period to be extended was refused.[84] In fairness, the CDB was limited in its financial decisions by the Treasury, which would not allow an extension of the payment period, but it also had unrealistic expectations of the settlers.[85] It was not a propitious beginning.

More requests followed this, firstly for an increased loan for buildings, then for seed oats and potatoes and finally for fencing.[86] The CDB agreed to most of these requests, but assiduously added the balance to the settlers' accounts.[87] The frustration of the settlers was shatteringly clear:

> I regret to inform your Honourable Board that the crop is to be a failure this year again and to crown matters, the river yesterday has flooded over the most of my holding and destroyed anything that has grown . . . There is not even value on my holding for the rates I have to pay besides <u>rent</u> and <u>interest</u> etc. Things are at present it is impossible to meet the Board's demands [sic].[88]

This sense of frustration, even desperation, characterises much of the correspondence from the Syre settlers to the CDB through the history of the settlement. Two settlers renounced their crofts and left the settlement entirely, both because they could not make the place pay, and as the years passed, all the settlers fell into arrear with the CDB, some by only a few pounds, others up to £50.[89]

In 1908, the dissatisfaction of the Syre settlers came to a head; the Small Landholders (Scotland) Bill was being debated clause by clause in Parliament, promising further benefits to crofter tenants.[90] The Syre

---

[83] NAS, AF42/1016, Syre settlers to CDB, 7 Nov. 1901.

[84] NAS, AF42/1016, CDB to Syre settlers, 20 Dec. 1901.

[85] NAS, AF42/1016, Minute by William Mackenzie, 27 Nov. 1901.

[86] NAS, AF42/1060, Syre settlers to CDB, Jan. 1902; AF42/1137, Syre Holdings Committee to CDB, 3 Mar. 1902; AF42/1296, 'As to fencing of Syre common grazing', 7 Jul. 1902.

[87] NAS, AF42/1672, CDB to Syre settlers, 16 Jun. 1903; AF42/2708, Question in Parliament on Syre settlers' failure to meet obligations, 1905.

[88] NAS, AF42/1717, D. MacLeod, Syre settler to CDB, 6 Jul. 1903.

[89] NAS, AF42/3784, A. Mackintosh to CDB, list of Syre arrears, 7 May 1907.

[90] E. A. Cameron, 'Politics, Ideology and the Highland land issue', *Scottish Historical Review*, 72 (1993), 70.

settlers petitioned the CDB, asking to be allowed to revert back to tenants: 'that your petitioners can entertain no hope of being successful in their holdings unless they are included in the number of those who are to come under the scope of the Small Holdings (Scotland) Bill.'[91] It is not clear what they thought the Small Landholders Bill would do for their immediate financial situation, but their petition is not surprising.[92] As owners they had to pay more tax, had no security on their crofts if they failed and they could not extend their holdings, which they complained were too small to be able to meet the demands of the CDB. This must have been a bitter irony to the CDB, who had reluctantly curbed the larger size of the original holdings because the local crofters did not have the means to take them. The CDB denied this request with a reminder that the settlers had made their bed and should now lie in it quietly: 'I am directed by the Board to point out that the Board offered for sale – and the purchasers, of their own free will, agreed to buy – their holdings after all the circumstances and conditions were fully and carefully disclosed to them.'[93]

The long-term future of Syre was not addressed again until 1911, the year the CDB was wound up and replaced by the Board of Agriculture for Scotland. Conditions on the Syre settlement had not improved materially since 1908 and the settlers were falling further into arrear with the CDB. This time, the CDB approached the Syre settlers and gave them a choice; they could submit to a re-valuation of their crofts with the possibility of a lower annuity to pay, or they could relinquish their ownership of the holdings and become rent-paying tenants of the new BoAS.[94] The answer of the Syre settlers was speedy and unanimous; they would become tenants, as long as fair terms for the building loans could be reached.[95] To thrash out these details, in a process Lord Pentland, Secretary for Scotland, dubbed 'as bad as the House of Commons', a meeting was held in Syre between six members of the CDB and the settlers.[96] The settlers wanted the loans to be waived and eventually the CDB agreed to cancel some of the debt in order to reach a quick and amicable agreement.[97]

The Syre experiment encapsulates the problems faced by the CDB when trying to meet its obligations in finding land for the crofters.[98] The 4th Duke,

[91] NAS, AF42/4401, Syre settlers to CDB, 1 Jan. 1908.

[92] Peter Keith, factor on the Ulbster estates, identified this issue in the Board of Agriculture for Scotland's plans for land under his jurisdiction: Ulbster Estate MSS, Factor's Letterbook 1909–11, Keith to Sir Tollemache, 10 Jan. 1911; Hunter, *Making of the Crofting Community*, 185–6.

[93] NAS, AF42/4401, CDB to Syre settlers, 1 Jun. 1908.

[94] NAS, AF42/8836, CDB to Syre settlers, 26 Sep. 1911; Cameron, *Land for the People*, 96.

[95] NAS, AF42/8888, Syre settlers to CDB, 6 Oct. 1911.

[96] NAS, AF42/8924, 'Minutes of meeting between CDB and Syre settlers', 13 Oct. 1911. Lord Pentland also travelled to Uig, Skye, to resolve a similar difficulty; Lady Pentland, *The Right Honourable John Sinclair, Lord Pentland, G. C. S. I.: a memoir* (London, 1928), 110.

[97] NAS, AF42/9324, 'Schedule for Agreement with Syre settlers', 29 Feb. 1912.

[98] Cameron, *Land for the People*, 90, 94–6.

like most Highland landlords, refused to see farms broken up on his estate while he was still the owner, and the CDB had to purchase land before it could be given to crofters. This put financial pressure on the CDB, which toiled under a very limited budget in addition to the political burden of expectations it carried. In an attempt to square this circle, the CDB put the burden of the purchase price and the costs of setting up on the settlers.[99] This almost inevitably led to the failure of the scheme, as those crofters or cottars most attracted by the promise of land were exactly those who could not possibly afford the heavy costs. As a result, it was mainly well-to-do crofters who took the crofts at Syre, who perhaps needed help less than the land-hungry crofters and cottars crammed around the north and west coasts of Sutherland, and even those crofters struggled to make ends meet. The Syre experiment collapsed because it not only failed to meet the demands of the landless cottars of Sutherland for holdings, but also failed to improve the living standards of those crofters who risked change and chose to become owner-occupiers.

'Get the farm for the people': Melness, 1911–12[100]

Just as the Syre experiment was in the process of being wound up by the CDB, the 4th Duke approached the Board with a new scheme, for the farm of Melness on the north coast. The farm's lease was due to end in 1912 and the tenants were not going to renew it.[101] The duke, in a surprising *volte face*, wrote to the CDB for assistance in breaking up the farm himself, in the manner of Sir Arthur Orde.[102] At the estate's invitation, two CDB inspectors went to Melness, including Mr Angus Mackintosh, the Syre farm manager, and there they inspected the ground and met the Tongue factor, John Morrison. Their report was not especially favourable:

> the farm is not a subject that, apart from special considerations, would appeal to us as a suitable one for the formation of small holdings, but the land is similar to much of what is under crofters in the north and west of Sutherland, and it is the only land available for the crofters of the Melness district which is largely congested.[103]

This sums up the problem faced by the CDB, and by its successor the BoAS, in Sutherland. The crofters were desperate for more land, but government experts considered the land too poor to be successfully settled, while acknowledging at the same time that there was nothing better locally.[104]

99   These problems were common to all CDB purchases: Cameron, 'Politics and Ideology', 69; J. Brown, 'Scottish and English Land legislation, 1903–11', *Scottish Historical Review*, 47 (1968), 73; Hunter, *Making of the Crofting Community*, 186; Cameron, *Land for the People*, 101.
100 NLS, Acc. 10225, Crofters, C/a, duchess to Macaulay, 23 Nov. 1911.
101 NAS, AF42/8563, duke to CDB, 14 Jun. 1911.
102 NAS, AF42/8563, duke to CDB, 14 Jun. 1911.
103 NAS, AF42/8857, 'Report on Melness', 25 Sep. 1911.
104 NLS, Acc. 10225, Factor's Correspondence, 1546, Morrison to Macaulay, 14 Oct. 1911.

With this in mind, the CDB decided not to take up the scheme, writing to the duke that 'there is not sufficient substance in this proposal for the Board to entertain it. It can therefore be wound up.'[105] The CDB had seen no hard evidence that the crofters even wanted the farm, and as they were coming to the end of their tenure, they decided against taking up such a complex scheme.[106] This rejection had a most unexpected effect on the Sutherland estate management, which was furious at the rebuff, calling it 'far from satisfactory', and determined to get 'a definite answer from the Board'.[107] The estate would have preferred to set up a scheme under the auspices of the CDB on its own terms, rather than have schemes forced on it by the compulsory purchase powers of the new BoAS in the future. Additionally, the estate management and ducal family may have had a political agenda after the narrow defeat of Lord Stafford in the December 1910 election.[108]

The Sutherland estate was certainly not going to give way without a fight, and was led in this, rather extraordinarily, by the Duchess Millicent. 'Meddlesome Millie', as she was known in some quarters, the 'Red Duchess' in others, she was far more active in persecuting the CDB than the duke could ever have been.[109] The duke was in Canada throughout the extended correspondence between the duchess and the CDB, and she was advised by the Sutherland factors and lawyers. This was not the first instance of activity on her part to benefit the crofters; she was probably the most socially and politically active duchess of Sutherland since the countess and first duchess Elizabeth. Since becoming duchess in 1892, she had campaigned on behalf of and held the presidency of the Scottish Home Industries Association and established the Golspie Technical School to provide training in trades for crofters' sons and daughters.[110] She was often at odds with the estate management, mainly because her projects required spending large sums of money. As she wrote to MacLean in 1900:

> I fear you consider me a very expensive item to the estate expenditure! I confess I shall always feel there is so much that <u>should</u> be done . . . The Duke always says 'alright' when I tell him a thing might be done!! then <u>you</u> say, I fear, its 'all wrong' as regards the estimates and

[105] NAS, AF42/8857, CDB to Morrison, 27 Oct. 1911.
[106] PP LXVII, 1907, *Ninth Annual Report of the Congested Districts Board*, 5; Cameron, *Land for the People*, 95–6.
[107] NLS, Acc. 10225, Factor's Correspondence, 1546, Morrison to Macaulay, 28 Oct. 1911.
[108] A. Tindley, 'The Sword of Avenging Justice': Politics in Sutherland after the Third Reform Act', *Rural History*, 19 (2008), 190–2.
[109] *Highland News*, 6 Jul. 1912.
[110] *Highland News*, 14 Oct. 1893, 25 Mar. 1899, 13 Jul. 1901, 26 Oct. 1901; NLS, Acc. 10225, Policy Papers, 107, MacLean to duchess, 4 Sep. 1894; 5th Duke of Sutherland, *Looking Back: the autobiography of the Duke of Sutherland* (London, 1957), 45–6; D. Stuart, *Dear Duchess: Millicent, Duchess of Sutherland, 1867–1955* (London, 1982), 91–6; J. Helland, 'Rural women and urban extravagance in late nineteenth century Britain', *Rural History*, 13 (2002), 182, 187–90.

then there is confusion and weariness of the flesh! Seriously I know expenses are heavy enough, but I would gladly forego some of my luxuries to use the money in ventures and improvements. I don't want to pauperise the people, but I do want to enlighten them.[111]

The duchess was occasionally mocked in crofting circles for her gushing approach, 'the Duchess is awfully sorry: sheds tears over the poor crofters', but she set to the CDB with a vengeance over Melness.[112] After gathering advice from the estate factors, she wrote personally to Lord Pentland, perhaps thinking that this might produce a more satisfactory result.[113] Lord Pentland had made it clear that the active support of the crofters of Melness, in the form of an official application to the CDB or Crofters Commission, had been missing from the estate's scheme and therefore the CDB could not take it any further.[114] The duchess rejected this in very strong terms, asking Lord Pentland, 'Don't you think it is very unfair that the Board should endeavour to ride off on these technicalities? . . . I maintain that these technical grounds do not in common fairness apply to the case.'[115] The collapse of the Melness scheme was skilfully used by the Sutherland estate to generate political goodwill, demonstrated in early December 1911 when the duchess had all of the correspondence published.[116]

This must have been extremely galling for the CDB; it was not a popular institution with the general public and was widely perceived to have failed in its task of redistributing land to crofters since 1897.[117] It was an easy target, but for the estate it was a hollow victory. Few were impressed by its attempts to get a scheme going; after all, it could have gone ahead without the CDB and taken the financial loss itself. Lord Pentland continued the correspondence with the duchess, defending the actions of the CDB, but to no avail.[118] The duchess replied only that, 'I am persuaded that the Board really has no heart to help anything in Sutherland. I consider I am putting this conviction very mildly.'[119] Lord Pentland ended the correspondence by saying, 'I must content to differ', and promised that if any application from the crofters was received he would bear all of the duchess's comments in mind.[120] When the crofters' petition arrived at the CDB, the Board wrote back, rejecting the scheme on the basis that the applicants could not pay

[111] NLS, Acc. 10225, Crofters, B/e, duchess to MacLean, 12 Nov. 1900.
[112] *Highland News*, 2 Dec. 1911.
[113] NLS, Acc. 10225, Crofters, C/a, duchess to Macaulay, 10 Nov. 1911.
[114] NLS, Acc. 10225, Crofters, C/a, Lord Pentland to duchess, 9 Nov. 1911.
[115] NLS, Acc. 10225, Crofters, C/a, duchess to Lord Pentland, 17 Nov. 1911.
[116] NLS, Acc .10225, Crofters, C/a, Lord Pentland to duchess, 30 Nov. 1911; *Scotsman*, 5 Dec. 1911.
[117] Hunter, *Making of the Crofting Community*, 185; Cameron, *Land for the People*, 101, 122.
[118] NLS, Acc. 10225, Crofters, C/a, Lord Pentland to duchess, 19 Dec. 1911.
[119] NLS, Acc. 10225, Crofters, C/a, duchess to Lord Pentland, 27 Dec. 1911.
[120] NAS, AF42/9256, Lord Pentland to duchess, 3 Jan. 1912.

for the stocking of the land: Melness farm was re-let privately by the estate in early 1912.[121]

The CDB had ended its tenure in Sutherland on a very sour note, having failed to come out of the Melness negotiations with its reputation intact, despite Lord Pentland's best efforts. This record was not entirely the fault of the CDB, however; it was constricted from its inception by a budget insufficient for its schemes all over the Highlands.[122] It was doubly unfortunate then that the 4th Duke would only sell Syre, forcing the CDB to spend a third of its annual budget and passing the entire risk of the settlement, financial and political, onto the Board. The nature of the land also dictated decisions about schemes in Sutherland, as it was rough, poor and generally agreed to have deteriorated under eighty years of intensive sheep farming. The nature and extent of the clearances which had created those sheep farms were also a barrier to increasing the amount of land under crofters.[123] Most of Sutherland's crofters were mired in poverty, with no capital for stocking new land or fencing and building. The main cry of the crofters was for more land, and in this the CDB had failed to provide.

'I prefer to establish myself in my own colony': the new Sutherland Estate, 1899–1920[124]

Increasing government intervention in the administration of Highland estates from 1886, in the finances of great landowners and the increasing loss of their political influence after 1906 drove the 4th Duke to radically re-structure his estate financially and territorially. For the duke and his contemporaries, the instinct was to shore up their estates, their fortunes and their political powers.[125] The 4th and 5th dukes were part of this trend and took active steps to re-mould the Sutherland estates into a structure that would survive the twentieth century. This included freeing up vast sums of sleeping capital through land sales in Britain and investing that money in safer ventures, away from the Treasury sniffer dogs. In many ways these efforts were unsuccessful; the 5th Duke had to live a relatively more frugal life than his father or grandfather.[126] But it was a fundamental success in one way; the Sutherland family is still a major landowner in the north of Scotland. True, these are the remnants of a former unimaginable wealth,

---

[121] NLS, Acc. 10225, Factor's Correspondence, 1547, Morrison to Sutherland Board of Management, 3 Feb. 1912; perhaps the CDB did not want another Syre.

[122] Cameron, *Land for the People*, 84.

[123] Leneman, *Fit for Heroes*, 53.

[124] *Highland News*, 2 Sep. 1911.

[125] Cannadine, *Decline and Fall*, 35–7.

[126] See 5th Duke, *Looking Back*, 86, 98, 164; the fact the 5th Duke even wrote an autobiography says much; D. Spring, 'The Role of the Aristocracy in the Nineteenth century', *Victorian Studies*, 4 (1960), 63.

but the family survived.[127] This success depended on four key factors: a cushion of broad acres, resilience in the face of agricultural depression, the ability to re-structure assets and debts, and the opportunity to exploit non-agricultural sources of income.[128] All will be examined here.

Immediately on his accession to the estate in 1892, the 4th Duke was exercised about expenditure. This concern initially stemmed from the ruinous settlement he had made in 1895 with his father's widow, the Duchess Mary Caroline, but years after that payment had been made, he regularly worried his factors with instructions to cut down estate expenditure.[129] He was working against the prevailing tide within his family, however; his wife was a keen worker for charity, frequently requiring large sums of money, and was also one of the 'fast' set, unwilling to accept the 4th Duke's curbs on family expenditure. She was stonily unsympathetic towards her husband's worries: 'Strath [the 4th Duke] has a mad lust for destruction on the plea of death duties . . . S. is a pitiable figure, mooning about like Scrooge and muttering about money.'[130]

The duke not only had to work against his own family in preserving the Sutherland fortune; he had the government to contend with as well. A new and aggressive Liberal administration from 1906 was a blow to both the duke's confidence in his wealth, and in the political power of his class. One of the duke's biggest worries came in 1909 with Lloyd George's People's Budget, which included a measure for the taxation of land values, as well as increased death duties and a super tax, all calculated to strike fear into the hearts of patrician landowners like the duke.[131] The prospect of this legislation caused a flurry of panic:

> In the face of such a Budget both my son and I should have power and freedom to sell land. I should not like to consent to hand my son down

[127] F. M. L. Thompson, 'English Landed Society in the Twentieth century: I: Property: Collapse and Survival', *Transactions of the Royal Historical Society*, 5th ser., 40 (1990), 10, 13; F. M. L. Thompson, 'English Landed Society in the Twentieth century: II: New Poor and New Rich', *Transactions of the Royal Historical Society*, 6th ser., 1 (1991), 11.

[128] A. Adonis, 'Aristocracy, Agriculture and Liberalism: the politics, finances and estates of the third Lord Carrington', *Historical Journal*, 31 (1988), 882.

[129] NLS, Acc. 10853, Policy Papers, 52, duke to MacLean, 15 Nov. 1907. Finances were a problem for many Highland estates in this period, often much more so than for the Sutherland estate; see, for example, Ulbster Estate MSS, Factor's Letterbook, 11, Keith to Sir Tollemache, 31 Mar. 1911; Armadale Castle, Macdonald MSS, 3611, Macdonald lawyers to Malcolm of Invergarry, 14 Sep. 1908.

[130] Duchess to Lord Esher, cited in Stuart, *Dear Duchess*, 118; J. Yorke, *Lancaster House: London's greatest town house* (London, 2001), 153.

[131] B. Murray, *The People's Budget 1909/10: Lloyd George and Liberal Politics* (Oxford, 1980), 173; I. Packer, *Lloyd George, Liberalism and the Land: the land issue and party politics in England, 1906–1914* (Woodbridge, 2001), 61–2; Cannadine, *Decline and Fall*, 48; Thompson, 'I: Property: Collapse and Survival', 2; Thompson, 'II: New Poor and New Rich', 6–7; Yorke, *Lancaster House*, 154; Newby, *Ireland, Radicalism and the Scottish Highlands*, 182–3; A. Offer, *Property and Politics, 1870–1914: landownership, law, ideology and urban development in England* (Cambridge, 1981), 327.

to an overtaxed estate. If the country as a whole determines to break up big estates so it must be but I would not consent to an impoverished owner being tied to land from which other people get the revenue.[132]

The duke's attitude was one of outraged paranoia, and he regarded the new legislation as totally unfair; he spoke of being 'burdened' by a large estate, while damning the chancellor: 'I daresay you will have noticed the wild way the Chancellor of the Exchequer has been behaving and there can be no doubt he will bring forward a very sensational Budget, which may be a serious thing.'[133] The duke feared that the new taxes would put off potential buyers of land, and with new legislation coming into force in 1911 to take land for crofters on compulsion, he feared for the future of landowners in Britain. As the *Highland News* put it, rather less sympathetically:

> The Duke of Sutherland, like other great landed proprietors, is taking fright at the trend of present legislation, and, instead of continuing the old frozen up style of refusing to listen to applications for land, is pleading with Government Boards to take the hot potato out of his hands . . . Meantime Dukes and Duchesses should be allowed to feel a little of the anxiety crofters and small farmers have been feeling for ages.[134]

The duke, as well as supporting Conservative candidates in both 1910 elections in Sutherland to stem the tide of this radical Liberalism, used another tactic in common with many other landowners; land sales.[135] He also ruthlessly cut back the family houses, as they simply could no longer be afforded; Trentham was offered to Staffordshire County Council as a gift in 1907 but they refused to take it and it was bulldozed in 1911.[136] Most symbolically, Stafford House, the great London palace of the Sutherlands, was sold to Lord Leverhulme in 1912 for £60,000.[137]

The 4th Duke sold three main lots of land in Sutherland before his death. In 1898, Andrew Carnegie, the fantastically wealthy industrialist, was

[132] NLS, Acc. 10225, Policy Papers, 105, Prowse to MacLean, 7 May 1909.
[133] NLS, Acc. 10225, Policy Papers, 169, duke to Morrison, 10 Jan. 1909.
[134] *Highland News*, 10 Feb. 1912; this refers to the unsuccessful Melness scheme.
[135] In Jan. 1910, Cameron of Lochiel stood as the Tory candidate and in Dec. 1910, as already mentioned, Lord Stafford, the future 5th Duke, also stood unsuccessfully. The 4th Duke had taken a Liberal Unionist stance in 1886 and over the years had turned to the Conservative party as the Liberals, as he saw it, attacked landowners' interests. This conversion was made between 1901 and 1906 in common with many aristocratic families from a Whig background; Tindley, 'The Sword of Avenging Justice', 189–92; Cannadine, *Decline and Fall*, 133.
[136] Yorke, *Lancaster House*, 159.
[137] Stuart, *Dear Duchess*, 56, 116–17; National Archives, TI/11564, Treasury, Office of Works, file 13936; F. M. L. Thompson, 'English Landed Society in the Twentieth century: III: Self-Help and Outdoor Relief', *Transactions of the Royal Historical Society*, 6th ser., 2 (1992), 13; Cannadine, *Decline and Fall*, 116.

looking for a Scottish estate and found it at Skibo; he bought the castle and 19,448 acres from the duke for £76,000.[138] A further 100,000 acres in the Tongue management were advertised, to be purchased by W. E. Gilmour, a wealthy Scotsman who owned a large dye-works in Dunbartonshire.[139] He bought the land from the duke for £100,500 in 1900.[140] The duke also sold his estates in Yorkshire in 1911; these were the heart of the Leveson-Gower family, the original landed estates granted to the family centuries ago, and their sale marked the end of an era.[141] They freed up £45,745 in capital, however, which represented £28 per acre, as compared to £1 per acre for that sold in Sutherland.[142] The duke also sold land in Shropshire, the land in the south fetching much higher prices than that in Sutherland.[143] The duke affected all of these sales without any objection from his heir; many of their contemporaries were doing the same, it being no longer viable to maintain large estates in the teeth of government legislation and decades of family debt.[144] The landowning community had been pessimistic since the agricultural depression of the 1880s, but add to this generally decreasing incomes, increased exactions and eroded political confidence and the 4th Duke's re-structuring does not look out of place in his social and financial context.[145] The duke was very keen to sell the poorest-quality land, and that with the most crofters on it, as advised by his factors: 'crofts are the barrier and when they come in any number they no doubt severely deteriorate the value of the whole property and I fear in most cases render the property unsalable'.[146] In 1913, just before he died, the duke completed the sale of Assynt for £50,000 to Mr J. W. Stewart, the son of an Assynt cottar who had emigrated to Canada, made a fortune in railway contracting and returned to buy 50,000 acres of his homeland.[147] These sales took poor land with troublesome crofters off the duke's hands and gave him hard cash instead, a conversion he was very happy with; in 1899, he had been obliged to take

---

[138] NLS, Acc. 10225, Sales, 1, 'Disposition by 4th Duke of Sutherland to A. Carnegie and Spouse', 27 May 1899; P. Krass, *Carnegie* (Hoboken, NJ, 2002), 350–3.

[139] McIver, *Memoirs*, 148; Habakkuk, *Marriage, Debt and the Estates System*, 671–3; *Northern Times*, 7 Feb. 1924, obituary of Gilmour.

[140] NLS, Acc. 10225, Sales, 1, 'Disposition of 4th Duke of Sutherland in favour of W. E. Gilmour', 29 Mar. 1900; McIver, *Memoirs*, 123–4, 150.

[141] *Highland News*, 25 Feb. 1911.

[142] *Highland News*, 8 Jun. 1912.

[143] *Highland News*, 3 Feb. 1912.

[144] Cannadine, *Decline and Fall*, 98–9.

[145] Cannadine, *Decline and Fall*, 98; J. Beckett and M. Turner, 'End of the Old Order? F. M. L. Thompson, the Land Question and the burden of ownership in England, c.1880–c.1925', *Agricultural History Review*, 55 (2007), 273, 283. Interestingly, Beckett and Turner point to the period 1896–1903 as a boom in land sales close to that of the 'revolutionary' period 1918–20.

[146] NLS, Acc. 10225, Sales, 3, MacLean to Box, 22 Jan. 1897.

[147] NLS, Acc. 10225, Sales, 1, 'Disposition by the 4th Duke of Sutherland and Lord Stafford in favour of John William Stewart', 25 Apr. 1913; again, this represents £1 per acre; *Highland News*, 8 Mar. 1913.

a private loan of £100,000 at 3% interest and despite his land sales, in 1912 the total debt on the Sutherland estate stood at £194,131.[148]

The duke was outraged by what he saw as destructive trends in British government and society, all aimed at eradicating the landowning class. His land sales had been for a very specific purpose, as he told an interviewer in 1911: 'if it becomes necessary to submit to mob rule as the outcome of Lloyd George's Government, I prefer to establish myself in my own colony, where political relations do not enter into the dealings between landlord and tenant'.[149] Through land sales, he was extracting sleeping, taxable capital from Britain and moving it to Canada through land purchases of over 100,000 acres, for which he paid £250,000.[150] As the *Highland News* pointed out: 'they [landlords] have a suspicion that landlordism is about to be played out in this country, and are making preparations to flit. Landlordism is a paying game while it lasts, and the Duke thinks it will last a while yet in the new country across the sea.'[151]

The duke had big plans for his land in Canada; as well as building his own permanent residence there he wanted to offer the rest in lots to emigrants from Britain, particularly Sutherland, to purchase on favourable terms.[152] By this time he was deeply involved in promoting settlement in the Empire generally, having founded both the British Empire Association and the Imperial Colonisation Corporation of Canada to further these ends.[153] He found an agent to manage his lands in Canada and instructed his factors to encourage any Sutherland crofters with capital to apply for a farm.[154] In the duke's eyes, the scheme had two advantages. Firstly, it removed the trouble and expense of a crofting tenantry from him and passed it onto either the emigrants or Canadian government. Secondly, it would appear that he was working for the good of the crofters, and would thereby stem public criticism. Unsurprisingly, there were few applicants from Sutherland for the duke's scheme; the required capital was too much for most to afford, and for many it smacked of the clearances: 'this is indeed adding insult to injury – this progeny of a noble family whose ancestors burned the poor Highlanders' cottages etc. about their ears, evicted them without remorse, and now has the impudence to offer a "settlement" in some far off country for the remnant of those whose forefathers escaped the Sutherland

---

[148] NLS, Acc. 10225, Sales, 1, 'Bond and disposition of 4th Duke for a loan of £100,000', May 1899; 'Abstract of total amount of bonds secured over the whole estates', 30 May 1912.

[149] *Highland News*, 2 Sep. 1911. The duke was not the only landowner to express these sentiments: Thompson, 'I: Property: Collapse and Survival', 13; 'II: New Poor and New Rich', 12–14.

[150] *Highland News*, 3 Sep. 1910; 5th Duke of Sutherland, *Looking Back*, 58–9; Cannadine, *Decline and Fall*, 103, 108, 134; Habakkuk, *Marriage, Debt and the Estates System*, 667–8.

[151] *Highland News*, 16 Jul. 1910.

[152] *Northern Times*, 2 Nov. 1911.

[153] *Highland News*, 22 Jun. 1912.

[154] NLS, Acc. 10853, Policy Papers, 54, Alex. Simpson to MacLean, 24 May 1911.

Clearances'.[155] Another correspondent asked, 'Why not give 5000 acres in Sutherlandshire? There is plenty of land there available for small holdings. It would be to our benefit in travelling expenses alone, and, again, it would give us the privilege of being situated upon our native heath.'[156] Whether the Canadian scheme would have succeeded is unknown; just as it began, the 4th Duke died, and from 1913 the Sutherland Canadian Lands Company, set up to administer the land, halted any further investment, and under the direction of the 5th Duke, sold off all the land over the following thirteen years.[157]

When the 5th Duke inherited in 1913 he immediately set about continuing what his father had begun. Pressed by existing debts of nearly £200,000 and with fresh Death Duties to pay, no less than 114,569 acres were advertised for sale in 1914, but due to the outbreak of war later that year, the auction was postponed until October 1919.[158] By this time, the 5th Duke had increased the amount of land for sale in Sutherland to a staggering 445,000 acres, which was sold for roughly £639,000 at auction in 1919.[159] Some of this immense sum went on paying off debts and Death Duties; the rest was invested in a variety of government stocks, including War Loans and National War Bonds.[160] The 5th Duke had learnt his father's lesson and sunk the financial future of the estate into safe government investments, away from risky imperial ventures, and, most ironically of all, land in Britain.

'For he will return to Dunrobin no more': conclusion, 1897–1920[161]

The tenures of the 4th and 5th dukes of Sutherland over the estates were overshadowed by the parallel power of government agencies in the region; the Crofters Commission, the CDB and the BoAS. The CDB saw thirteen years of activity in Sutherland, but this resulted in little change in the structure of land holding there or elsewhere in the Highlands.[162] Its scheme at Syre was a failure, a result of both the duke's unwillingness to accept less than the market price for land and the economic problems of the

[155] *Highland News*, 15 Oct. 1910, letter to the editor from 'A Highland Land Leaguer'.
[156] *People's Journal*, 11 Nov. 1911, letter to the editor from 'N. F.'; 5th Duke, *Looking Back*, 58.
[157] 5th Duke, *Looking Back*, 58.
[158] *Times*, 4 Apr. 1914; NLS, Acc. 10225, Sales, 7, brochure of land divisions for sale, 1914; the auctioneers were Knight, Frank and Rutley who handled many of the great estate sales in the period; Cannadine, *Decline and Fall*, 108–9; Acc. 10225, Sales, 8, printed notice, 1914; Acc. 10225, Factor's Correspondence, 480, Morrison to Knight, Frank and Rutley, 30 Nov. 1914.
[159] NLS, Acc. 10225, Sales, 6, 'Note of sales made at auction, 1919'; the most expensive lot, at £85,000, was the Reay Forest, bought by the Duke of Westminster.
[160] NLS, Acc. 10225, Factor's Correspondence, 501, Macaulay to duke, 4 Nov. 1919; 26 Nov. 1919.
[161] *Highland News*, 12 Jul. 1913.
[162] Cameron, *Land for the People*, 122–3.

crofting community. For most crofters and cottars in Sutherland, purchase was not a realistic option; they wanted more land, but could not possibly pay market prices for it and afford stock and buildings. Their wish was to remain tenants, with the benefits that status conferred, such as security of tenure, lower taxes and low rents.[163] Very few crofters, especially the poorest whom the CDB was supposed to assist, had a few hundred pounds of capital to spend on purchasing small crofts of low value; if they did, they would not have needed the CDB at all.

The ducal family were also adjusting to a new financial future. The 4th and 5th dukes regarded themselves and their class as under attack from both crofters and government. As a result of this siege mentality, large tracts of land in Britain were sold off and invested firstly, and unsuccessfully, in Canada, and later in government stocks and bonds. The 5th Duke spent much of his life retrenching estate finances in an effort to keep his head above water, and was largely successful. Although the model of 'decline and fall' is applicable to the Sutherland estate, it was not obliterated entirely; indeed, the family still holds Dunrobin castle and 100,000 acres in the north of Scotland. This relative success was only possible because of the vast cushion of wealth and resources behind the ducal family, built up by luck and marriage from the late eighteenth century. Adverse financial and governmental circumstances from the late 1880s provided the catalyst for a radical adjustment in the form of that fortune. Between 1898 and 1919, the Sutherland estates were reduced in area by a staggering 615,000 acres; but this still left 385,000 acres, keeping the family within the top bracket of patrician landowners.

[163] Hunter, *Making of the Crofting Community*, 185–6.

CHAPTER SIX

'Let them understand that they must submit to rule': Clashmore and the Sutherland Estate, 1850–1909[1]

Introduction

In 1869, the 3rd Duke of Sutherland was busy planning land reclamation in Sutherland. Although centred on Lairg and Kildonan, the Scourie management was not excluded from the improving mania: £200 per annum was set aside for the creation of a model farm at Clashmore in Assynt.[2] The management was also looking for ways to create employment for the local population, which had been suffering under a severe economic downturn since 1868. As Evander McIver, Scourie factor, related to the Napier Commission in 1883:

> Clashmore was a township with a lot of small tenants in it. They cultivated the lots very partially, and the Duke of Sutherland one day, standing on the hill pasture, asked me, would it not be a good thing for the employment of the people if we were to set a-going a small farm here, on which we could show the people what crops could be grown by proper trenching and drainage and farming on the regular rotation. I said I thought it would be a very good thing indeed, and would give a great deal of employment to the people of this place, Clashmore was fixed upon as suitable for the purpose.[3]

This decision would precipitate decades of strife and agitation between the estate management and the crofters. The extent of the disruption there was unique in Sutherland, which generally saw very little violent agitation compared to areas such as Skye, Lewis or Tiree. It is, therefore, important to put Clashmore into its wider Highland context, in terms

---

[1] National Library of Scotland [hereafter NLS], Sutherland Estates Papers, Acc. 10225, Policy Papers, 215, McIver to Kemball, 22 Jan. 1886.

[2] NLS, Acc. 10225, Policy Papers, 212, McIver to Loch, 10 Sep. 1869 and 7 Feb. 1870; E. Richards and M. Clough, *Cromartie: Highland life, 1650–1914* (Aberdeen, 1989), 257.

[3] PP 1884, XXXII–XXXVI, 1884, *Evidence and Report of the Commissioners of Inquiry into the condition of the Crofters and Cottars in the Highlands and Islands of Scotland* [hereafter *Napier Commission Evidence*], Evander McIver, 1763. Before 1882, the estate would often initiate works projects to provide employment and thereby encourage payment of rents: see E. McIver, *Memoirs of a Highland Gentleman: being the reminiscences of Evander McIver of Scourie*, Rev. G. Henderson (ed.) (Edinburgh, 1905), 79; Richards and Clough, *Cromartie*, 287.

of the course and methods of crofter agitation and the response of the estate and of the authorities.[4] In this way, although Clashmore stands out in a Sutherland context, it slots into wider events in the Highlands in this period. The involvement of several different authorities, from the Crofters Commission to the Congested Districts Board and various legal bodies, produced a rich seam of records separate from those of the estate that can be utilised. This allows both a detailed case study of one township not possible elsewhere in this book, while exposing the wider Highland and national context.

Clashmore also throws the Sutherland estate management into sharp relief. The township saw the worst of the crofters' agitation in Sutherland and would put a huge strain on relations between estate staff, resulting in two actual and two threatened resignations. This may be partly explained by the prevalence of strong personalities in the estate management in this period. The Scourie factor from 1845 to 1895 was Evander McIver, a well-educated Lewis-man and son of a prosperous fish merchant, who believed in maintaining strict discipline over the crofters, earning the bitter soubriquet, the 'King of Scourie'.[5] McIver had a rather tragic personal life, which may have had some bearing on his attitude towards the crofters. He had eleven children, only one of whom outlived him; six died in childhood and of the four who survived, two were killed in India, one died of tuberculosis and the last in a riding accident in South Africa.[6] In his later years he became unpopular among the crofters for his despotic methods of management, his consistent advocacy of emigration as a solution to the social and economic problems of his management, and his rejection of the crofting system.[7] McIver, like many of his colleagues in Sutherland and across the Highlands, was energetic, emotional though not sentimental, and impatient when faced with the active and passive resistance of crofters to what he saw as measures of improvement instituted for their benefit. His advocacy of emigration was a personal as well as a policy matter; his sons had made their way in the world and before being appointed factor, McIver 'was quite anxious to emigrate to Australia'.[8] He regarded the new Clashmore farm as a boon for the crofters, and would never understand their objections to it. He was also frequently in conflict with his superiors over what the estate response to this conflict should be. These tensions weakened and occasionally paralysed the management, making Clashmore

---

[4] T. M. Devine, *Clanship to Crofters' War: the social transformation of the Scottish Highlands* (Manchester, 1994), 218.

[5] Ironically, Evander's father, Lewis, was constantly at loggerheads with Sir James Matheson's infamous factor, Donald Munro; J. Shaw Grant, *A Shilling for your Scowl: the history of a Scottish legal mafia* (Stornoway, 1992), 42–8; Devine, *Clanship to Crofters' War*, 217–18.

[6] McIver, *Memoirs*, 97–100.

[7] PP XXXVIII–XXXIX, 1895, *Royal Commission (Highlands and Islands, 1892), Report and Evidence* [hereafter *Deer Forest Commission Evidence*], McIver, 718.

[8] His father did not allow him to go, however; McIver, *Memoirs*, 32.

an instructive case study of the Sutherland estate and its relations with its
tenantry, the churches and government.

Genesis: 1850–74

'You will lose and not gain by your conduct.'[9]

Clashmore was a clearance township, established in the early nineteenth
century, its population substantially added to in 1851. The Clashmore
tenants had petitioned McIver to prevent the influx of more tenants, which
would lead to greater congestion in already difficult circumstances:

> That your petitioners beg to remark that they were promised by Mr
> Gunn factor when their houses were built before and Clashmore lotted
> [divided into crofts] that they would never be desired to change their
> houses or make any further lots as long as they would be able to pay
> their rents. That your petitioners most respectfully ask that you would
> lay their distressed case before his Grace the Duke of Sutherland and
> also that you would use your influence to prevent the contemplation
> [sic] change.[10]

The petition was rejected and the township was added to, greatly increasing
congestion and reducing the value of the land for the existing tenants.

After the upheaval of 1851, the estate left the township alone until the
land was chosen as a site for reclamation in 1869. George Loch, the commissioner, was not without qualms about the proposed reclamations at
Clashmore, raising as they did the old spectre of clearance.[11] He cautioned
McIver over and over again about the proper way to treat the tenants
who had to be moved: 'I am very glad to hear that it will not be necessary
to move more than six tenants, and that, during five years . . . We must
always be careful to have some place to offer to each of the tenants before
removing them.'[12]

McIver agreed, and re-assuring Loch, sent Mr Humphrey, a surveyor,
to Clashmore to begin measuring the ground for the farm in February
1870. Foolishly, McIver had not informed the Clashmore tenants of the
estate's intentions and, unsurprisingly, the tenant of the croft, widow Janet
Mackenzie, reacted strongly. As McIver reported to Loch,

> Her sons, two big fellows came and kicked down his [Humphrey's]
> pole and told him no one would be permitted to interfere with their lot
> without their mother's permission or authority. Humphrey called for the
> mother who told him she had also desired her sons to act as they did.[13]

[9] NLS, Acc. 10225, Factor's Correspondence, 1941, McIver to Janet Mackenzie, 18 Aug. 1870.
[10] NLS, Dep. 313, 1397, Clashmore crofters to McIver, 1851.
[11] Richards and Clough, *Cromartie*, 267–8.
[12] NLS, Acc. 10225, Policy Papers, 186, Loch to McIver, 15 Feb. 1870.
[13] NLS, Acc. 10225, Policy Papers, 212, McIver to Loch, 16 Feb. 1870.

The estate had not informed any of the tenants that a farm was going to be established on their township, and in fact, as McIver admitted, until they served removal summonses they had no legal right to start any work on the crofts at all.[14] Despite Loch's pleas for delicacy in dealing with the Clashmore tenants, McIver had blundered. He suggested that Janet Mackenzie be served with a summons so that work could proceed and an example be set. He reported to Loch that if he could find a replacement lot at Whitsunday, 'they deserve to be removed to it'.[15]

Loch was disheartened, but supported his factor: 'there is no reason why the summons may not be served, so as to place you in a position legally to commence the improvement, but no steps may be taken to remove her, until there be some other place for her to go'.[16] The widow Mackenzie did not give up so easily; she wrote to Loch personally and also had the Free Church minister in Stoer write on her behalf to the duke, asking for a reprieve.[17] She was given a new lot to occupy in the nearby township of Balchladich, but nevertheless continued to occupy her old house at Clashmore. She was soon joined in her protests by another tenant, a second widow Mackenzie, who 'has behaved very improperly and has actually frightened the trenchers so much by her noise and denunciations that none of them will return and begin on her lot'.[18] The resistance would worsen, however, as when Humphrey did finally persuade a man to start trenching on her lot, 'they at once set upon him with stones . . . [and] hurt and bruised him so that he had to fly'.[19]

McIver's response was to write personally to the offending crofters to warn them about their behaviour and to serve summons of removal: 'I am most displeased with you for your own and your children's conduct about the trenching . . . You will lose and not gain by your conduct.'[20] Overall, six summonses were issued, the budding agitation quietened down and Humphrey worked on the cleared lots in relative peace.[21] The duke had been kept informed but was more concerned with the growing expense of the project. Clashmore was employing between forty and sixty men a day, but 'it will be very expensive before it is fenced and drained and with houses be fit for a crop and occupation. It will give very favourable employment to a number of poor men who would otherwise be much

---

[14] NLS, Acc. 10225, Policy Papers, 212, McIver to Loch, 16 Feb. 1870.

[15] NLS, Acc. 10225, Policy Papers, 212, McIver to Loch, 16 Feb. 1870.

[16] NLS, Acc. 10225, Policy Papers, 186, Loch to McIver, 21 Jul. 1870.

[17] NLS, Acc. 10225, Policy Papers, 186, Loch to McIver, 26 Jul. 1870.

[18] NLS, Acc. 10225, Policy Papers, 212, McIver to Loch, 18 Aug. 1870.

[19] NLS, Acc. 10225, Policy Papers, 212, McIver to Loch, 30 Sep. 1870.

[20] NLS, Acc. 10225, Factor's Correspondence, 1941, McIver to Janet Mackenzie, 18 Aug. 1870; 5 Apr. 1870; McIver to widow Flora Mackenzie, 16 May 1870; McIver to John Mackenzie, 25 Jan. 1871.

[21] NLS, Acc. 10225, Policy Papers, 212, McIver to Loch, 30 Sep. 1870; episodes of resistance in the Highlands at this time were usually dealt with in this way; see Highland Council Archive [hereafter HCA], Papers of Christie and Ferguson, solicitors, Kilmuir Estate MSS, D123/1v, William Fraser to Alex. Macdonald, 3 Mar. 1865.

in want.'[22] The creation of Clashmore farm was often defended in these terms in future years, but the crofters soon realised that the loss of their lots would be more significant than short-term employment.[23]

Work continued relatively peacefully until 1873, when the next round of removals was planned. In March, Humphrey and his workers complained to McIver of a renewal of violent conduct by the tenants and so McIver, with one of his sons in tow, went to Clashmore to investigate. As he reported to Loch,

> There were some women hovering about us, but with the exception of one who came up towards Humphrey and two of the workmen and threw some clods at them, we were not interfered with . . . That night the whole of the sods and moss thrown out of the ditch by the workmen were thrown back in the ditch. Next day the 26th March Humphrey and his workmen returned . . . when the whole people of Clashmore, men and women, young and old, in a body came and said to Humphrey and his men that they must immediately desist from the work and that if they did not do so peaceably and quietly they would at once proceed to drive them away by force.[24]

This was a new tactic: unity. As the whole township had turned out, the estate could not identify ringleaders to punish and make an example of. McIver was outraged by this latest round of resistance, writing, 'it really is a very bad state of matters and among ignorant rude people such as the Stoer district is full of it has the most injurious effect on the habits and ideas of the people . . . Unless some strong measure of this kind [removals] be taken I must cease to attempt to exercise authority over the people of Assynt.'[25] This would not be the last resignation threat McIver would make over Clashmore. He demanded the full force of the estate's power to be brought against the crofters. He argued that

> All the tenants have been summoned to remove at the approaching term of Whitsunday on account of their misconduct and interference about the lots proposed to be improved . . . I think this affords an opportunity of considering the subject of an increase in rent in this township, a subject which circumstances compel us now in my opinion to seriously take up . . . I think two or three of the ringleaders in the late disturbances there should be deprived of their lots altogether, and that the rental of all the other lots should be increased annually . . . 25 per cent at least should be added.[26]

22 NLS, Acc. 10225, Policy Papers, 212, McIver to Loch, 1 Jul. 1870.
23 *Napier Commission Evidence*, McIver, 1763.
24 Staffordshire County Record Office [hereafter SCRO], Sutherland Estates Papers, D593, K/1/3/62, McIver to Loch, 13 Oct. 1873.
25 SCRO, D593, K/1/3/62, McIver to Loch, 26 Mar. 1873.
26 SCRO, D593, K/1/3/62, McIver to Loch, 5 May 1873; the view that examples had to be made to maintain discipline was common to many Highland estates: HCA, Kilmuir Estate MSS, D123/2e, Fraser to Alex. Macdonald, 24 Dec. 1882.

Loch concurred that 'it is quite certain that these acts of violence cannot be allowed to pass without serving notice'.[27] He suggested that two of the ringleaders should be deprived of their lots entirely and McIver obliged by sending him a list of no fewer than ten deserving candidates.[28]

Fourteen of the Clashmore crofters petitioned the duke in 1873, asking for the removals to be halted and for a reduction in the newly increased rents. They were careful to express their faith in the duke, 'in whom we always had the greatest confidence . . . being confident that whatever grievances were experienced by tenants on the estate were not to be traced either to you or your most noble family'.[29] They clearly saw the duke as a sympathetic and benevolent figure and knew that the Sutherland family was sensitive about its public reputation: 'we beg moreover respectfully to state that some who knew how unevenly we have been treated recommended us to bring our grievances before the public through the press'.[30] They received no reply and the removals went ahead. Loch argued they should continue as soon as possible, so 'that the people be convinced you are quite in earnest in carrying out the works of improvement'.[31] Seventeen crofters were summoned and fourteen had their rents increased, although Loch was uneasy that 'it be seen that we do so out of temper or to punish them'.[32] This put an end to the agitation and by 1874 it had died away completely.[33]

The reclamations at Clashmore sparked off some surprisingly stiff resistance from the crofters, and the sustained nature and variety of tactics they used was unusual in the wider Highland context of the early 1870s. More famous cases of crofter resistance included Bernera in 1874 and Leckmelm in 1879, but Clashmore did not attract the same publicity.[34] In the early 1870s, public opinion was very favourable towards the duke and his land reclamation projects, and he was held up as an example to his peers for ploughing vast sums of money into improving his estate.[35] Also, the resistance was never so bad that the estate had to call in the forces of law and order to help deal with it. The powers the estate had to hand, such as removal at forty days' notice and arbitrary rent increases, were enough to quell the agitation in the early 1870s, even though Loch and the duke were uneasy about using them.[36] The work had been done with few qualms at

[27] NLS, Acc. 10225, Farms, Clashmore 1873–88, Loch to McIver, 31 Mar. 1873.
[28] NLS, Acc. 10225, Crofters, ZN/h, McIver to Loch, 14 Apr. 1873.
[29] NLS, Acc. 10225, Crofters, ZN/h, Clashmore crofters to duke, 26 Sep. 1873.
[30] NLS, Acc. 10225, Crofters, ZN/h, Clashmore crofters to duke, 26 Sep. 1873.
[31] NLS, Acc. 10225, Farms, Clashmore 1873–88, Loch to McIver, 1 Apr. 1873.
[32] NLS, Acc. 10225, Farms, Clashmore 1873–88, Loch to McIver, 22 May 1873.
[33] SCRO, D593, K/1/3/62, McIver to Loch, 3 Mar. 1874, 6 Mar. 1874.
[34] I. M. M. MacPhail, *The Crofters' War* (Stornoway, 1989), 127; J. Hunter, *The Making of the Crofting Community* (Edinburgh, 1976), 141; Devine, *Clanship to Crofters' War*, 223–4.
[35] For example, *Highlander*, 8 Jan. 1876; *Glasgow Herald*, 19 Sep. 1876; A. Tindley, 'The Iron Duke': land reclamation and public relations in Sutherland, 1868–95', *Historical Research*, 82 (2009), 314–16.
[36] NLS, Acc. 10225, Policy Papers, 216, McIver to Brereton, 23 Jan. 1888.

the time, however, and in 1874 it seemed to the estate management that the resistance was over, the people were settling into their new lots and the farm was coming together.

'A nursery for Paupers': 1875–86[37]

In 1877, the new farm was completed and in 1880 let to its first tenant, Mr Burns Brown.[38] The estate had spent the huge sum of £4,964.9.2 on reclaiming the ninety-two acres of Clashmore farm, but it was unlikely to make its money back very quickly, as the farm was let at only £90 per annum, this figure decreasing to £50 per annum by 1896.[39] It had at least been let, which many of the estates other reclaimed farms in the east of the county had yet to be, and so any income, however small, was seen as better than nothing.

The Clashmore crofters and cottars, however, were not so well pleased with the farm. Those crofters that had been removed to make way for it had to start from scratch, despite Loch's exhortations that they be put on equally good lots. Some had to build new houses, with only a small grant of ten pounds from the estate to help them.[40] None received compensation for the improvements they had made on their old lots or for having to move elsewhere. Two families were evicted entirely, as a punishment for their role in the disturbances of March 1873. One of those evicted was Kenneth Campbell, whose widow was still petitioning the estate for a house in 1896, having been reduced to a poverty-stricken cottar for nearly thirty years.[41] The new farm caused greater congestion in the township than ever before, as the next generation began to squat on their parents' crofts or on the common pasture to survive. It would be these cottars, often the children of the original Clashmore crofters who had lost out to the farm, who would lead the agitation of the 1880s.[42]

The estate management noted with concern the rise in numbers of cottars.[43] Delegates to the Napier Commission in 1883 detailed the increase, one from Clashmore describing how '[the people] were disposed of by crowding them in corners of the place near about, upon others'.[44] At the

---

[37] SCRO, D593, K/1/3/70/c, McIver to Kemball, 2 May 1884.

[38] *Napier Commission Evidence*, McIver, 1764.

[39] SCRO, D593, N/4/3/4, 'Memo on the outlay on the reclamation of 92 acres of land at Clashmore, Assynt, 1877'; NLS, Acc. 10225, Factor's Correspondence, 1920, McIver to David MacBrayne, 13 Dec. 1888; Farms, 25, Clashmore farm lease, 1896. This was at least partly the result of agricultural depression in Britain generally; R. Perren, *Agriculture in Depression, 1870–1940* (Cambridge, 1995), 4–5.

[40] NLS, Acc. 10225, Factor's Correspondence, 1941, McIver to Flora Mackenzie, 16 May 1870.

[41] NLS, Acc. 10225, Crofters, ZB/c, J. Simpson to MacLean, 8 Sep. 1896.

[42] This was in common with other areas of the Highlands and Islands; Devine, *Clanship to Crofters' War*, 222–3.

[43] SCRO, D593, K/1/3/72/e, McIver to Kemball, 29 Dec. 1884.

[44] *Napier Commission Evidence*, William Matheson, 1730.

same hearing, the Free Church minister of Assynt pointed out that Assynt as a whole had only 360 crofters but 200 cottars, burdening the already marginal land.[45] In Clashmore, the growing numbers of cottars, who supported themselves by fishing, were becoming an intolerable burden on the crofters, especially when the local economy suffered a downturn in the early 1880s.[46] This situation not only led to tension between the cottars and the estate, but with the Clashmore crofters as well, and would be one of the key obstacles preventing a solution to the land hunger issue in the early twentieth century. The combination of difficult economic circumstances, acute congestion and raw grievance created a tense situation that could ignite at any time. Added to this was the agitation spreading across the Highlands from 1882; crofters' grievances were being debated in the highest circles, and the Napier Commission had radicalised, organised and politicised the crofters.[47]

In 1884, the Clashmore crofters took action. Mr Burns Brown's lease was due to expire that year, and the crofters saw an opportunity to get the land back. They petitioned the duke for the farm:

> That your petitioners having been brought up in Clashmore before it was cleared and being now much in need of land, beg to offer your Grace the present rent for the farm. That your petitioners sincerely trust that your Grace will regard us as having a preferable claim to all others to becoming tenants of Clashmore, seeing that we, or our fathers were deprived of it.[48]

This petition illustrates the fact that the crofters regarded the land under Clashmore farm as inalienably theirs and, at this point, they were willing to pay for it.[49] The crofters took further steps to secure the lease by warning off prospective tenants who visited the farm. One such, a Mr Davis and his wife, visited Clashmore in February 1884:

> On their arrival there they were met by a crowd of men in number about forty who came up to Mr Davis . . . A spokesman came forward from among them and addressing Davis said he was desired by the Tenants of Clashmore to warn any offerer of Clashmore farm as now held by Brown that the people of Clashmore were determined to get it for themselves and if they did not get it from the Duke they would get it with swords and bayonets and that all the other tenants in Stoer

---

[45] *Napier Commission Evidence*, Rev. N. N. MacKay, 1714.

[46] Hunter, *Making of the Crofting Community*, 131.

[47] A. G. Newby, *Ireland, Radicalism and the Scottish Highlands, c.1870–1912* (Edinburgh, 2007), 101; Hunter, *Making of the Crofting Community*, 144–5; Armadale Castle, Macdonald MSS, 4675, J. D. Brodie to Alexander Macdonald, 6 Feb. 1882.

[48] SCRO, D593, K/1/3/70/c, Clashmore tenants to duke, 19 Feb. 1884.

[49] The Clashmore crofters regarded the land as theirs, by moral if not legal right; C. W. J. Withers, '"Give us land and plenty of it": the ideological basis to land and landscape in the Scottish Highlands', *Landscape History*, 12 (1990), 46–7, 52–3.

would turn out to assist them if necessary . . . that if anyone ventured to come and take it he would soon be a corpse.[50]

The crofters later wrote to McIver denying the accusation that they had threatened the life of Mr Davis, probably advised to do so by the Free Church minister of Assynt, Rev. Norman N. MacKay.[51] The situation at Clashmore remained tense, despite the refutation, and the Assynt ground officer, Robert Ross, was uneasy in the presence of the crofters. McIver, impatient with Ross, reported him as being 'quite nervous and timid among them and says he has no one to support or assist him'.[52] Ross would not have an easy time over the next few years, as he was ostracised and frequently threatened by the Clashmore tenants. McIver knew his ground officer needed support, especially against the power of MacKay, like himself a well-educated man, with great moral influence over the crofters.[53] He told Kemball, commissioner since 1879, that 'I think I must go and spend a fortnight in Assynt myself and go among the people to judge for myself, to strengthen and assist the Ground Officer and try to counteract the evil influences doing such mischief among these poor ignorant people.'[54] McIver may have misjudged his adversary, MacKay; it is likely that he actually kept violence off the agenda and looked for a compromise with the estate over Clashmore farm.[55] McIver and Kemball were unhappy that MacKay had set himself up as a mediator between the estate and the crofters, in case he promised them too much, a possibility which could only lead to disappointment and further, perhaps violent, agitation: 'unless he is strictly restrained and limited, he is sure to exceed his commission and be very likely to lead the people astray and raise extravagant expectations in their minds not to be realised'.[56]

Kemball, the duke and Lord Stafford were in principle willing to give the farm to the crofters, but only if they could pay the £500 valuation costs for stock, crops and implements, as well as the £70 rent per annum. It was the valuation cost that was the obstacle, as none of the crofters had any capital. McIver, however, did not agree: he was against giving extensions of land to

[50] SCRO, D593, K/1/3/70/c, McIver to Kemball, 22 Feb. 1884. Most ground officers, including Ross, came from the crofter class and were often intensely disliked by their neighbours as a result.

[51] NLS, Acc. 10225, Crofters, ZN/h, Clashmore tenants to McIver, 4 Mar. 1884.

[52] SCRO, D593, K/1/3/70/c, McIver to Kemball, 22 Feb. 1884.

[53] A. W. MacColl, *Land, Faith and the Crofting Community: Christianity and social criticism in the Highlands of Scotland, 1843–1893* (Edinburgh, 2006), 113.

[54] SCRO, D593, K/1/3/70/c, McIver to Kemball, 22 Feb. 1884.

[55] MacColl, *Land, Faith and the Crofting Community*, 113; D593, K/1/3/70/c, MacKay to Kemball, 16 May 1884; MacKay to Stafford, 16 May 1884.

[56] SCRO, D595, K/1/3/70/c, McIver to Kemball, 17 May 1884; concern about the impact of agitators, local or 'outsiders', was present on other Highland estates, for instance, HCA, Kilmuir Estate MSS, D123/2e, Fraser to Alex. Macdonald, 23 Jan. 1882.

the crofters on principle.[57] He argued that the crofting system merely generated poverty, and giving more land to crofters would simply spread that
poverty over a greater area. He pointed out to Kemball that most crofters,
and certainly those agitating for land at Clashmore, were penniless, in
arrears of rent and with no capital for stock:

> The parties signing the Petition are men of no means . . . these tenants
> would soon form a nursery for Paupers to be put on the Poor Roll . . .
> There are too many small tenants already in Assynt – it will be better
> to assist some of them to emigrate and to endeavour to consolidate the
> existing crofts as opportunities occur.[58]

Kemball was more inclined to attempt some reform and grant crofters
land, if it meant no financial loss to the estate to do so.[59] But the crofters
could not possibly meet the valuation price and the farm was eventually
re-let to Burns Brown.

The Clashmore crofters did not give up their campaign, however,
moving their focus to land in the cleared township of Unapool, which had
been annexed to Achmore sheep farm. Unapool's proximity to fishing
grounds in Loch Glendhu made it a more attractive economic prospect
than Clashmore.[60] The estate management debated long and hard about
letting this land to the crofters; McIver was, unsurprisingly, firmly against
it. He argued that the land was unsuitable, 'it is full of rocks and bogs',
and that the people were unsuitable also: 'the truth is that there is not in
Assynt any tenants possessing the knowledge or the capital to fit them for
being tenants of small pastoral farms'.[61] He complained that his years of
experience and knowledge were being ignored and his authority in the
district undermined.[62] The arguments rumbled on through 1885, McIver
desperately clinging on to what he believed to be the best system of rule in
Assynt, in the face of mounting criticism from Kemball: 'I have ever considered it a kindness towards the crofter population of the district to treat
them with firm decision . . . to let them understand that they must submit to
rule. They are Celts and by no other system can order be preserved among
them.'[63] Kemball disagreed: nothing had been done to satisfy the demands
of the crofters and as a result the estate management was ostracised from
them and had to rely on Rev. Norman MacKay as an intermediary.[64] McIver

[57] SCRO, D593, K/1/3/70/c, McIver to William Matheson, Clashmore tenant, 8 Mar. 1884;
      other Highland estates maintained the same policy; see Armadale Castle, Macdonald MSS,
      2979, Sconser tenants to Alexander Macdonald, 1 Jun. 1885.
[58] SCRO, D593, K/1/3/70/c, McIver to Kemball, 2 May 1884.
[59] NLS, Acc. 10225, Policy Papers, 195, Kemball to McIver, 27 Mar. 1884.
[60] NLS, Acc. 10225, Crofters, ZN/h, Clashmore cottars to Stafford, 7 Dec. 1885.
[61] SCRO, D593, K/1/3/70/c, McIver to Kemball, 8 July 1884.
[62] SCRO, D593, K/1/3/70/c, McIver to Kemball, 8 July 1884.
[63] NLS, Acc. 10225, Policy Papers, 215, McIver to Kemball, 22 Jan. 1886; of course, McIver, as
      a Lewis-man, was also a 'Celt'.
[64] NLS, Acc. 10225, Crofters, ZN/a, Kemball to McIver, 3 Jul. 1884.

and Kemball would not resolve this issue; Kemball resigned in 1886, and McIver never wholly reconciled himself to the changing political, social and legislative circumstances of the 1880s.

The Clashmore crofters saw nothing of these splits, but felt their effect through the inaction of the estate: accordingly, they went on rent strike in December 1884.[65] By doing so, they were not demanding lower rents, but rather defying the estate and trying to force it to grant them more land.[66] They certainly succeeded in infuriating McIver, as they continued the strike into 1885: 'it was distressing to witness the change which has come over the people in that parish. Their minds are diseased – in fact agitation and the recent canvas and election excitement has quite demoralised them.'[67] Additionally, the 1885 election and Lord Stafford's candidature had an effect on the situation at Clashmore. As part of his canvass, Lord Stafford visited many townships, promising changes and accepting petitions. In this spirit, the Clashmore cottars again petitioned Stafford for Unapool township, supplemented with a letter from the crofters urging him to grant the land, 'as doing so would free us from a great burden and benefit the petitioners'.[68] The cottars' petition was swiftly followed by one from the crofters, also asking for a land grant.[69] The estate was able to avoid making a decision by deciding to wait until the government passed its expected land legislation.[70]

In 1886, the Crofters Holdings Act was finally passed. Crucially for the Clashmore crofters, the clauses relating to the extension of holdings were very limited and there was absolutely nothing in the Act to help the position of the cottars.[71] The security of tenure clause gave the crofters a more secure platform on which to agitate for land, but overall, the Act would only lead to greater frustration for the tenants.[72] The Clashmore crofters nevertheless applied to the Crofters Commission to have their rents fixed and for land extensions, but would be unhappy with the results.[73] The tension this created would manifest itself in 1887, but McIver saw earlier signs of trouble, through the continuing refusal of the Clashmore tenants to pay their rents: much worse was to follow.[74]

[65] NLS, Acc. 10225, Policy Papers, 215, McIver to Kemball, 6 Dec. 1884.
[66] Again, this was a common tactic in Highland land agitation in the 1880s; Hunter, *Making of the Crofting Community*, 133–5; MacPhail, *Crofters' War*, 30.
[67] NLS, Acc. 10225, Policy Papers, 215, McIver to Kemball, 28 Dec. 1885.
[68] NLS, Acc. 10225, Crofters, ZN/h, Clashmore cottars to Stafford, 7 Dec. 1885.
[69] NLS, Acc. 10225, Policy Papers, 215, McIver to Kemball, 22 Jan. 1886.
[70] NLS, Acc. 10225, Crofters, ZN/h, Kemball to Clashmore cottars, 3 Feb. 1886.
[71] E. A. Cameron, *Land for the People? The British Government and the Scottish Highlands, c.1880–1925* (East Linton, 1996), 37–8; Hunter, *Making of the Crofting Community*, 162–4; Devine, *Clanship to Crofters' War*, 231, 235.
[72] This was the case elsewhere, particularly Lewis and Tiree; Hunter, *Making of the Crofting Community*, 165.
[73] NLS, Acc. 10225, Policy Papers, 216, McIver to Brereton, 20 Nov. 1886.
[74] NLS, Acc. 10225, Policy Papers, 216, McIver to Kemball, 9 Jun. 1886; J. Hunter, 'The

1887–9: agitation and 'the Last of the Mohicans'

'It is the people's intention to make the farm a complete rag.'[75]

Once the Clashmore tenants realised the 1886 Act could do nothing to meet their demands for land, they abandoned their previous policy of negotiating with the estate management and declared war on it. A crofters' meeting resolved 'that this meeting of the inhabitants of Stoer, Assynt are disappointed, as well as displeased, at the action of the Land Court, in not reducing rents . . . seeing all improvements were executed by the tenants, and in not cancelling all arrears, and it is our opinion that their decisions are out of harmony with the spirit of the Crofters Act'.[76] The Clashmore crofters, like many others in Sutherland and across the Highlands, were not satisfied by the decisions of the Crofters Commission, and the cottars received no benefit at all.[77] Land hunger was the dominating grievance in Clashmore, and this was not being addressed.

The estate management was in a weak position, unable to come to any internal agreement on what its policy should be. The new commissioner, R. M. Brereton, was still settling in, but it became clear almost immediately that he and McIver would disagree regarding the crofters. McIver wanted to resist all of the crofters' applications to the Commission, but Brereton and the duke, on the advice of the Scottish Office, argued the opposite position.[78] Brereton further angered McIver by visiting Assynt without informing him; a snub, and perhaps a reflection of McIver's dire reputation among the crofters, which Brereton wished to dissociate himself from.[79]

McIver had other issues to worry about, including the accumulating arrears of the Assynt crofters. He was especially angry about the Clashmore rents, as he knew they were being withheld deliberately.[80] He wrote to Brereton, and argued that those tenants more than two years in arrear should be served with summonses of removal. Brereton was cautious: 'I find you do not clearly follow my view of the action we should follow in these matters. I wish to avoid playing into the hands of the Land League Agitators, and to work as much as we can upon the lines of the Crofters Act 1886.'[81] The Commission would not visit Assynt until late 1888, but it was McIver's plan to use the summonses to frighten the crofters into paying up their

Politics of Highland Land Reform, 1873–1895', *Scottish Historical Review*, 53 (1974), 56; Hunter, *Making of the Crofting Community*, 180–1.

[75] *Scottish Highlander*, 15 Dec. 1887.
[76] *Scottish Highlander*, 10 Feb. 1887.
[77] Cameron, *Land for the People*, 50, 55; Hunter, *Making of the Crofting Community*, 164.
[78] NLS, Acc. 10225, Policy Papers, 198, Brereton to McIver, 28 Mar. 1887.
[79] NLS, Acc. 10225, Policy Papers, 216, McIver to Brereton, 14 Mar. 1887.
[80] Rent strikes were common in other flashpoints of agitation; Armadale Castle, Macdonald MSS, 4694/1/2, tenants of Tockavaig, Tarskavaig and Stonefield to Alex. Macdonald, 3 Dec. 1884.
[81] NLS, Acc. 10225, Policy Papers, 198, Brereton to McIver, 9 Apr. 1887.

arrears before the Commission wiped them out. He also wanted to assert the authority of the estate: 'there is a common belief now that the Duke is afraid to issue summons of removal – my wish to have done is to remove this impression [sic]'.[82] McIver assured Brereton that he expected no agitation to result from serving removal summons, and the inexperienced Brereton eventually agreed to the policy.[83] The crofters were holding out for a visit from the Crofters Commission, however, and saw the decision (rightly) as the estate trying to bully them. The removal summons itself was an emotive tool and massively unpopular among the crofting community, especially in Clashmore, where it had been used with devastating effect by the estate only thirteen years before.[84] Its reappearance would spark off real trouble.

On 22 April 1887, a sheriff officer, Alexander Sandieson, accompanied by the Assynt ground officer, Robert Ross, went to Clashmore to serve the summonses and was deforced.[85] He was met at Clashmore by fifty or sixty men, the summonses were burnt and the crofters made Sandieson 'come out and go on his bended knees, promising never to come back that way again on the same errand'.[86] The ground officer, in an interesting role reversal, was also made to kneel before the crofters.[87] One of the ringleaders in this incident was a cottar-fisherman, Hugh Kerr, who would later become a symbol of resistance in Clashmore.

This deforcement, by turning a civil matter into a criminal one, took the agitation at Clashmore onto a new level. Now the authorities were called in, and four crofters, including Hugh Kerr, were cited to stand trial.[88] Brereton did not let the matter rest entirely in the hands of the authorities, however, and in early May he travelled to Assynt, and again, he did not ask McIver to accompany him. McIver was furious and concerned:

I feel hurt that you did not inform me of your intention, as I would have asked to accompany you . . . The crofters are so given to exaggerate and misrepresent that one must hear all they say with doubt . . . You could not have done anything more calculated to injure my authority and position here – it is sure to be construed as a want of confidence . . . this being the first time during the 42 years I have been here that

---

[82] NLS, Acc. 10225, Policy Papers, 216, McIver to Brereton, 8 Apr. 1887; the Macdonald estate tried a similar tack; Armadale Castle, Macdonald MSS, 4725, 'Notice to crofter tenants on the Macdonald estate', 8 Dec. 1886.

[83] NLS, Acc. 10225, Policy Papers, 216, McIver to Brereton, 8 Apr. 1887.

[84] Using removal summons to enforce estate policy was common across the Highlands; Hunter, *Making of the Crofting Community*, 116–17; MacPhail, *Crofters' War*, 31.

[85] NLS, Acc. 10225, Policy Papers, 216, McIver to Brereton, 26 Apr. 1887; MacPhail, *Crofters' War*, 144.

[86] *Scottish Highlander*, 28 Apr. 1887.

[87] For other examples of similar deforcements, see MacPhail, *Crofters' War*, 40–1; Hunter, *Making of the Crofting Community*, 135–6.

[88] This follows a similar pattern on other Highland estates; Armadale Castle, Macdonald MSS, 4745, Alexander Macdonald to Lord Lothian, 12 Oct. 1888.

either Landlords or Commissioners came to any part of the district without informing me of their intention and asking me to visit them you must not be surprised that I felt your doing so as a slight and likely to injure my authority and my usefulness here.[89]

McIver was right to be concerned, as Brereton was highly critical of his past management decisions: 'if the statements made to me by some of the Clashmore people are correct, and from what I heard from outside sources and from Mr Gordon and the G. O. [ground officer] I think there must be more or less truth in them, great injustice was done to several of the tenants, when the Clashmore farm was created'.[90] McIver's fears that Brereton had no confidence in him seemed to be materialising. In May, the unfortunate Constable Sandieson was ordered to serve writs on the crofters who had been involved in the April deforcement to stand trial at Dornoch. He managed to serve two before the crofters realised what he was doing and 'the women turned out in full force'.[91] The writs were burnt in front of him, and he was told to leave or be thrown in the river. He left, declaring himself deforced.[92]

By deforcing another official, the Clashmore crofters were demonstrating pure defiance to the estate and authorities, protected by the remoteness of their township. The authorities recognised the practical difficulties, but also the necessity to impose some order.[93] The Under-Secretary for Scotland was determined that the offences should not go unpunished: 'I think that we have treated these viragos too chivalrously in the past – and that we should, in this case . . . make an example of some of them.'[94] It would be difficult to enforce this command, however; of the four Clashmore men who were cited to appear for trial in Dornoch in June for the original April deforcement, only one turned up. The Sheriff was unable to make an example of him, as he had a defender in none other than the 3rd Duke of Sutherland himself:

Just as the Sheriff was about to pass sentence, His Grace the Duke of Sutherland, who was present in the Court, requested the opportunity of interposing on behalf of the panel [accused]. His Grace said that considering Mackenzie had surrendered himself, and submitted to the law by accepting the citation in a peaceable way . . . he wished to express the hope that his lordship would make the sentence as lenient as possible, for he felt convinced that Mackenzie did not of his own accord really mean to break the law, but whatever he did was

[89] NLS, Acc. 10225, Policy Papers, 216, McIver to Brereton, 7 May 1887.
[90] NLS, Acc. 10225, Policy Papers, 198, Brereton to McIver, 6 May 1887.
[91] *Scottish Highlander*, 26 May 1887.
[92] National Archives of Scotland [hereafter NAS], Lothian Muniments, GD40, 16/4, Constable Sandieson to Sheriff Cheyne, 23 May 1887; *Scottish Highlander*, 26 May 1887.
[93] MacPhail, *Crofters' War*, 145.
[94] NAS, GD40, 16/4, Francis Sandford to Lord Lothian, 27 May 1887.

prompted by outside influence – by people who, while professing to be friends of the crofters, were really their worst enemies – and he thought a lenient sentence would adequately meet the circumstances of the case and have a good effect.[95]

This was wishful thinking on the part of the duke, but the sheriff did take note of his words and sentenced Mackenzie to only fifteen days' imprisonment.[96] If this was intended to try to calm the agitation in Clashmore by presenting the estate management as sympathetic to the crofters, it failed.[97] The authorities were still determined to bring the three remaining April deforcers to trial but when Constable Sandieson went to Clashmore to serve citations against them, he was attacked by Hugh Kerr and a group of women, who stripped him and confiscated the documents.[98] Clearly, Mackenzie's sentence had done little to stem the agitation.

There was a lull in the violence at Clashmore over the summer of 1887 until the cottars made a sudden and unexpected move; they petitioned the estate for land, once again at Unapool. This surprising reversal of tactics stemmed from the fact that cottars had no rights under the Crofters Act, and remained dependent on the estate for land extensions. McIver thought this sufficient reason to reject their application.[99] This of course did not prevent an estate from independently coming to an agreement with cottars, but McIver quickly pointed out that Unapool would be a bad site: 'these people would be sure to injure the shooting held by Mr Whitehead and would be very disagreeable neighbours for the Duke of Westminster'.[100] Brereton was calculating on the influence of the Crofters Commission to keep the Clashmore crofters in line: 'I do not think the Clashmore crofters will take forcible possession . . . as they know well enough that that course would not help them with the Crofters Commission.'[101] He had never been more wrong about the 'course' the crofters would take.

November 1887 would see the worst of the agitation at Clashmore. That month saw the transfer of the Clashmore farm lease to David MacBrayne, the shipping entrepreneur.[102] He would have little success with the farm from the very start: 'the people of Clashmore and Achnacarnin interfered

[95] *Scottish Highlander*, 2 Jun. 1887; MacPhail, *Crofters' War*, 144.

[96] *Scottish Highlander*, 2 Jun. 1887.

[97] What the duke's other motives for this action were is not clear, but sensitivity over his family's historical reputation is one possibility: there are no other sources for the trial, the relevant records of Dornoch Sheriff Court not surviving.

[98] *Scottish Highlander*, 2 Jun. 1887.

[99] NLS, Acc. 10225, Policy Papers, 216, McIver to Brereton, 11 Oct. 1887.

[100] NLS, Acc. 10225, Policy Papers, 216, McIver to Brereton, 11 Oct. 1887.

[101] NLS, Acc. 10225, Policy Papers, 198, Brereton to McIver, 29 Oct. 1887.

[102] By 1887, the let of Clashmore farm was added to that of the Culag Hotel, Lochinver, the idea being that hay and oats for the guests' horses could be grown cheaply. It was of course the hotel, and not the farm, that MacBrayne was interested in, which might explain his relaxed attitude to future events.

with the valuation and transference of Clashmore farm to Mr MacBrayne on Friday and that on Saturday the Clashmore tenants in a body broke into the Parks at Clashmore farm and drove in their cattle in a body'.[103] The raid on the farm was an assertion of ownership of the land, if not in a legal sense then in a moral one, and was also a warning to the new tenant that they were determined to have the land.[104] The crofters had 'marked out lots [crofts] for themselves on the land with stones taken from the dykes'.[105] They quickly withdrew their cattle from the Clashmore parks, but a statement of intent had been made. On 24 November, the Clashmore farm steading, mill and offices were set on fire, causing massive damage.[106] The estate was unable to identify the perpetrators or bring them to trial, despite the repairs being estimated at £1000. The duke, however, seemed less concerned, writing in his diary for that day, 'Doing well. Clashmore farm burnt down.'[107]

Meanwhile, the estate management became involved in an argument with the authorities over whether the raid on the farm in November was a civil or criminal offence. The estate management regarded it as a criminal one, but both the Sheriff of the County, Cheyne, and the Sheriff Substitute, William Mackenzie, disagreed, and it was treated as a civil case, to the immense frustration of the estate.[108] The friction between the estate and the legal authorities was further increased in December when a row broke out over the serving of interdicts on the Clashmore crofters. The estate had tried to do this by post, to prevent a potential deforcement, but the crofters refused to open them and so they remained officially unserved. The estate lashed out, looking for someone to blame.[109] It focused on Sheriff Mackenzie and its own lawyer in Sutherland, G. G. Tait. Brereton and McIver suspected that they were sympathetic to the crofters' demands and Brereton accused the sheriff of being more concerned about his public image than upholding the law:

> There is much mischief brewing, and this is why I am so annoyed with the authorities for not dealing with these Clashmore outrages more speedily and upon the criminal procedure. Both Sheriffs are so funky of incurring any personal liability, as Sheriff Ivory's case has so frightened them . . . I am afraid both Tait and Sheriff Mackenzie sympathise with the Clashmore people.[110]

[103] NLS, Acc. 10225, Policy Papers, 216, McIver to Brereton, 21 Nov. 1887.
[104] Withers, 'Give us land', 46–7.
[105] *Scotsman*, 6 Dec. 1887.
[106] *Scotsman*, 6 Dec. 1887; *Scottish Highlander*, 24 Nov. 1887.
[107] SCRO, D593, P/24/4/A.79, diary of the 3rd Duke, 1887.
[108] The Clashmore episode was one of many flashpoints between Highland proprietors and local and national legal authorities: HCA, Kilmuir Estate MSS, D123/32, Fraser to lord advocate, 10 Jun. 1884; Armadale Castle, Macdonald MSS, 4680/2, lord advocate to Sheriff Ivory, 3 Nov. 1882.
[109] NLS, Acc. 10225, Policy Papers, 198, Brereton to McIver, 5 Dec. 1887.
[110] NLS, Acc. 10225, Policy Papers, 198, Brereton to McIver, 24 Dec. 1887. Brereton's comments referring to the wretched Sheriff Ivory reflected the intense criticism and legal

Despite the doubts of the estate management, the authorities were in fact active, if unsuccessful, in Clashmore through December. On 1 December, the gunboat *Jackal* sailed to Assynt, with the object of arresting Hugh Kerr, 'the man whose capture I was chiefly anxious to effect, as, not only was he according to my information the ringleader in the deforcement which occurred in April last, but he is also reported to me as being one of the leading agitators in the district'.[111] Without the element of surprise, however, they failed to find him. They had attempted to land at Clashmore, but the weather was too rough, and they had landed at Lochinver instead. As reported in the *Scottish Highlander*, this gave Kerr warning, and he 'bolted up the hill'.[112] The remoteness of the district meant the crofters could rarely be taken by surprise, and they posted boys as lookouts on the surrounding hills as an extra precaution, perhaps to match the constant police watching of the area.[113]

Meanwhile, the situation at Clashmore was spiralling out of control. Dykes were broken and the crofters had been regularly running their stock onto the parks.[114] On 15 December, James Gordon, the Assynt sub-factor, the farm grieve, Donald Forbes, and MacBrayne's clerk, Angus Kerr, were at Clashmore farm, trying to poind the invading cattle in order to identify who had breached their interdicts, when they were attacked by a group of women and men dressed as women.[115] Gordon got a black eye in the ensuing brawl, and he and the others were eventually chased off the farm entirely.[116] The attack on Gordon signalled the estate's lowest point in Clashmore.[117] The authorities were not faring much better: twelve police constables had been stationed at Clashmore to watch for further lawbreaking and to try to formally identify the perpetrators, but were assaulted:

action he had recently undergone with reference to his law-enforcement activities on Skye in 1885–6: MacPhail, *Crofters' War*, 198–9.

[111] NAS, AF67/36, Report by Sheriff Cheyne on expedition to Clashmore, 3 Dec. 1887. Although military forces were deployed, their leadership remained in civil hands, as in the Highlands generally and in contrast to Ireland; E. A. Cameron, 'Communication or Separation? Reaction to Irish Land Agitation and Legislation in the Highlands of Scotland, c.1870–1910', *English Historical Review*, 487 (2005), 639–41.

[112] *Scottish Highlander*, 8 Dec. 1887.

[113] NAS, AF67/36, Report PC George Murray to Sheriff Cheyne, 5 Dec. 1887; MacPhail, *Crofters' War*, 145.

[114] NAS, AF67/36, Report PC George Murray to Sheriff Cheyne, 10 Dec. 1887.

[115] This transvestism was common to crofter protest across the Highlands and many theories have been put forward to explain it; to avoid harsh retaliation, for example; I. J. M. Robertson, 'The role of women in social protest in the Highlands of Scotland, c.1880–1939', *Journal of Historical Geography*, 23 (1997), 194–6.

[116] NLS, Acc. 10225, Policy Papers, 216, McIver to Brereton, 16 Dec. 1887; *Scottish Highlander*, 22 Dec. 1887; NAS, AF67/36, Sheriff Cheyne to Lord Lothian, 16 Dec. 1887; AF67/37, Report PC Murray to Sheriff Cheyne, 17 Dec. 1887.

[117] Concern and outrage rippled through the estate management on receiving news of the attack; NAS, GD 305, Cromartie Estate Papers, Estate Correspondence, 1890, Gunn to Brereton, 11 Jan. 1888; Richards and Clough, *Cromartie*, 327.

'a serious attack had last night been made by crofters on the lodgings occupied by the Police which had been battered with stones . . . and that another attack was expected tonight'.[118] McIver boiled in frustration, and blamed the mess on Sheriff Mackenzie, 'for any advice we could give would not be taken by the Sheriff'.[119]

He was also concerned about Gordon after the attack, believing that he had lost his confidence, informing Brereton that 'he requires not only the material but all the moral support we can give him'.[120] Gordon's position was certainly not enviable: as the representative of the Sutherland estate in the township, he was the focus of the Clashmore crofters' anger.[121] Gordon was also abandoned by the Assynt ground officer, Robert Ross. Ross was even more exposed than Gordon, coming from the crofter class, and therefore seen as a greater traitor. At the end of December he wrote to McIver, 'resigning his situation because he is in peril of his life . . . You will observe Gordon confirms the statement, he has cause as he was assaulted.'[122] Gordon must have felt completely exposed by late December 1887; he had been attacked by the crofters and none had yet been arrested, his ground officer had resigned in fear of his life, and the twelve policemen who had been stationed at the farm were withdrawn at the end of the month, provoking fury among the estate management.[123] Additionally, the nine watchers hired by the estate to patrol the Clashmore farm buildings at night 'told Mr Gordon that they were not to watch any longer as they were afraid of their lives'.[124]

It had been a bad year for the Sutherland estate in Clashmore. The 1886 Crofters Act had failed to satisfy the Clashmore crofters' demand for land or quiet their grievances and resentment against the estate. McIver was in no doubt as to who was behind the agitation: 'it is the children of the parents [who were evicted in the 1870s] who are now giving so much trouble at Clashmore'.[125] The leadership of this bout of agitation was confused; certainly, Norman MacKay had little or nothing to do with it, after his negotiations with the estate in 1884 failed to come to fruition. Like many Free Church ministers in the Highlands in this period, he may not have wished to condone any violence and took on a conciliatory role instead.[126]

[118] NAS, AF67/37, Sheriff Cheyne to Under-Secretary for Scotland, 22 Dec. 1887.

[119] NLS, Acc. 10225, Factor's Correspondence, 1963, McIver to Gordon, 24 Dec. 1887.

[120] NLS, Acc. 10225, Policy Papers, 216, McIver to Brereton, 17 Dec. 1887.

[121] NLS, Acc. 10225, Policy Papers, 201, Lord Stafford to McIver, 23 Jan. 1889.

[122] NLS, Acc. 10225, Policy Papers, 216, McIver to Brereton, 30 Dec. 1887; resignations of estate staff were not uncommon in the years of turbulent agitation: Dunvegan Castle, MacLeod of MacLeod MSS, 1406/3, Alex. Macdonald to MacLeod, 26 Nov. 1882.

[123] NLS, Acc. 10225, Policy Papers, 216, McIver to Brereton, 14 Feb. 1888; NAS, AF67/38, Sheriff Mackenzie to Lord Lothian, 7 Jan. 1888.

[124] NAS, AF67/37, Report PC Murray to Sheriff Cheyne, 17 Dec. 1887.

[125] NLS, Acc. 10225, Policy Papers, 216, McIver to Brereton, 23 Jan. 1888.

[126] MacColl, *Land, Faith and the Crofting Community*, 113; I. J. M. Robertson, 'The Historical Geography of social protest in Highland Scotland, 1914–c.1939', unpublished Ph.D. thesis (University of Bristol, 1995), 27–9.

Hugh Kerr was certainly the symbol of the agitation, but his long absences on the run from the authorities meant that he could have provided little practical leadership after May 1887. It seems that much of the agitation was spontaneous or opportunistic in nature and led by women, notably Kerr's wife Mary, and used tactics common across the Highlands at this time: deforcement, running stock onto farm land and dyke breaking.[127]

The estate was frustrated with the authorities' failure to resolve the difficulties at Clashmore, but there were limits to what the authorities could do. Clashmore was part of a wider context of agitation in the Highlands in 1887 and 1888, the bulk of which was concurrent with trouble on Lewis, at the Park Deer Forest (November–December 1887) and the farm of Aignish (January 1888).[128] The authorities had limited resources, and had to be seen to be punishing criminal activity, while avoiding accusations of heavy-handedness. Overall, the strategy of the authorities seemed to have been reactive, rather than pro-active, and there was no long-term plan for Clashmore. By January 1888, it seemed as if the Clashmore crofters well and truly had the upper hand. In that month, the authorities made another attempt to capture Hugh Kerr with a gunboat and marines. They failed in this, but did make four other arrests, for mobbing and rioting and the assault on Gordon the previous month.[129] One of those arrested was Mary Kerr, wife of Hugh, who stated in her defence, 'it was on account of the Clashmore land having been taken from the Clashmore tenants, that I threw the mud at Gordon and the others'.[130]

The arrests halted trouble at Clashmore: serious friction transferred into the estate management. McIver and Brereton had been in disagreement over whether to grant land to the Clashmore crofters for some time, but open hostilities broke out in January 1888. Brereton took the extraordinary step of visiting Clashmore with Angus Sutherland, Liberal MP for the county and not a man held in high esteem by McIver, who reported that 'he accomplished nothing. I heard they [the Clashmore crofters] spoke most violently to him and also that they abused myself and Gordon violently for doing our duty and opposing them.'[131] This was the third time Brereton had slighted McIver in this way, and it precipitated a major fallout. Brereton was in favour of land grants to law-abiding crofters, to satisfy their demands and halt the agitation.[132] He was frustrated by McIver's unbending views, arguing – fruitlessly – that the agitation would continue until the estate made some concessions:

[127] Robertson, 'The role of women in social protest', 194–6; Robertson, 'Historical Geography', 36–8; Devine, *Clanship to Crofters' War*, 220.
[128] MacPhail, *Crofters' War*, 199–201, 202–4; Cameron, *Land for the People*, 56, 64–6.
[129] *Scottish Highlander*, 5 Jan. 1888.
[130] NAS, JC26/1888/202, declaration of Mary Kerr, 29 Dec. 1887; Withers, 'Give us land', 52–3.
[131] NLS, Acc. 10225, Policy Papers, 216, McIver to Wright, 17 Jan. 1888.
[132] NLS, Acc. 10225, Policy Papers, 200, Brereton to McIver, 6 Jan. 1888.

It is the duty and the business of the Estate Management to try and find out what is best for the people as well as for His Grace's interests, both present and future. Nothing can be worse for the estate than a chronic feeling of discontent and spirits of mischief. It would become like the west coast of Ireland, if we did not take care. I cannot get you to realise the fact that legal force is no remedy. The disease will go on smouldering and flare out from time to time. The Sheriffs and the authorities are clearly averse to taking any active measures, and mischief, which cannot be remedied, is done before any precautionary measures are taken by the authorities. We are, therefore, left entirely to ourselves to work out a remedy for the bad and lawless feeling which you say is common to all. Your gospel appears to be no forgiveness, no enlargement of existing crofts and nothing but the cold steel. This won't do in the present age.[133]

Brereton worked hard to impose his authority on McIver, a difficult task when facing an estate official used to getting his own way for over forty years. Brereton made frequent reference to 'changed times' and the 'present age', identifying McIver as a relic of the past, unable to realise that he could no longer wield arbitrary power: 'you should not worry about the policy I, as Commissioner, think to follow out in these days of discontent and agitation. In these days it is not the business of the Estate Management to add to the punishment which the authorities may inflict; or to visit the sins of the Father upon the children.'[134]

Brereton made it clear that he supported the crofters' assertions that they had been ill treated, laying the blame for the current agitation at McIver's door, jolting him into putting together a hasty defence: 'I cannot help feeling very anxious about all matters connected with this farm – considering how much I have been mixed up with it I must be much interested in all that occurs regarding it – and the future action of His Grace's advisors in regard to it. No one connected with the estate liked the Removal policy.'[135] But despite some guilty doubts, McIver had spent the past decade fighting tooth and nail against any extensions of land in Assynt and would continue to do so.[136] The stand-off could not long continue, and, in June, McIver was threatening to resign rather than be involved in extending crofters' holdings: 'I would prefer to resign my factorship rather than be a party to such measures or be any hindrance to you carrying them out. I thought after what happened at Clashmore it was not a time to grant

[133] NLS, Acc. 10225, Farms, Clashmore 1873–88, Brereton to McIver, 8 Feb. 1888.
[134] NLS, Acc. 10225, Farms, Clashmore 1873–88, Brereton to McIver, 21 Jan. 1888: fears about the Highlands becoming 'another Ireland' were common; Dunvegan Castle, MacLeod of MacLeod MSS, 1372/2, Joseph Chamberlain to MacLeod, 10 May 1887.
[135] NLS, Acc. 10225, Policy Papers, 216, McIver to Brereton, 23 Jan. 1888.
[136] NLS, Acc. 10225, Policy Papers, 216, McIver to Brereton, 9 Jan. 1888. McIver's attitude was common to many factors of Highland estates faced with new demands from the crofters: Richards and Clough, *Cromartie*, 298, 300–1, 338.

concessions to the crofters, and this led me to express my dissent to you.'[137] The duke and his London staff sided with McIver and Brereton was forced to resign in June 1888; ironically, it was after Brereton's departure that land was granted to the crofters through the Crofters Commission.

January 1888 saw a sustained campaign of dyke breaking begin at Clashmore. This was a tactic common across the Highlands, and the crofters' reasoning was that they would harry the farm until the tenant gave it up as a losing concern, forcing the estate to give it to them.[138] The estate estimated that 1000 yards of dykes were broken in January and February 1888, all of which had to be repaired to honour MacBrayne's lease.[139] It drove McIver to distraction, as nothing could be done except to offer a reward for information as to the perpetrators. Of course, no informers came forward, and the estate was left with the cost of the repairs.

In February 1888, McIver would receive some consolation when the Clashmore crofters arrested for attacking Gordon in December 1887 were brought to trial in Edinburgh. They were tried at the High Court of Justiciary together with the Aignish rioters from Lewis under Lord Craighill, notorious for having little sympathy for the crofters' grievances.[140] He dished out sentences of unprecedented severity, ranging from nine to fifteen months each.[141] In reading the sentences, Lord Craighill particularly castigated the women for their part in the violence, characterising it as 'unwomanly and degrading'.[142] Not everyone disapproved, however; a South African émigré sent two medals to Mary Kerr and Johan MacLeod, 'for their bravery at Clashmore, Sutherlandshire, Scotland, 15 December 1887, wishing them long life, health and happiness . . . and considers them far superior to the Duchess of Sutherland that is brought up on Ill Got in Dunrobin Castle'.[143]

Clashmore was further calmed by the arrest of Hugh Kerr in August 1888, after eighteen months on the run. It was reported that he gave himself up, perhaps because his wife Mary Kerr had been released from prison early, along with the other Clashmore prisoners.[144] The pair made a triumphant tour around Sutherland and were treated to a heroes' welcome, to the disgruntlement of James Gordon: 'Did I think they were in the least penitent I should rejoice . . . but there is no evidence of this on their or their supporters' part and as we are compromised – thereby I am disgusted.'[145]

---

[137] NLS, Acc. 10225, Policy Papers, 216, McIver to Brereton, 16 Jun. 1888.

[138] *Scottish Highlander*, 15 Dec. 1887; Hunter, *Making of the Crofting Community*, 141.

[139] NLS, Acc. 10225, Policy Papers, 200, Brereton to McIver, 28 Feb. 1888.

[140] NAS, records of the High Court of Justiciary, JC26/1888/202, AD14/88/225, JC8/82, JC4/84; MacPhail, *Crofters' War*, 207–10; Robertson, 'Historical Geography', 62; Hunter, *Making of the Crofting Community*, 176–7.

[141] *Scotsman*, 4 Feb. 1888.

[142] *Scotsman*, 4 Feb. 1888.

[143] *Scottish Highlander*, 7 Jun. 1888.

[144] *Scottish Highlander*, 16 Aug. 1888.

[145] NLS, Acc. 10225, Factor's Correspondence, 1972, Gordon to McIver, 9 Aug. 1888; *Northern Ensign*, 29 Aug. 1888.

McIver was sympathetic and tried to cheer Gordon up: 'if in your position I would think very little about it, for the poor creatures never heed a severe punishment'.[146] Hugh Kerr was tried at Dornoch in December, and in spite of his infamy, received a sentence of only sixty days' imprisonment, a good eight months less than his wife received.[147] The *Scottish Highlander* remarked that 'Kerr was thankful for small mercies'.[148]

Another reason for a reduction in agitation was the visit of the Crofters Commission in December 1888. McIver had not changed his mind about extensions of land, but the Commission demanded it and there was little he could do.[149] On top of this defeat, the evidence given to the Commission was a shock to McIver, who genuinely thought the Clashmore crofters had no grievances and that their demands were unreasonable. He came face to face with his real reputation at the sittings:

> We have had a bad time of it here before the Crofter Commissioners for the last few days . . . Clashmore has been a trying subject and griev-ances and cruel treatment described by people on oath made me stare – shocked me more than I can express, for I had never heard of many of them before. I discovered from what occurred before the Commissioners that they were disposed to concede a slice of the west side of Clashmore farm. This includes a pasture park of 20 acres and arable field of 10 acres below it down to the Loch and about 30 or 40 acres of the hill pasture opposite.[150]

Despite McIver's best efforts, the Clashmore crofters had finally got back some of the land under Clashmore farm.[151]

In fairness to McIver, he also had the duke's and the tenant's interests to look after. McIver was worried that after all the damage the crofters had inflicted on the farm, this division by the Commission might be the last straw for his long-suffering tenant. MacBrayne was unconcerned, however, and was very patient, both with his neighbours and the estate's slow rate of repairs.[152] Gordon characterised his attitude as 'rather careless', and he was satisfied to keep the lease at a small reduction of £10 per year.[153] McIver was relieved that the estate had not lost its tenant altogether, which would have not only entailed financial loss, but perhaps would have had the effect of renewing crofter agitation for the rest of the farm.[154]

By the beginning of 1889, the main phase of agitation at Clashmore was over, but the township remained problematic. Firstly, the land hunger of

[146] NLS, Acc. 10225, Factor's Correspondence, 1963, McIver to Gordon, 10 Aug. 1888.
[147] *Scottish Highlander*, 11 Oct. 1888.
[148] *Scottish Highlander*, 11 Oct. 1888.
[149] McIver remained bitter about this decision: McIver, *Memoirs*, 80–1.
[150] NLS, Acc. 10225, Policy Papers, 216, McIver to MacBrayne, 7 Dec. 1888.
[151] PPLX, 1889, *Second Report of the Crofters Commission*, 10–11, 130.
[152] NLS, Acc. 10225, Factor's Correspondence, 1972, Gordon to McIver, 4 Feb. 1888.
[153] NLS, Acc. 10225, Factor's Correspondence, 1972, Gordon to McIver, 23 Jan. 1888.
[154] NLS, Acc. 10225, Policy Papers, 217, McIver to Lord Stafford, 12 Dec. 1888.

the cottars had not been dealt with, and secondly, the Clashmore crofters were unhappy with the rent fixed on their new pasture and the fences they were required to build before they could use it. The crofters were frustrated and hesitated over accepting the decisions:

> It was only last week we got their [the Crofters Commission] decisions which they at the same time intimated to the crofters – who have been much disgusted on receipt of this. They expected the Commissioners would have put little or no rent on this additional pasture and numbers of them declare they will not take possession or interfere with it . . . The refusal to accept these decisions is very awkward for the Duke.[155]

The crofters could not afford the increased rents and would get little benefit from the extra pasture if they did not have the capital to stock it immediately. Frustration on both sides turned the situation into a stalemate. For the crofters, the disappointment must have been acute; all the more so, when it seemed their goal had been so nearly reached, but could not be secured for lack of capital.[156] Eleven of the twenty crofters participating in the land extension failed to pay their rents; hardly surprising when they were receiving no benefit from the land.[157] The situation was at a standstill until 1891, when the Commission returned to Assynt. The appeals of the crofters were rejected and the Commission, which had been looked to by both the crofters and the estate as a final remedy to the open sore of Clashmore, had instead incited further frustration, and for the cottars it had held out no hope at all.[158]

The crofters' response was more dyke breaking. In all, 700 yards were pulled down over the next two years, on top of the 1000 yards that had come down in 1887–9, but as Wright, the 3rd Duke's personal secretary, commented bitterly, 'the authorities seem very lax about it. I fancy they do not look upon it as a political agitation and therefore do not mind so much.'[159] The estate did as much as it could, offering a reward for information and setting up watchers to guard the walls at night, but this was costly and futile, as offences continued to be committed.[160] McIver's frustration was reminiscent of his rage at the height of the Clashmore agitation: 'I am sorry and vexed . . . the expense of watching and repairing what is thrown down is enormous and the annoyance and vexation connected with these outrages together try one's patience and equanimity.'[161]

---

[155] NLS, Acc. 10225, Policy Papers, 217, McIver to Wright, 26 Feb. 1889.

[156] NLS, Acc. 10225, Factor's Correspondence, 1963, McIver to Gordon, 22 Mar. 1889.

[157] NAS, AF67/14, Jamieson, Sutherland estate Edinburgh lawyer, to Lord Lothian, 18 Feb. 1891.

[158] NLS, Acc. 10225, Policy Papers, 217, McIver to Wright, 17 Jul. 1891. These frustrations were common across the Highlands: Cameron, *Land for the People*, 55–6.

[159] NLS, Acc. 10225, Policy Papers, 205, Wright to McIver, 4 Jan. 1892.

[160] NLS, Acc. 10225, Policy Papers, 217, McIver to Wright, 8 Dec. 1891.

[161] NLS, Acc. 10225, Policy Papers, 217, McIver to Wright, 7 May 1892.

In late 1892, the cottars in desperation again petitioned the estate for Unapool, but the estate refused.[162] McIver remarked that

> Assynt is already overburdened with crofters and our policy would be to reduce them and if possible not to add to them . . . they have no capital to build houses or stock a farm and are men of no reputation suspected of complicity in the recent outrages at Clashmore – it would be mere folly to entertain their request.[163]

This petition shows, apart from how little McIver's views had mellowed, that land hunger in Clashmore was not going to go away. Agitation fizzled out after 1892, but the old grievances rumbled on. In 1895, an opportunity for agitation arose when the Clashmore farm lease was transferred to a new tenant, Mr John Mackenzie, but the cottars remained quiet.[164] Mackenzie would be left in peace initially, but in a few years the Clashmore cottars would renew their demands for the farm.

Resolution: 1902–9

For seven years, Clashmore was quiet, but its problems had not gone away. Land hunger was built into the structure of the township and the grant of the grazing parks to the crofters in 1888 had done little to change that. This demand was demonstrated by regular petitions for land which flowed into the estate management from the cottars.[165] It was the petition sent in December 1902 that was to be the opening salvo in a renewed and organised campaign by the Clashmore cottars to get more land.[166]

One of these, Hugh MacLeod, would become the *de facto* leader of the Clashmore cottars, writing their petitions and organising their demands. His father had been evicted from Clashmore in the 1870s and this may have given MacLeod both the standing in the community and the real need for land necessary to be an effective leader. He was also an elder and precentor in the local United Free Church, giving him moral authority.[167] In the renewed campaign for land, all of the petitions sent in were signed by five persons, including MacLeod. There were certainly more than five cottars in Clashmore and competition between MacLeod's group and the others, who felt deliberately left out of the negotiations, would increase as the estate took the petitions seriously.

In 1904, the five cottars stepped up their campaign for land and handed in a letter to the farm tenant, John Mackenzie:

[162] NLS, Acc. 10225, Policy Papers, 217, McIver to Wright, 18 Nov. 1892.
[163] NLS, Acc. 10225, Policy Papers, 217, McIver to Wright, 18 Nov. 1892.
[164] NLS, Acc. 10225, Factor's Correspondence, 1976, Gordon to McIver, 1 Apr. 1895.
[165] NLS, Acc. 10225, Crofters, ZB/c, James Simpson to MacLean, 8 Sep. 1896.
[166] NLS, Acc. 10225, Farms, 25, Clashmore cottars to duke, 14 Dec. 1902.
[167] NAS, AF67/58, PC Ross to Chief Constable of Sutherland, 1 Feb. 1904.

We the undersigned beg to ask you, not to plough any more on Clashmore farm, or to put yourself into more expenses as we expect to have it from His Grace the Duke or take it with our own hands. We were deprived of Clashmore farm thirty years ago . . . we bind ourselves to have Clashmore farm one way or the other, we only want part of Ardvar farm . . . we rather it than Clashmore as we would expect to take the half of our living out of the sea, as there is a good harbour, but seeing it is refused we are bound to stick to Clashmore farm . . . we will be compelled to take forcible possession of Clashmore farm, as we consider it more honourable to suffer in the struggle than to allow ourselves and our families starve. We intend to put all our petitions and replies in the newspapers to show the world the justice of our demand.[168]

There were a number of unusual aspects to this letter. Firstly, it was written to the farm tenant, rather than the estate, perhaps in the belief that the tenant would take it more seriously, as it threatened to take over his farm. Secondly, although the cottars emphasised the land they actually wanted was in Ardvar, their target would be Clashmore; by linking themselves to the famous agitation of the past, they could hope for a swifter response from the estate and remind it of the origins of their grievance.

Mackenzie, who lived at Clashmore, was understandably alarmed; the night he received the letter, he showed it to the Chief Constable of Sutherland, who happened to be in the area. Enquiries were made and the chief constable reported,

Mackenzie says that they [the cottars] have been breaking down pieces of the dykes and fences and putting in their sheep on the farm for some time back . . . I also understand through Mr Gordon, late sub-factor, that the wording of the letter referred to, is similar to the one received at the time of the last Clashmore disturbances and these cottars took a very active part in the last Clashmore riots.[169]

It is clear the authorities took the threat seriously, and that the history of agitation on the farm fed that concern. Recent disturbances elsewhere in the Highlands, at Vatersay for instance, meant that land raids were a possibility again and this lent the Clashmore threat extra urgency.[170] The estate management took a very different view, however, led now by McIver's successor in Assynt, the moderate Donald MacLean. He believed the threat would not have been acted on, but was simply intended to generate interest in the cottars' situation, and was angry that the authorities had been

---

[168] NAS, AF67/58, Clashmore cottars to John Mackenzie, 20 Jan. 1904.

[169] NAS, AF67/58, chief constable to Under-Secretary of Scotland, 30 Jan. 1904; sheriff to under-secretary, 27 Jan. 1904.

[170] Cameron, *Land for the People*, 120–2: Hunter, *Making of the Crofting Community*, 187–91.

dragged into the matter.[171] The estate was willing to address the demands of the cottars, and the 4th Duke agreed that an arrangement could be made, as long as the cottars agreed to retract the threat to raid first.[172] They did so, and Mackenzie agreed to give up the lease whenever it was convenient for the estate.[173]

In February 1904, the estate was moving quickly to offer Clashmore farm to the cottars. The estate knew they had no capital, and most were in arrears of rent, but was optimistic: 'very likely the Congested D. Board would help in this matter if asked, and perhaps help with houses for them . . . I think it would be advisable to get the Crofters Commission or the Congested D. Board to divide the parks among the people. If we do it there are sure to be complaints afterwards.'[174] The estate was too optimistic, both as regards the cottars' means and the potential involvement of the CDB. The estate offered the cottars the farm, provided they met the valuation costs, in February 1904, and were swiftly rejected: 'you know very well that we are not able to take Clashmore farm at valuation which will come to few hundred £ pounds sterling [sic] we are only poor men'.[175] The negotiations ground to a halt; both the estate and the cottars wrote to the CDB asking for help, but none was immediately forthcoming.[176]

Meanwhile, a new conflict was brewing over Clashmore, this time between the cottars themselves. Hitherto, only five of the Clashmore cottars had applied for land, but in March 1904, four others applied to the estate, accusing the first group of secrecy and unfair dealing: 'whereas five cottars – or alleged cottars – have secretly applied to your Grace for Clashmore farm last spring, and, as it is rumoured to be broken up, we the undersigned approach your Grace with a view to participating in the farm. We are all cottars in the strictest sense of the word.'[177] The original group responded furiously; MacLeod wrote to the estate denying the others were true cottars: 'I may also say that anyone who does not belong to Clashmore has not any claim for any part of it when dividing the farm.'[178] Clashmore farm was not very large: the more applicants there were, the less everyone would receive, and so conflict was breaking out.

Negotiations between the estate and the CDB were carried on at a slow pace, as had been the case at Syre. The difficulty was that the CDB did not regard Clashmore as a good farm for division because it had no pasture, that having been divided among the crofters in 1888. Ironically, what had benefited the crofters had made the circumstances of the landless cottars

[171] NLS, Acc. 10225, Factor's Correspondence, 434, MacLean to duke, 3 Jan. 1904.
[172] NLS, Acc. 10225, Farms, 25, duke to MacLean, 30 Jan. 1904.
[173] NLS, Acc. 10225, Farms, 25, Clashmore cottars to duke, 5 Feb. 1904.
[174] NLS, Acc. 10225, Farms, 25, Simpson to MacLean, 13 Feb. 1904.
[175] NLS, Acc. 10225, Farms, 25, Hugh MacLeod to MacLean, 22 Feb. 1904.
[176] NLS, Acc. 10225, Farms, 25, CDB to MacLean, 3 Mar. 1904.
[177] NLS, Acc. 10225, Farms, 25, Clashmore cottars to duke, 26 Oct. 1904.
[178] NLS, Acc. 10225, Farms, 25, Hugh MacLeod to MacLean, 29 Nov. 1904.

even more intolerable later.[179] This, combined with the problem of fluctuating numbers of applicants, brought the negotiations to a virtual standstill
until early 1905, when an inspector for the CDB came to visit Clashmore.
The outcome was that the CDB still did not consider Clashmore suitable for
division, but would give some help 'to assist five or six tenants in the erec-
tion of new buildings and in meeting the outgoing tenant's valuation'.[180]
This would be in the form of a loan that would cover most of the £218 valuation costs, but the estate was concerned: it was still unsure how many applicants there were, which would have a significant bearing on how the land
would be divided up. In 1905, nothing was resolved and the estate had to
negotiate a £10 rent reduction with Mackenzie to compensate the trouble
he had endured.[181] Nothing more could be done about Clashmore by the
estate or CDB until the cottars had worked out their differences. By 1909,
this had been achieved and Mackenzie had given up his lease. Despite
some misgivings, the estate, the Crofters Commission and the CDB all came
together to divide the farm up among the applicants, finally numbering
twenty. The Commission made the divisions and set the rents on them, and
the CDB granted £60 towards the valuation costs.[182]

All the groups involved in the division had to compromise in order to
come to a settlement, something that took seven years to happen. The
estate management did become frustrated: with the CDB for being slow
and inflexible, and with the applicants for repeatedly rejecting what it
considered to be reasonable terms. The CDB was an underfunded and
overstretched institution and its concerns about Clashmore's suitability
for division were practical and well founded. But it was really the crofters
and cottars of Clashmore who faced the greatest frustration. Having been
deprived of land without compensation forty years previously, they had
since been caught in a vicious circle of intense land hunger and lack of
capital. The division of 1909 did nothing to solve these deep-rooted problems, but the victory was symbolic: Clashmore farm had been liquidated
and the land given back to the crofters and cottars, many of whom were
direct descendants of those who had been moved in 1870.

Conclusion: Clashmore in context

This chapter has used Clashmore as a case study, using one township to
provide an indepth view of the Sutherland estate not possible elsewhere
in this book. Clashmore gives a cross-section of the estate management
from ground officer to duke, through forty years of radical change in the

---

[179] NLS, Acc. 10225, Farms, 25, Scottish Office (Reginald MacLeod) to duke, 6 Dec. 1904;
MacLean to CDB, 29 Nov. 1904, CDB to MacLean, 25 Nov. 1904.
[180] NLS, Acc. 10225, Factor's Correspondence, 438, MacLean to Simpson, 10 Feb. 1905.
[181] NLS, Acc. 10225, Factor's Correspondence, 439, MacLean to Mackenzie, 29 Apr. 1905.
[182] Copy Order by Crofters Commission, R. N. 983, 31 Dec. 1909; NAS, AF42/6037,
AF42/6102, AF42/6171.

management of Highland estates, and illustrates the changes and conflicts in that management as it evolved after the watershed of 1886. It is vital, however, to put Clashmore in a wider estate and Highland context. The reclamations that sparked agitation in Clashmore were unique to the Sutherland estate, being the 3rd Duke's own personal vision, but the agitation of the 1880s was reflected across the Highlands.[183] Land hunger dominated the region; whether it had been caused by clearance or reclamation, the result was the same.[184]

The wider economic context was the same in Clashmore as in the rest of the Highlands. The early 1880s saw a sharp downturn for the crofting economy; the 1881 harvest was poor and the fishing, a key source of income for crofters and cottars, failed.[185] These difficulties made dependence on land even heavier at a time when it was a scarce resource. Crofters also demanded security from eviction at forty days' notice, something especially relevant to the Clashmore case, where removal summons had been used with devastating effect in both 1851 and 1870–4. For the cottars, the situation was even more unstable; in legal terms they were merely trespassers and could in theory be removed without any notice served at all. The methods used by the Clashmore crofters in their dealings with the estate after 1882 were the same as those used elsewhere: petitioning, rent strikes, and finally violence in the form of deforcement, dyke breaking and attacks on estate staff, as well as land raids.[186] The social and economic background of local leaders was also similar. In Clashmore, the local Free Church minister was initially key in negotiating with the Sutherland estate and articulating the demands of the crofters.[187] Similarly, in Lewis, a local schoolmaster was central to the organisation of the raid on Park Deer Forest.[188] There was one aspect of the Clashmore agitation which was unique in the Highlands, and this was the role of that 'modern-day Rob Roy' Hugh Kerr.[189] His offences were relatively minor, but the fact that he eluded the authorities for so long made him a hero for many and exercised the authorities, civil and military, local and central, by his audacity. Nowhere else was there such a figure, a leader who was a cottar, not a minister or schoolmaster, who defied the authorities for so long.[190]

The response of the Sutherland estate to agitation at Clashmore was

---

[183] Hunter, *Making of the Crofting Community*, 176.
[184] Hunter, *Making of the Crofting Community*, 119–20, 124–5, 190–1.
[185] Hunter, *Making of the Crofting Community*, 131–2; Devine, *Clanship to Crofters' War*, 221.
[186] Devine, *Clanship to Crofters' War*, 218; Hunter, *Making of the Crofting Community*, 153.
[187] MacColl, *Land, Faith and the Crofting Community*, 113.
[188] Hunter, *Making of the Crofting Community*, 172.
[189] Incidentally, Kerr was given his nicknames by the *Scottish Highlander*, a newspaper which supported his activities: *Scottish Highlander*, 11 Oct. 1888.
[190] Norman Stewart or 'Parnell' of Valtos, Skye, was a similar figure, although he was a crofter and his tactics differed: he never went on the run from the authorities and, rather, used his court appearances as a platform; MacPhail, *Crofters' War*, 28–9, 120–2.

similar to that of other Highland estates, despite its many unique qualities.[191] Before the Crofters War broke out, the Sutherland estate management dealt with resistance in Clashmore as other estates did: by issuing
and enforcing summonses of removal. The estate was perfectly within the
law to do so, and it nipped agitation in Clashmore in the bud in the early
1870s. By the 1880s, however, the situation had changed; the Sutherland
estate was sensitive to public criticism and anxious to stay out of the newspapers.[192] After years of conflict within the management, the estate did
compromise with the Clashmore crofters, firstly in 1888 and latterly in
1909. The sacrifice of the estate was hardly crippling, however; Clashmore's
annual rent by 1909 was only £40. The bitter history of Clashmore farm,
however, and the removals associated with it meant that when the estate
finally divided it among the crofters, it was a sharper victory.

The response of the authorities to the agitation in Clashmore was also
very similar to that in other parts of the Highlands; using tactics such as
sending in gunboats and contingents of marines to back up the local police
force in serving interdicts and making arrests.[193] Despite some sensational
newspaper reporting, the gunboats and soldiers never stayed for more than
two days at a time and operations were still led by the local police. The most
effective tool the authorities had in halting violence, both in Clashmore
and Lewis, were trials in the High Court of Justiciary in 1888.[194]

The situation in Clashmore was unique in one way, and that was in the
achievements of the crofters and cottars. The creation of the farm had
thrown up problems common all over the Highlands: land hunger, a sim-
mering resentment against the estate management and a desperate cottar
problem. But the agitation there achieved more in a shorter time than
elsewhere, almost certainly because it focused on only one tiny township,
not a whole island population. The resolution of the Clashmore agitation
in 1909 prevented the type of acute land agitation seen elsewhere in the
Highlands in the inter-war period, as crofters continued to struggle to gain
what the Clashmore crofters had already achieved.

---

[191] Compare to, for example, Armadale Castle, Macdonald MSS, 4675, J. D. Brodie to
Alexander Macdonald, 6 Feb. 1882; 4745, Alexander Macdonald to Lord Lothian, 12 Oct.
1888; Ulbster Estate MSS, Factor's Letterbook, 1880–7, Logan to Sir Tollemache, 29 Mar.
1883.

[192] E. Richards, *The Highland Clearances: people, landlords and rural turmoil* (Edinburgh, 2008,
new edn), 362–4. Other Highland estates had similar concerns: see Ulbster Estate MSS,
Factor's Letterbook 1880–7, Logan to Sir Tollemache, 8 Jan. 1884; Armadale Castle,
Macdonald MSS, 4675, J. D. Brodie to Alexander Macdonald, 25 Apr. 1882.

[193] Hunter, *Making of the Crofting Community*, 150, 165; Armadale Castle, Macdonald MSS,
3181, Lord Macdonald to Alex. Macdonald, [?] 1886.

[194] *Scotsman*, 4 Feb. 1888.

Conclusion: 'Neither forgotten nor forgiven'[1]

This book has given an overview of the Sutherland estate management during one of the most sustained periods of crisis and flux in its history. It has examined the background and reasoning behind the many important, and frequently controversial, policy decisions it made over the years and dissected the often tortuous structure of the management. It has been written primarily from an estate-centric viewpoint and demonstrates the dedication and effort that the lower estate management put into preserving the ducal family's financial and political interests, however they were perceived. The decline of the power of the family and estate – political, territorial and financial – has been tracked.

The Highland context of the Sutherland estate is vitally important when looking at its changing fortunes and structure from 1850 to 1920. The vast size and wealth of the estate made it unique in a Highland, or even British, context, and as such, has been labelled as unworthy of the level of academic attention it has received.[2] It is argued here, however, that behind the screen of wealth, the trajectory of the Sutherland estate closely matched that of other Highland estates. The breakdown of traditional authority and discipline over the small tenants, their influence to be replaced by government agencies, and the decline of political power and capital wealth has been tracked. The key difference between the Sutherland estate and other Highland estates lay in the vast personal wealth of the ducal family from land, property and investments outwith Sutherland, which cushioned their decline, a safety net that most other Highland estates did not have.

'A debt of honour due our ancestors': the clearances[3]

The clearances have been the ghost at the feast in this book: although the only evictions that took place between 1851 and 1920 were those at Clashmore, there is no escaping the wholesale clearances of the early nineteenth century and their evolving meaning in this period. According

---

[1] *Highland News*, 17 Jan. 1914.
[2] R. H. Campbell, 'Too much on the Highlands? A plea for change', *Scottish Economic and Social History*, 14 (1994), 69–70.
[3] *Highland News*, 17 Jan. 1914.

to the rhetoric of the improvers, the clearances would pluck crofters out of the cycle of grinding poverty they subsisted in, providing employment and opportunities.[4] This did not materialise, however, and acute poverty and periods of occasional destitution remained the norm. The crofters were moved to poor land on the coasts, where little provision was given for their participation in the fishing industry, followed by a population boom, creating intolerable congestion. The interior of Sutherland was almost completely cleared, presenting another long-term legacy – the difficulty, if not impossibility, of their reversal.[5] The sheep farms and the rents they generated had been so large, the later temptation for afforestation and the rents the forests generated was so immediate and the capital of the crofters so small, that the government found it very difficult to negotiate a solution after 1886.

By and large ignoring these practical difficulties, crofter champions and the crofting press were guilty of relying on tired rhetoric about the clearances. The ducal family was very sensitive to this criticism, while refusing to accept personal blame.[6] The estate, in front of several royal commissions and in the press, refused to discuss the clearances, considering them to be outwith the remit of contemporary discussion. They were in the past and the present-day estate management would accept no responsibility for them. Despite this refusal to discuss the clearances in public, they nevertheless had a profound effect on later generations of the ducal family, by making them intolerant of public criticism. This aversion directly affected estate policy, generating strife within the estate management over how the ducal family's reputation should best be defended. After 1882, the 3rd and 4th dukes preferred to be conciliatory towards the crofters, rather than face renewed criticism, but the estate factors were often opposed to policies which, as they thought, encouraged lawlessness in the crofters.

The period 1886 to 1920 was one of acute and continuing crisis for the Sutherland estate. Along with all other Highland estates, the Sutherland estate had to face a fundamental change: direct government intervention in the administration of crofting tenancies, a massive ideological and practical imposition.[7] In addition, but not related to this, the 1880s saw the end of the family tradition of spending on large capital projects, and the estate went into a period of retrenchment. The consequences of a legacy of vast expenditure, combined with low land values, a depressed agricultural market after 1879, and government intervention, irrevocably changed the nature of the Sutherland estate.

---

[4] J. Loch, *An Account of the Improvements on the Estates of the Marquis of Stafford* (London, 1820).

[5] L. Leneman, *Fit for Heroes? Land Settlement in Scotland after World War One* (Aberdeen, 1989), 53.

[6] 5th Duke of Sutherland, *Looking Back: the autobiography of the 5th Duke of Sutherland* (London, 1957), 31–2.

[7] E. McIver, *Memoirs of a Highland Gentleman: being the reminiscences of Evander McIver of Scourie*, Rev. G. Henderson (ed.) (Edinburgh, 1905), 81.

**'The still backward and rather neglected county': the government and the
Sutherland Estate, 1886–1920**[8]

This book has examined the impact of direct government intervention
in the running of the Sutherland estate after 1886, from its attempts
to impose order in Clashmore, to setting rents and purchasing land.
Government agency did generate some important changes in Sutherland,
though it was never an unqualified success. The government's aim to
manage and then halt de-population, and reverse the chronic poverty in
Sutherland failed: indeed, dramatic de-population began in Sutherland
from 1890, *after* government agency had been introduced.[9] This failure was
compounded by the continuing endemic poverty of many of Sutherland's
crofters, as the following petition painfully demonstrates. It was written in
1910 by a young boy with tuberculosis, living in poverty with his disabled
father. It could have been written in 1810, and shows that for many small
tenants, especially on the north and west coasts, standards of living had
changed very little over a hundred years:

> Noble Sir I am writing your lordship to inform you of my condition I
> have nobody to look after me my sister went away before your letter
> came they were saying your lordship was to have me sent away I am
> writing your lordship to have pity on a poor helpless lad like me who
> can not do anything to help himself in the goodness of his heart send
> me to a sanatorium and God would guide you in your work in the
> future. I humbly beg pardon for this letter I do hope your lordship will
> send me away soon.[10]

Lord Stafford sent him to a sanatorium and paid the fees, perhaps also demonstrating that local expectations of the paternalistic duties of landlordism
had not entirely disappeared in early twentieth-century Sutherland.

Was the estate partly at fault for this deplorable situation? Crofter poverty
was, and remained, an accepted part of estate life in the Highlands until
well after the First World War. As crofters' rents represented only a small
proportion of the Sutherland estate's income, little was done to remedy their
poverty. Over the period 1850 to 1920 there was minimal change to crofters'
rents; in 1914, for example, crofters' rents represented 13% of a total rental of
£58,634, and 59% of this sum was unpaid.[11] Following government intervention in Highland estates after 1886, the estate became very unwilling to make
any financial sacrifices for the crofters, regarding that as the government's

8 5th Duke, *Looking Back*, 65.
9 *Census of Scotland*, 1921 (Edinburgh, 1923), 1867; M. Anderson and D. J. Morse, 'High
  fertility, high emigration, low nuptuality: adjustment processes in Scotland's demographic
  experience, 1861–1914, Part I', *Population Studies*, 47 (1993), 12, 21.
10 National Library of Scotland [hereafter NLS], Sutherland Estate Papers, Acc. 10225,
  Buildings, 40, no. 60, Duncan MacRae to Lord Stafford, 16 Oct. 1910.
11 NLS, Acc. 10853, 113, Rental Abstract, 1914.

responsibility.[12] The estate certainly did not obstruct government attempts to improve the living conditions of crofters, although the obstacles were numerous and the government had little success. Perhaps the social and economic problems on the Sutherland estate were too fundamental for the state to tackle effectively. The undercapitalised nature of the crofting economy and the constantly criticised standards of crofter husbandry were key factors in this failure, as was the tension between the crofters and cottars over scarce resources and patchy government attention. Add to this the legacy of the clearances on an estate where they had been executed with a rigour and thoroughness which made re-settlement difficult, if not impossible, under the economic and legislative framework of the time. The remoteness of the north and west of the county and the poor quality of land also told against the government. The poverty of the Sutherland crofters would remain a thorny problem for the government throughout the twentieth century.

'The grand old estate': the Sutherland Estate in flux[13]

It is clear that the Sutherland estate had a very poor public reputation in the period analysed here. Much of this reputation was predicated on historical responsibility for the clearances and a widespread assumption that the estate resembled a well-oiled machine: monolithic, united, powerful. This book shows that in this particular, its reputation was inaccurate. The large and elaborate management structure was often racked with disagreement, leading to breakdowns in working relations. These collapses could be seen at all levels, from the implosion of the ducal family between 1892 and 1894 to the resignation of Alex Ross, the Assynt ground officer, in 1888. The vast size and wealth of the Sutherland estate and the thoroughness of the clearances in the early nineteenth century generated an image of unity and power which, after 1882 at least, the estate simply did not have.

Evander McIver, for instance, was never reconciled to changing Highland society after 1882. He criticised the 1886 Crofters Act, as it 'set up a barrier between the crofters and their landlords, with whom it was their wisdom to be on happy and pleasant terms'.[14] He rejected both the 1886 Act and the 1897 Congested Districts Act for their provisions to provide more land for the crofters: the extension of the crofting system, he believed, would only spread poverty further and be detrimental to landlords' interests.[15] The

---

[12] The clearest articulation of this belief came from the 4th Duke in 1900, when commenting on the Syre scheme and the government's responsibility towards the crofters; National Archives of Scotland, Congested Districts Board files, AF42/633, 4th Duke to Lord Balfour, 22 Sep. 1900.

[13] McIver, *Memoirs*, 124.

[14] McIver, *Memoirs*, 82.

[15] PP XXXII–XXXVI, 1884, *Evidence and Report of the Commissioners of Inquiry into the condition of the Crofters and Cottars in the Highlands and Islands of Scotland* [hereafter *Napier Commission Evidence*], Evander McIver, 1710.

final blow came in his retirement, as he watched the 4th Duke sell 100,000 acres for as many pounds to W. E. Gilmour. McIver bitterly noted that the Sutherland family had paid £300,000 for the land in 1827 and, 'I cannot but conclude that the price paid by Mr Gilmour is low and inadequate and that the sale made to him is a great mistake financially.'[16] McIver's regret was based on more than what he saw as the financial folly of the duke, but rather on the breaking up of 'the grand old estate' he had spent so much of his career trying to preserve, order and shape.[17] He observed discontentedly in 1898, 'I am vexed and broken in spirit by the sale of so much of this fine estate that I cannot think, speak or write about it with patience.'[18]

When he retired in 1895, McIver was one of a dying breed: unable to accept the changes in the fortunes of either crofters or landlords, he fought tooth and nail against his colleagues and was gradually isolated. He gratefully accepted the 4th Duke's offer of retirement in 1895, perhaps realising how ineffectual his protests against the new world of crofting rights had become. Despite a rather nostalgic view of his past relations with the Scourie crofters, McIver never gave up hope that things would revert to better and happier times:

> The crofters on the Sutherland estates had been treated with kindness . . . and for thirty years after I became factor, they were easily managed in the Scourie agency. They had confidence in my sense of fairness and justice as their factor, and rents were paid, as a rule, with regularity; in short, it was satisfactory as compared with most Highland estates with crofter tenants. But once the excitement and agitation sprung up, the Sutherland crofters became dissatisfied. The subject of the removals from Strathnaver in times long gone by was revived and rehearsed in exaggerated colours and open rebellion broke out . . . Time will open the eyes of the crofters to the fact that their ideas and expectations as to the benefits and advantages they were to obtain, and which had been so grossly and extravagantly exaggerated by agitating land leaguers, are not to be realised.[19]

McIver never changed his views about the Sutherland crofters: after fifty years of complete domination over them, he could not accept their new political confidence and legislative rights. He ended his career a disappointed man: all he had worked for had been rejected by the ducal family in the 1880s and 1890s and he could only look on in sadness.

The ducal family have provided important points of reference in this book. Their vast wealth – the Sutherland fortune put them in the top

---

[16] McIver, *Memoirs*, 150.

[17] McIver, *Memoirs*, 124.

[18] McIver, *Memoirs*, 281; J. Shaw Grant, *A Shilling for your Scowl: the history of a Scottish legal mafia* (Stornoway, 1992), 164, 198–200, 211; I. M. M. MacPhail, *The Crofters' War* (Stornoway, 1989), 13–14.

[19] McIver, *Memoirs*, 82.

rank of British aristocrats – and the field of their investments after 1880, meant their influence stretched far beyond Sutherland, into almost every continent.[20] The financial heyday of the ducal family was short, however, beginning with the marriage of Countess Elizabeth to Lord Stafford in 1785 and ending with the 5th Duke's massive land sales in 1919. Much of the fortune was lost on the way in bad investments, and in the dynastic strife of the 1890s. With a fortune the size of the Sutherlands' it was almost inevitable that an argument over inheritance would crop up at some point, but the losses sustained by the estate in the crisis of 1892–4, perhaps as much as £750,000, were a huge blow.[21] The payout to the dowager duchess was part of the decline of the Sutherland fortune from the 1890s, but the trend had begun earlier, and, despite the paranoia of the 4th Duke, the decline was not entirely the fault of the crofters or the government, but of the ducal family itself.

The Sutherland estate was unique in many ways: primarily, in its size, structure and wealth, especially when viewed in a Highland context. The significance of the Sutherland fortune in the day-to-day running of the estate is notable. Other landowners were dependent to a far greater degree on the incomes from their estates than the Sutherland family was and this manifested itself in how those estates were run. A positive press reputation was more important to the dukes than a healthy rental roll, for instance, whereas the opposite was true for struggling or financially embarrassed estates elsewhere in the Highlands. This is not to say that the Sutherland estate did not suffer financially, but it had other resources which allowed for complex cross-subsidisation of assets and provided the northern estates with a financial crutch. The family sold off 615,000 acres in Sutherland by 1919, for instance, but that still left them with 385,000 acres. Further, although by 1914 both Stafford House in London and Trentham house in Staffordshire had been sold, that still left Dunrobin, Cliveden and Lilleshall houses for the family. The pattern of sale and losses is the same as on many other Highland estates, therefore, it was just that as the Sutherland family started with so much land and property, the scale of their loss was disguised.

The Sutherland factors had much in common with their contemporaries on other Highland estates. They differed with the ducal family and commissioners on many points of principle over the crofters: they were unhappy about rent arrears, for instance, believing the crofters should be pressed to pay up to maintain discipline.[22] The same can be said about the factors'

[20] D. Cannadine, *The Decline and Fall of the British Aristocracy* (London, 1990), 710; 5th Duke, *Looking Back*, 58; J. Forbes Munro, *Maritime Enterprise and Empire: Sir William Mackinnon and his business network, 1823–1893* (Woodbridge, 2003), 213–20, 233; E. Richards, 'An Anatomy of the Sutherland Fortune: income, consumption, investments and returns, 1780–1880', *Business History*, 21 (1979), 54.

[21] D. Stuart, *Dear Duchess: Millicent Duchess of Sutherland, 1869–1955* (London, 1982), 44–5.

[22] *Napier Commission Evidence*, Evander McIver, 1707.

response to the loss of their traditional political powers through the Poor and School Boards: their failure to retain these seats in the 1880s or get onto the new County Council after 1889 led them to make doom-laden statements about the future of landed estates. All of these issues point to something much more fundamental, however: an inability on the part of the older generation of estate staff to adapt to their new position in relation to the crofters. Accustomed to, and believing it to be absolutely necessary to have, complete dominance over the crofters to maintain 'order', older factors were repelled by the new-found confidence of the crofters after 1882. There was little they could do to retain their status and as representatives of the landlord class, matched their 'decline and fall', moving from being local 'kings' in the mid-nineteenth century to land managers by 1920. A bitter aftertaste surrounded twentieth-century Sutherland estate managers, and they faced an increasingly difficult balancing act between their landlord, the government and the crofters, on a much tighter budget and with reduced status.

The Sutherland estate, far from being a smooth-running, united machine, was in fact an often tortured, overelaborate structure, ill equipped to deal with the challenges of the period. The sheer number of people it took to run the estate resulted in many competing and often opposing priorities, periodically bringing the management to a standstill. Like all Highland estates, the Sutherland estate had to learn, reluctantly, how to adapt to the new world of crofters' rights after 1886, as well as the government bodies that administered them. But the Sutherland estate faced an additional challenge: the memory of the clearances and the direct impact they had on ducal and estate policy. In spite of the unique extent of the lands held by the ducal family, and their extraordinary wealth, the central narrative of the estate matches that of most other Highland estates: decline. Politically, financially and territorially, the Sutherland estate was a shadow of its former self by 1920. The fact that it was still a large estate was a result of the vast Sutherland fortune of the early nineteenth century, not of successful management of that fortune or the estate from 1850.

Appendix
The Sutherland Estate Management, 1812–1920

The Dukes of Sutherland

2nd Duke, 1833–61
3rd Duke, 1861–92
4th Duke, 1892/4–1913
5th Duke, 1913–63

The Commissioners

James Loch, 1812–55
George Loch, 1855–79
General Sir Arnold Burrowes Kemball, 1879–86
R. M. Brereton, 1886–9

The Factors

Dunrobin	*Tongue*	*Scourie*
Joseph Peacock 1859–85	John Horsburgh 1837–59	Evander McIver 1845–95
Donald MacLean 1885–1912	John Crawford 1859–85	Donald MacLean 1895–1912
Col. John Morrison 1912–c.1925	John Box 1885–1902	
	Col. John Morrison 1902–12	

Bibliography

MANUSCRIPT SOURCES

A. The Sutherland Estates Papers
The Sutherland Estates Papers consist of two main deposits: one in the National Library of Scotland, under five separate Accession or Deposit numbers, and the other in Staffordshire County Record Office. In addition, papers relating to the period after 1920 and some private family papers have been retained by the Sutherland family at Dunrobin Castle and the Estate Office, Golspie.

National Library of Scotland
Sutherland Estates Papers: Acc. 10225; Acc. 10853; Acc. 12173; Dep. 313; Dep. 314
Papers relating to the dukes of Sutherland's Scottish estates, on deposit since 1980. Deposits 313 and 314 relate to the period c.1300–1861, Accessions 10225 and 10853 to the period 1861–1920 and Acc. 12173 consists of Scottish material moved from Staffordshire County Record Office to the NLS as part of a rationalisation exercise between the two institutions.

Staffordshire County Record Office
Sutherland Estates Papers, D593
The collection includes material relative to the period c.1200–c.1900 and is mainly concerned with the family's English estates. It consists of material originally stored at Stafford House, London and Trentham House, Staffordshire.

B. Estate and personal papers
Armadale Castle, Skye
   Papers of the Macdonald Estate, Skye.

Bodleian Library
   Harcourt Papers.
   Hughendon Papers.

Dunvegan Castle, Skye
   Papers of MacLeod of MacLeod.

Highland Council Archives
  Papers of Christie and Ferguson, solicitors, Kilmuir Estate MSS, D123.

House of Lords Record Office
  Lloyd George Papers, LG/C-F.

National Archives of Scotland
  Lothian Muniments, GD 40.
  Cromartie Estate Papers, GD 305.
  Reay Papers, GD 84.
  Papers of the Scottish Landowners Federation, GD 325.

National Library of Scotland
  Papers of John Stuart Blackie, Acc. 2634.
  Papers of Rev. James Cumming, Acc. 5931.
  Papers of Sir William Mackinnon, Mg. 2.

Ulbster Estate Office, Thurso
  Papers of the Sinclair of Ulbster Estate, Caithness.

C. Government records
National Archives of Scotland
  Crofting Files, AF67.
  Congested Districts Board Files, AF42.
  Scottish Home and Health Department Miscellaneous Files, HH1.
  Scottish Office, Emigration Files, HH55.

The National Archives
  Treasury Records, Office of Works.

D. Legal papers
National Archives of Scotland
  Papers of the High Court of Justiciary, JC26/1888/202.
  Papers of the Sheriff Court of Dornoch, SC9/47/2.

The National Archives
  Justiciary Records, J 165/13–14, 1891 Will case.

PRINTED PRIMARY SOURCES

A. Public reports
Crofters' Commission Annual Reports, 1886–1912
Congested Districts Board Annual Reports, 1898–1912
Fishery Board for Scotland Annual Reports, 1903–1906

B. *Parliamentary papers*

1884, XXXIII–XXXVI, *Evidence and Report of the Commissioners of Inquiry into the condition of the Crofters and Cottars in the Highlands and Islands of Scotland.*

1890, XXVII, 1890–1, XLIV, *Reports of the Committee appointed to inquire into certain Matters affecting the interests of the population of the Western Highlands and Islands of Scotland.*

1895, XXXVIII–XXXIX, *Royal Commission (Highlands and Islands, 1892), Report and Evidence, 1895.*

HANSARD, *Parliamentary Debates, House of Commons.*

C. *Newspapers*
Crofter
Highland News
Inverness Courier
John O'Groat Journal
Northern Ensign
Northern Times
Scottish Highlander
Scotsman
Times

D. *Contemporary commentaries*

ALISON, W. P., *Letter to Sir John MacNeill on Highland Destitution and the Adequacy or Inadequacy of emigration as a remedy* (Edinburgh, 1851).

Observations on the Famine of 1846–7 in the Highlands of Scotland and in Ireland, as illustrating the connection of the principle of population with the management of the poor (Edinburgh, 1847).

Observations on the reclamation of waste lands and their cultivation by croft husbandry considered with a view to the productive employment of destitute labourers, paupers and criminals (Edinburgh, 1850).

ARGYLL, 8th Duke of, 'A Corrected Picture of the Highlands', *Nineteenth Century*, 16 (1884).

'On the Economic Condition of the Highlands of Scotland', *Journal of the Royal Statistical Society of London*, 26 (1883).

'The Prophet of San Francisco', *Nineteenth Century*, 15 (1884).

BEDFORD, Duke of, *A Great Agricultural Estate: being the story of the origin and administration of Woburn and Thorney* (London, 1897).

CAMPBELL, R., 'On Land Tenure in Scotland and England', *Law Quarterly Review*, 2 (1885).

'CONFERENCE of landlords in Inverness', *Transactions of the Gaelic Society of Inverness*, 11 (1884–5).

FARQUARSON, R., *The House of Commons from Within* (London, 1912).

In and Out of Parliament: Reminiscences of a Varied Life (London, 1911).

JOHNSTON, T., *Our Scots Noble Families* (Glasgow, 1909).

KEMP. D., *The Sutherland Democracy* (Edinburgh, 1890).

LOCH, J., *An Account of the Improvements on the Estates of the Marquis of Stafford* (London, 1820).

MACKENZIE, A., *A History of the Highland Clearances* (Inverness, 1883).

MACLEOD, D., *Gloomy Memories in the Highlands of Scotland* (Toronto, 1857).

MALLOCK, W. H., 'The Arch-depopulator of the Highlands', *Nineteenth Century and After*, 75 (1914).

MARX, K., 'Sutherland and Slavery, or the Duchess at home', *People's Paper* (London, 1853).

MCIVER, E., *Memoirs of a Highland Gentleman: being the reminiscences of Evander McIver of Scourie*, Rev. George Henderson (ed.) (Edinburgh, 1905).

MITCHELL, J., *Reminiscences of my Life in the Highlands, vols I and II* ([private print, 1884] Newton Abbot, 1971).

PENTLAND, Lady, *The Right Honourable John Sinclair, Lord Pentland, G. C. S. I.: a memoir* (London, 1928).

ROBERTS, C. G., 'Sutherland Reclamation', *Journal of the Royal Agricultural Society*, 2nd ser., 15 (1879).

RUSSEL, A., 'The Highlands – Men, Sheep and Deer', *Edinburgh Review*, 106 (1857).

SELLAR, T., *The Sutherland Evictions of 1814: former and recent statements respecting them examined* (London, 1883).

SUTHERLAND, 5th Duke of, *Looking Back: the autobiography of the Duke of Sutherland* (London, 1957).

SECONDARY SOURCES

ADONIS, A., 'Aristocracy, Agriculture and Liberalism: the politics, finances and estates of the third Lord Carrington', *Historical Journal*, 31 (1988).

Making Aristocracy Work: the peerage and the political system in Britain, 1884–1914 (Oxford, 1993).

'THE Survival of the Great Estates: Henry 4th Earl of Carnarvon and his dispositions in the 1880s', *Historical Research*, 64 (1991).

ANDERSON, M. and MORSE, D. J., 'High Fertility, high emigration, low nuptuality: adjustment processes in Scotland's demographic experience, 1861–1914, Part One and Part Two', *Population Studies*, 47 (1993).

ARCHER, J. E., *Social Unrest and Popular Protest in England, 1780–1840* (Cambridge, 2000).

AULD, J. W., 'The Liberal Pro-Boers', *Journal of British Studies*, 14 (1975).

BECKETT, J. and TURNER, M., 'End of the Old Order? F. M. L. Thompson, the Land Question and the burden of ownership in England, c.1-880–c.1925', *Agricultural History Review*, 55 (2007).

BIAGINI, E. F., *Liberty, Retrenchment and Reform: popular liberalism in the age of Gladstone, 1860–1880* (Cambridge, 1992).

BLACKDEN, S., 'The Board of Supervision and the Scottish Parochial Medical Service, 1845–95', *Medical History*, 30 (1986).

BLEWETT, N., *The Peers, the Parties and the People: the general elections of 1910* (London, 1972).

BONNETT, H., *The Saga of the Steam Plough* (Newton Abbot, 1965).

BREATHNACH, C., *Framing the West: images of rural Ireland, 1891–1920* (Dublin, 2007).

BROWN, J., 'Scottish and English Land legislation, 1905–11', *Scottish Historical Review*, 47 (1968).

BROWN, S. J., '"Echoes of Midlothian" Scottish Liberalism and the South African War, 1899–1902', *Scottish Historical Review*, 71 (1992).

BUSH, M. L. (ed.), *Social Orders and Social Classes in Europe since 1500: Studies in Social Stratification* (London, 1992).

CAMERON, E. A., *Land for the People? The British Government and the Scottish Highlands, c.1880–1925* (East Linton, 1996).

    The Life and Times of Charles Fraser Mackintosh, Crofter MP (Aberdeen, 2000).

    'The Political Influence of Highland Landowners: a reassessment', *Northern Scotland*, 14 (1994).

    'Politics, Ideology and the Highland Land Issue', *Scottish Historical Review*, 72 (1993).

CAMPBELL, R. H., *Owners and Occupiers: changes in rural society in south-west Scotland before 1914* (Aberdeen, 1991).

    'Too much on the Highlands? A Plea for change', *Scottish Economic and Social History*, 14 (1994).

CANNADINE, D., 'Aristocratic Indebtedness in the nineteenth century: the case re-opened,' *Economic History Review*, 2nd ser., 30 (1977).

    Aspects of Aristocracy: grandeur and decline in modern Britain (London, 1994).

    The Decline and Fall of the British Aristocracy (London, 1990).

    (ed.), *Patricians, Power and politics in nineteenth century towns* (Leicester, 1982).

CHAMBERS, J. D. and MINGAY, G. E., *The Agricultural Revolution, 1750–1880* (London, 1966).

CHECKLAND, O., *Philanthropy in Scotland: social welfare and the voluntary principle* (Edinburgh, 1980).

CHESHIRE, G. C. and BURN, E. H. (eds), *Modern Law of Real Property* (15th edn, London, 1994).

COLLINS, E. J. T., *The Agrarian History of England and Wales, vol. VII, 1850–1914* (Cambridge, 2000).

COULL, J. R., *The Sea-Fisheries of Scotland: a historical geography* (Edinburgh, 1996).

CRAGOE, M., 'The Anatomy of an eviction campaign: the General Election of 1868 in Wales and its Aftermath', *Rural History*, 9 (1998).

    An Anglican Aristocracy: the moral economy of the landed estate in Carmarthenshire, 1832–1895 (Oxford, 1996).

'Conscience or Coercion? Clerical Influence at the General Election of 1868 in Wales', *Past and Present*, 149 (1995).

CRAIG, F. W. S., *British Parliamentary Election Results, 1885–1918* (London, 1974).

DAVIDSON, N., 'Marx and Engels on the Scottish Highlands', *Science and Society*, 65 (2001).

DEVINE, T. M., *Clanship to Crofters' War: the social transformation of the Scottish Highlands* (Manchester, 1994).

Clearance and Improvement: land, power and people in Scotland, 1700–1900 (Edinburgh, 2006).

Conflict and Stability in Scottish Society, 1700–1850 (Edinburgh, 1990).

Farm Servants and Labour in Lowland Scotland, 1770–1914 (Edinburgh, 1984).

The Great Highland Famine: hunger, emigration and the Scottish Highlands in the nineteenth century (Edinburgh, 1988).

(ed.), *Scottish Elites* (Edinburgh, 1994).

DONNELLY, J. S., 'The Irish Agricultural Depression of 1859–64', *Irish Economic and Social History*, 3 (1976).

The Land and the People of Nineteenth Century Cork: the rural economy and the land question (London, 1975).

DRAYTON, R., *Nature's Government: Science, Imperial Britain and 'the Improvement of the world'* (New Haven, 2000).

DUNBABIN, J. P. D., 'Expectations of the new County Councils and their realisation', *Historical Journal*, 8 (1965).

ELLENBERGER, N. W., 'The Souls and London "Society" at the end of the Nineteenth century', *Victorian Studies*, 25 (1982).

FFORDE, M., *Conservatism and Collectivism, 1886–1914* (Edinburgh, 1990).

FLOUD, R. and McCLOSKEY, D. (eds), *The Economic History of Britain since 1700, vol. 2, 1860–1939* (Cambridge, 1994).

FORBES MUNRO, J., *Maritime Enterprise and Empire: Sir William Mackinnon and his business network, 1823–1893* (Woodbridge, 2003).

FRASER, D. (ed.), *The New Poor Law in the Nineteenth century* (London, 1976).

FRASER, W. H. and MORRIS, R. J. (eds), *People and Society in Scotland vol. II 1830–1914* (Edinburgh, 1990).

GOURVISH, T. R. and O'DAY, A. (eds), *Later Victorian Britain, 1867–1900* (Basingstoke, 1988).

GRAY, M., *The Fishing Industries of Scotland, 1790–1914: a study in regional adaption* (Oxford, 1978).

GREEN, E. H., *The Crisis of Conservatism: the politics, economics and ideology of the British Conservative Party, 1880–1914* (London, 1995).

'Radical Conservatism: the Electoral Genesis of Tariff Reform', *Historical Journal*, 28 (1985).

HABAKKUK, J., *Marriage, Debt and the Estates System: English landownership, 1650–1950* (Oxford, 1994).

HAMLIN, C., 'William Pulteney Alison, the Scottish Philosophy and the making of a political medicine', *Journal of the History of Medicine*, 61 (2005).

HASSAM, J. A., 'The Landed Estate: paternalism and the coal industry in Midlothian, 1800–1900', *Scottish Historical Review*, 59 (1980).

HELLAND, J., 'Rural Women and Urban Extravagance in late nineteenth century Britain', *Rural History*, 13 (2002).

HOBSON, P., 'Assynt Parish', *Scottish Geographical Magazine*, 65 (1949).

HORN, P., *High Society: the English Social Elite, 1880–1914* (Stroud, 1992).

 Ladies of the Manor: wives and daughters in country-house society, 1830–1918 (Stroud, 1991).

HUNTER, J., *The Making of the Crofting Community* (Edinburgh, 1976).

 'The Politics of Highland Land Reform, 1873–1895', *Scottish Historical Review*, 53 (1974).

 (ed.), *For the People's Cause: from the writings of John Murdoch* (Edinburgh, 1986).

HUTCHISON, I. G. C., 'The Nobility of Politics in Scotland, c.1880–1939', in T. M. Devine (ed.), *Scottish Elites* (Edinburgh, 1994).

 Scottish Politics in the Twentieth Century (Basingstoke, 2001).

JENKINS, T. A., *The Liberal Ascendancy, 1830–1886* (Basingstoke, 1994).

JOHNSTON, R., '"Charity that heals": the Scottish Labour Colony Association and attitudes to the able-bodied unemployed in Glasgow, 1890–1914', *Scottish Historical Review*, 77 (1998).

JONES, P., 'Swing, Speenhamland and rural social relations: the "moral economy" of the English crowd in the nineteenth century', *Social History*, 32 (2007).

KIRBY, M. W., *The British Coal-mining Industry, 1870–1946* (London, 1977).

KIRK, N., *Custom and Conflict in 'the land of the Gael': Ballachulish, 1900–1910* (Monmouth, 2007).

KRASS, P., *Carnegie* (Hoboken, NJ, 2002).

LAWES, K., *Paternalism and Politics: the revival of paternalism in early nineteenth century Britain* (Basingstoke, 2000).

LAWRENCE, J., *Speaking for the People: party, language and popular politics in England, 1867–1914* (Cambridge, 1998).

LEE, S. J., *British Political History, 1815–1914* (London, 1994).

LENEMAN, L., *Fit for Heroes? Land Settlement in Scotland after World War One* (Aberdeen, 1989).

LORIMER, H., 'Guns, game and the grandee: the cultural politics of deer-stalking in the Scottish Highlands', *Ecumene*, 7 (2000).

LUBENOW, W. C., *Parliamentary Politics and the Home Rule Crisis: the British House of Commons in 1886* (Oxford, 1988).

LYNCH, P., *The Liberal Party in rural England, 1885–1910: radicalism and community* (Oxford, 2003).

MACCOLL, A. W., *Land, Faith and the Crofting Community: Christianity and social criticism in the Scottish Highlands, 1843–1893* (Edinburgh, 2006).

'Religion and the Land Question: the Clerical evidence to the Napier Commission', *Transactions of the Gaelic Society of Inverness*, 52 (2000–2).

MACKAY, D., 'The Congested Districts Boards of Ireland and Scotland', *Northern Scotland*, 16 (1996).

MACINNES, A. I., *Clanship, Commerce and the House of Stuart, 1603–1788* (East Linton, 1996).

MACKENZIE, J. M., *Empires of Nature and the Nature of Empires: imperialism, Scotland and the environment* (East Linton, 1997).

MACKILLOP, A., *More Fruitful than the Soil: army, empire and the Scottish Highlands, 1715–1815* (East Linton, 2000).

MACPHAIL, I. M. M., *The Crofters' War* (Stornoway, 1989).

'The Highland Elections of 1884–86', *Transactions of the Gaelic Society of Inverness*, 50 (1976–8).

'The Napier Commission', *Transactions of the Gaelic Society of Inverness*, 48 (1972–4).

MATHER, A. S., 'The Congested Districts Board for Scotland', in W. Ritchie, J. C. Stone and A. S. Mather (eds), *Essays for Professor R. E. H. Mellor* (Aberdeen, 1986).

MEEK, D., 'The Catholic Knight of Crofting: Sir Donald Horne McFarlane, MP for Argyll, 1885–86, 1892–95', *Transactions of the Gaelic Society of Inverness*, 58 (1992–4).

MEEK, D. (ed.), *Tuath is Tighearna: Tenants and Landlords: an anthology of Gaelic poetry of social and political protest from the Clearances to the Land Agitation, 1800–1890* (Edinburgh, 1995).

MINGAY, G. E., *Land and Society in England 1750–1980* (London, 1994).

MURRAY, B., *The People's Budget, 1909/10: Lloyd George and Liberal politics* (Oxford, 1980).

NEWBY, A. G., *Ireland, Radicalism and the Scottish Highlands, c.1870–1912* (Edinburgh, 2007).

'"Scotia Major and Scotia Minor": Ireland and the birth of the Scottish land agitation, 1878–1882', *Irish Economic and Social History*, 31 (2004).

NICHOLAS, T., 'Businessmen and Landownership in late nineteenth century Britain', *Economic History Review*, 53 (2000).

OFFER, A., *Property and Politics, 1870–1914: landownership, law, ideology and urban development in England* (Cambridge, 1981).

OLECHNOWICZ, A. (ed.), *The Monarchy and the British Nation: 1780 to the present* (Cambridge, 2007).

ORR, W., *Deer Forests, Landlords and Crofters: the Western Highlands in Victorian and Edwardian times* (Edinburgh, 1982).

PACKER, I., *Lloyd George, Liberalism and the Land: the land issue and party politics in England, 1906–1914* (London, 2001).

PATON, D. M. M., 'Brought to a wilderness: the Rev. David Mackenzie of Farr and the Sutherland Clearances', *Northern Scotland*, 13 (1993).

PERREN, R., *Agriculture in Depression, 1870–1940* (Cambridge, 1995).

READMAN, P., 'The Conservative Party, patriotism and British politics:

the case of the General election of 1900', *Journal of British Studies*, 40 (2001).

'Jesse Collings and Land Reform, 1886–1914', *Historical Research*, 81 (2008).

REVILL, G., 'Liberalism and Paternalism: Politics and corporate culture in "railway Derby", 1865–75', *Social History*, 24 (1999).

REYNOLDS, K. D., *Aristocratic Women and Political Society in Victorian Britain* (Oxford, 1998).

RICHARDS, E., 'An Anatomy of the Sutherland Fortune; income, consumption, investments and returns, 1780–1880', *Business History*, 21 (1979).

The Highland Clearances: people, landlords and rural turmoil (Edinburgh, new edn, 2008).

'How Tame were the Highlanders during the Clearances?', *Scottish Studies*, 17 (1973).

The Leviathan of Wealth: the Sutherland fortune in the Industrial Revolution (London, 1973).

'The Military Register and the pursuit of Patrick Sellar', *Scottish Economic and Social History*, 16 (1996).

Patrick Sellar and the Highland Clearances: homicide, eviction and the price of progress (Edinburgh, 1999).

RICHARDS, E. and CLOUGH, M., *Cromartie: Highland life, 1650–1914* (Aberdeen, 1989).

ROBERTSON, I. J. M., 'The Role of Women in social protest in the Highlands of Scotland, c.1880–1939', *Journal of Historical Geography*, 23 (1997).

SHEPPERSON, G., 'Harriet Beecher Stowe and Scotland, 1852–53', *Scottish Historical Review*, 31 (1952).

SMITH, J. A., 'Landownership and Social Change in late nineteenth century Britain', *Economic History Review*, 2nd ser., 53 (2000).

SMOUT, T. C., 'The Highlands and the Roots of Green consciousness, 1750–1990', *Proceedings of the British Academy*, 76 (1991); also printed in *Scottish Natural Heritage, Occasional Paper*, 1 (1990).

Nature Contested: environmental history in Scotland and Northern England since 1600 (Edinburgh, 2000).

SPRING, D., 'The Role of the Aristocracy in the nineteenth century', *Victorian Studies*, 4 (1960).

STENTON, M. and LEES, S. (eds), *Who's Who of British MPs, vol. 1 and vol. 2* (Brighton, 1978).

STUART, D., *Dear Duchess: Millicent, Duchess of Sutherland, 1867–1955* (London, 1982).

SYKES, A., *Tariff Reform in British Politics, 1903–13* (Oxford, 1979).

THOMPSON, A. S., 'The Language of Imperialism and Meanings of Empire: Imperial discourse in British politics, 1895–1914', *Journal of British Studies*, 36 (1997).

THOMPSON, B., *Imperial Vanities* (London, 2002).

THOMPSON, F. M. L., 'English Landed Society in the twentieth century:

I: Property: Collapse and Survival', *Transactions of the Royal Historical Society*, 5th ser., 40 (1990).

'English Landed Society in the twentieth century: II: New Poor and New Rich', *Transactions of the Royal Historical Society*, 6th ser., 1 (1991).

'English Landed Society in the twentieth century: III: Self-help and Outdoor relief', *Transactions of the Royal Historical Society*, 6th ser., 2 (1992).

'English Landed Society in the twentieth century: IV: Prestige without power?', *Transactions of the Royal Historical Society*, 6th ser., 3 (1993).

'Moving frontiers and the fortunes of the aristocratic town house, 1830–1930', *London Journal*, 20 (1995).

TINDLEY, A., '"The Sword of Avenging Justice": Politics in Sutherland after the Third Reform Act', *Rural History*, 19 (2008).

TREBILCOCK, C., *Phoenix Assurance and the Development of British Assurance, vol. II* (Cambridge, 1998).

VAUGHAN, W. E., *Landlords and Tenants in Mid-Victorian Ireland* (Oxford, 1994).

WALLACE, S., *John Stuart Blackie: Scottish scholar and patriot* (Edinburgh, 2006).

WHATLEY, C., 'An Uninflammable People?', in Donnachie, I. and Whatley, C. (eds), *The Manufacture of Scottish History* (Edinburgh, 1992).

WHEELER, P. T., 'Landownership and the crofting system in Sutherland since 1800', *Agricultural History Review*, 14 (1966).

WITHERS, C. W. J., 'Destitution and migration: labour mobility and relief from famine in Highland Scotland, 1836–1850', *Journal of Historical Geography*, 14 (1998).

'"Give us Land and Plenty of it": the Ideological basis to Land and Landscape in the Scottish Highlands', *Landscape History*, 12 (1990).

'Rural Protest in the Highlands of Scotland and Ireland, 1850–1930', in Connelly, S. J., Houston, R. A. and Morris, R. J., *Conflict, Identity and Economic Development: Ireland and Scotland, 1600–1939* (Preston, 1995).

WOMACK, P., *Improvement and Romance: constructing the myth of the Highlands* (Basingstoke, 1989).

YORKE, J., *Lancaster House: London's greatest town house* (London, 2001).

YOUNG, J. D., *Women and Popular Struggles: A history of British working class women, 1560–1984* (Edinburgh, 1985).

THESES

HILDEBRANDT, R. N., 'Migration and economic change in the northern Highlands during the nineteenth century, with particular reference to the period 1851–1891', unpublished Ph.D. thesis (University of Glasgow, 1980).

MACCOLL, A., 'The Churches and the Land Question in the Highlands of Scotland, 1843–1888', unpublished Ph.D. thesis (University of Cambridge, 2003).

MACPHAIL, I., 'Land, Crofting and the Assynt Crofters' Trust: a Post-colonial Geography', unpublished Ph.D. thesis (University of Lampeter, 2002).

NEWBY, A., 'Shoulder to Shoulder? Scottish and Irish Land Reformers in the Highlands of Scotland, 1878–1894', unpublished Ph.D. thesis (University of Edinburgh, 2001).

PERREN, R., 'The Effects of the Agricultural Depression on the English Estates of the Dukes of Sutherland, 1870–1900', unpublished Ph.D. thesis (University of Nottingham, 1967).

ROBERTSON, I. J. M., 'The Historical Geography of Social Protest in Highland Scotland, 1914–c.1939', unpublished Ph.D. thesis (University of Bristol, 1995).

TINDLEY, A. M., 'Orkney and Shetland: Land Reform, Government Policy and Politics, c.1870–1914', unpublished M.Sc. thesis (University of Edinburgh, 2002).

Index

socialism, 13, 94, 101
Society for the Promotion of Scientific
    Industry, 38
Stafford, Marquis of (future 4th Duke
    of Sutherland), 43, 77, 80–3, 86,
    89, 95, 146, 148
Stafford House, 43, 64, 116, 133,
    172
steam plough, 37–9, 42, 49–50, 53
Stewart, John William, 115n, 134
Stoer, 97, 141–2, 145, 149
Strathan, 97–8
Strathnaver, 18, 70, 109–10, 115, 118,
    120–1, 123, 125, 171
Strathpeffer Spa, 36, 51
subdivision, 9, 17n, 27n, 28, 31–2
Sutherland, Angus, 66–8, 72n, 75n,
    80–1, 108, 114, 156
Sutherland Canadian Lands Company,
    136
Sutherland Farmer's Club, 31
Sutherland, Millicent Duchess of,
    129–30, 132
Sutherland, 2nd Duke of, 1, 3, 10, 20,
    174
Sutherland, 3rd Duke of, 4, 7, 23, 30,
    33–4, 36, 41, 44, 48–9, 50, 58–9, 81,
    88–9, 92, 95, 110, 120, 138, 151,
    165, 174

Sutherland, 4th Duke of, 4–5, 89–91,
    104, 108, 115, 119–20, 127–8,
    131–4, 136, 163, 168, 170n, 171–2,
    174
Sutherland, 5th Duke of, 4, 115, 120,
    129, 131, 133n, 136–7, 169, 172, 174
Syre, 115, 118, 120–8, 131, 136, 163,
    170n

Tait, G. G., 153
Tarbat, 97
Times, 54
Tongue management, 18, 60, 62, 105,
    116, 122, 134
Trentham House, 89, 133, 172, 175
Turkey, 36

Unapool, 30, 147–8, 152, 161

Vatersay, 121, 162
Victoria, Queen, 52

War Loans, 136
Westminster, dukes of, 3, 136n, 152
Wick Burghs, 29
Wright, Henry (secretary to 3rd Duke),
    98, 160

Young, William, 48